S0-BYU-230

DEFINING
DIALOGUE

DEFINING DIALOGUE

FROM

Socrates

TO THE

INTERNET

GEOFFREY ROCKWELL

an imprint of Prometheus Books
59 John Glenn Drive, Amherst, New York 14228-2197

Published 2003 by Humanity Books, an imprint of Prometheus Books

Inquiries should be addressed to
Humanity Books
59 John Glenn Drive
Amherst, New York 14228–2197
VOICE: 716–691–0133, ext. 207
FAX: 716–564–2711
WWW.PROMETHEUSBOOKS.COM

07 06 05 04 03 5 4 3 2 1

Library of Congress Cataloging-in-Publication Data

Rockwell, Geoffrey, 1959–
Defining dialogue : from Socrates to the Internet / Geoffrey Rockwell.
p. cm.
Includes bibliographical references and index.
ISBN 1–57392–954–9 (alk. paper)
1. Dialogue. I. Title.

PN1551 .R63 2002
302.3'46—dc21 2002068613

Printed in the United States of America on acid-free paper

CONTENTS

ACKNOWLEDGMENTS

I would like to acknowledge and thank all those who helped me with this book. I am very grateful for the encouragement of Paul Gooch who supervised my graduate studies and first suggested that we eavesdrop on dialogue. I am also grateful to Graeme Nicholson who advised me throughout, reading many early drafts. I would like to thank Will Crichton and John Bradley who patiently commented on early chapters, and Cynthia Rockwell who edited the text. I should also mention Paul and Rosemary Desjardins who first introduced me to dialogue and Plato. Without the love, patience, and support of Peigi, Peter, and Alethea Rockwell I would never have completed this book.

INTRODUCTION

> *Rhetoric:* Having conceived an inordinate affection for that bearded man in the mantle, Dialogue, who is said to be the son of Philosophy and is older than he (Lucian of Samosata) is, he lives with him. Showing no sense of shame, he has curtailed the freedom and the range of my speeches and has confined himself to brief, disjointed questions: and instead of saying whatever he wishes in a powerful voice, he fits together and spells out short paragraphs, for which he cannot get hearty praise or great applause from his hearers, but only a smile, or a restrained gesture of the hand, an inclination of the head, or a sigh to point his periods.[1]

In *The Double Indictment*, a charming dialogue by Lucian of Samosata, the author is brought to trial by his two loves, Rhetoric and Dialogue. Rhetoric, Lucian's first companion, accuses him of abandoning her for Dialogue, and Dialogue accuses Lucian of turning him into a monstrosity by combining him with comedy. This dialogue by Lucian marks an important moment in the history of the literary dialogue. Along with Plato and Cicero, who used the dialogue for philosophical purposes, Lucian is one of the three most influential dialogue writers. He adapted the form to mock the pretensions of ideologues of all sorts, including philosophers, showing the comic potential of the genre. After Lucian, the written dialogue was never again the sole preserve of philosophy. He opened the dialogue and reflected back, in *The Double Indictment*, on the justice of what he did to dialogue.

Today we, too, are turning from rhetoric to dialogue and adapting it to our own needs. As Giulio Ferroni noted in his introduction to a collection of papers on dialogue, "The dialogue is the order of the day: dialogue, dialogicity, dialogism are the constant points of reference for contemporary debates in the human sciences; and, as never before, dialogue traverses the space of the entire planet creating relationships between entities that until recently ignored each other completely, producing a tight net of voices, calls, and responses."[2] Dialogue has gone from being a minor literary form, representing a type of intellectual activity, to being a defining human activity. This, as Ferroni points out, may be due to the technological advances from the telephone to the Internet that have allowed us to listen in to each other and to enter into discussion with each other as never before. We are weaving a web of conversations that span the globe, and creating new communities unconstrained by distance. In this world of electric talk, dialogue has become the paradigm for virtuous activity. In the age of mass communication it has become the balm for conflict and intellectual difference. As we extend our ability to communicate, we hope we have created the conditions for the dialogues we imagine. Let me mention a few of the specific contexts in which discussion of dialogue has bloomed:

- When Bill Clinton was elected president in the United States, there was a marked increase in discussion, even in Canada, about the "information superhighway" championed by his vice president, Al Gore. This "infobahn" builds on the Internet, which has been exploding as a communications network for academics.[3] The Internet, unlike mass media such as television, encourages the exchange of information through Web sites, chat rooms, e-mail, and discussion lists. It adds to the communication technologies like the telegraph and telephone that we have at our disposal for dialogue. On the Internet there are thousands of open discussions on all sorts of topics that one can participate in. These electronic dialogues are beginning to replace traditional mechanisms for the publication of information.[4] We can now read messages posted by researchers and eyewitnesses without waiting for published news. We can dialogue with witnesses and colleagues rather than read reports.[5]

- Mass media like radio and television, which we would not normally think of as dialogical, are increasingly presenting us with information in the form of discussions which we are invited to overhear. Radio call-in shows that draw us into nationwide dialogues have been a fixture for some time. Television talk shows have been growing in popularity; now even the news is presented as a talk show where we listen daily to dialogues around events and their significance. Experts didn't tell us what to think about the Gulf War, they debated each other in panels set up by the networks. It should not surprise us that politicians routinely use these shows to sway the electorate. Given the importance of these shows in forming public opinion, their hosts, like Oprah, Geraldo, and Letterman, can be said to have become our Socratic gadflies, questioning the rich and famous in our living room.[6]
- Dialogue has become a valued practice in business. One of the better-known works on management, *The Fifth Discipline* promotes dialogue as one of the important practices of learning organizations in the information age. As author Peter Senge writes in the introduction, "Dialogue groups now are forming in a wide variety of settings, in the public and private sector. . . . We are learning that there is deep hunger to rediscover our capacity to talk with one another."[7]
- Statistical studies of bibliographic databases like the *Philosopher's Index* and the card catalogue of the University of Toronto show that the relative frequency of works on dialogue has increased substantially since the beginning of the 1960s, especially in the area of religious studies, politics, and philosophy.[8] Not only is more being published on dialogue, but a greater percentage of what is published is now on dialogue.
- Much of this growth in interest in dialogue can be traced back to the Vatican II *Decree on Ecumenism* (Unitatis Redintegratio), which exhorts Catholics "to take an active and intelligent part in the work of ecumenism." An essential step in this work of reconciliation and understanding between faiths is dialogue between their representatives.[9] Dialogue is not only the model for ecumenical work, but in theologians like Martin Buber it is presented as a paradigm for our relationship with our fellow men, god, and the natural world.[10]

- In education dialogue still holds a place of honor. Michael Oakeshott reminds us that "as civilized human beings, we are the inheritors, neither of an enquiry about ourselves and the world, nor of an accumulating body of information, but of a conversation, begun in the primeval forests and made more articulate in the course of centuries. It is a conversation which goes on both in public and within each of ourselves."[11] The National Endowment for the Humanities in the United States took this literally and sponsored national conversations about the humanities.[12]
- In philosophy dialogue is still alive and well as an activity and subject. In an article on the dialogue experiments of Ernesto Grassi, Michael Heim points out that, "for Phenomenology, 'dialogue' and 'being-together' are both subject and object of philosophical investigation."[13] Recent works like *Dialogue and Deconstruction* report and comment on the encounter between two of the most important recent Continental thinkers, Gadamer and Derrida, as the encounter of a philosophy of dialogue and one of deconstruction (as the title suggests). Associating Gadamer with dialogue is not unfair, since it was an important part of his teaching and thought.[14] On the other side of the Atlantic, in analytic circles, there is also a growing interest in dialogue, though in the context of argument and human-computer dialogue.[15]
- Advertisers have not missed this desire for dialogue. Labatt, a Canadian beer company, invited us in 1994 to open a dialogue about beer. Their print ad had a picture of a "handsome metal bottle-opener" with the line: "It isn't intended to open a bottle, but a dialogue." Alert dialogue watchers like myself rushed to call an automated voice system and answer a few questions about our favorite beers so that we could get the handsome dialogue opener. Labatt's advertising agency, no doubt, was aware of the connection between dialogue and drinking alcohol that goes back to Plato.

How are we to understand this explosion of dialogue? Lucian was twice accused, first by Rhetoric for abandoning her genre of persuasion for Dialogue, and then by Dialogue for opening him to laughter and corrupting him; I believe our culture should likewise face a double charge, first for abandoning other activities for dialogue, and then by those who think dialogue should be kept for serious tasks and not repurposed for everything from management to advertising. Who, then, is going to prepare the case? Communication scientists are studying the technologies that facilitate interaction while human-computer interface engineers are studying human-computer dialogue. Political scientists can discuss the merits of dialogue as a political activity while sociologists try to account for the growth of interest in dialogue. Literary historians have traced the history of the written dialogue, while authors continue writing them. It is left up to philosophy, the mother of dialogue, to ask anew what dialogue is and submit that for trial by discussion. We who gave birth to dialogue should, in the spirit of Socrates, hold our child up for examination, and ask if it is but a phantom. To do this we can draw from the history of philosophical dialogues and previous attempts to define dialogue, including Lucian's comical redefinition.

MONSTROUS DIALOGUE

Given the number of ways dialogue is used today, the first question we have to deal with is whether dialogue is one thing or many. It may be that what is considered dialogue in one context is not the same thing as what is called for in another. Dialogue could be a monster made up of very different parts, joined for convenience under one name.

This problem of the unity of dialogue can be seen in Lucian's dialogue where the author plays with the possible senses. First, he fashions dialogue into a character, tied to a particular content—that of philosophy, while at the same time retaining its other senses as an oral activity and a written genre. The character stands as the child of a community (philosophy) and a genre of writing. He is described as dour, awesome, and skeletal, due to all the questioning that takes place in dialogue—in contrast to full-bodied Rhetoric, seducer of young men. We have Lucian to thank for cleaning Dialogue up; before that he was not attractive to the public, who had previously "avoided taking hold of him as if he were a sea-urchin."[16] This description, which plays with the image of Socrates as an inquirer who did not care for his appearance and whose barbed questions could sting, no longer seems true given the present love of dialogue.

The second sense of dialogue is as an oral activity. The activity that Lucian represents is different from the character that participates in the trial. It is a way of conversing in short questions and paragraphs, conversing that invites not applause but a smile or slight gesture. It is a subtle activity that does not try to persuade in the direct way of rhetoric, but entertains and educates with irony and light comedy.

The third sense of dialogue is that of the written form. This form, as Lucian the author transforms it, is something else yet. It is a short and entertaining work of moral satire, one of the first of a rich tradition of "dialogues of the dead" where impossible combinations of characters (like Dialogue and Rhetoric) are combined, often in Hades. It is also a conscious repurposing of a form traditionally associated with philosophy that is designed to make fun of philosophy so that even the professional philosopher would be amused.

Dialogue the character complains that after being dressed up by Lucian he is "neither afoot nor ahorseback, neither prose nor verse, but seem to my hearers a strange phenomenon made up of different elements, like a Centaur."[17] Lucian's work makes a monster out of dialogue and admits it. It leaves us with an image of dialogue in general as a hybrid genre, neither serious philosophy nor comedy. Along with the character there are, in Lucian's work, two forms of dialogue, the oral conversation, and the written work that represents it. This last form is Lucian's real defense.

If we look at today's explosion of interest in dialogue we can discern three parallel uses of the word that we need to study if we are to understand it as one thing:

1. *Oral Dialogue.* Dialogue as an oral activity between two or more people who alternate asking and answering questions.
2. *Written Dialogue.* Dialogue as a written genre that represents oral dialogue and is usually not intended to be performed on stage.
3. *Ineffable Dialogue.* Dialogue as an exchange between individuals or communities through which comes something undefinable but meaningful.[18]

What is significant about all three of these uses of the word *dialogue* is that we rarely talk about being in dialogue at the time that it is happening. There is something sacred about dialogue, such that we use it sparingly for the untidy interactions we are actually in. Dialogue is something that is to be entered, called for, or read after. We talk about events as dialogues only when we are outside as witnesses, before they have begun or after they are finished. This suggests that one thing these uses have in common is that they refer to something that has a unity that a conversation need not have. Only when an interaction is over (or has not yet begun) can it be judged to have a unity similar to the artistic integrity of finished written work; then we are willing to call it a dialogue. While we are in a conversation we are hesitant to call it a dialogue; when two communities are in negotiation they rarely call it a dialogue; only the anticipated or completed work do we call dialogue. Even what we call for, though it hasn't happened, is imagined as something with the integrity of a finished work, not something confused and wandering like a conversation that could go astray at any moment.

All three of these uses of the word can be found in Lucian if one considers how the character Dialogue is the representative of a community of thinkers and writings. What has changed is the way the third sense has become common since the Second World War, accounting for much of the growth in interest in dialogue.[19] There are two facets to this sense that make it different from the other two. First, this sense of dialogue is used when people talk about the interaction that isn't necessarily between individuals or in the form of an oral conversation. It is this sense of dialogue that is used to talk about the interaction (in whatever form) between communities (as in "Arab-Israeli dialogue"), ideologies (as in "Marxist-Christian dialogue"), and with entities that don't talk in the normal way, like gods or books. Second, it is the hardest use of the word to pin down as it refers to an interaction which is (or should be) meaningful in a way that cannot be defined. The difference between dialogue in this sense and other types of interaction is precisely the undefinable quality of the event. One can't point to some formal element of a dialogue and say that that is what differentiates it from a conversation. A dialogue is an interaction where something valuable and meaningful took place that cannot be described, except by the dialogue. This is the dialogue that we hope for, call for, but rarely find. This is what we hope our fancy communication systems will facilitate.

This book will look at these three senses of the word dialogue, beginning with the last, in order to define dialogue. In chapter 1 I will deal with the ineffable in dialogue. I will conclude that while this sense of dialogue cannot be defined, it needs to be kept in mind when we discuss other senses of the word. In chapter 2 I look at oral dialogue, and in chapters 3 and 4 the written dialogue, showing how they are similar genres of persuasion. Chapter 5 and the conclusion propose a definition for the oral and written dialogue that opens the way for a discussion of the ideological baggage of dialogue. Simply put, the bulk of this work gathers up the senses of dialogue, so that I can suggest a definition that allows us to understand the possibilities for dialogue that make it so attractive.

I begin with the third sense of dialogue, rather than taking them in the order listed above, because the ineffable qualities that are associated with dialogue haunt all the senses of dialogue. Only once we understand what cannot be pinned down about dialogue can we safely go on to discuss the more mundane senses of dialogue and define it. The definition I eventually arrive at will not encompass the ineffable in dialogue; it is proposed to further conversation about what can be said about dialogue. This work will not answer the sociological question of why there has been such a growth of interest in dialogue and opening in its use; it is meant to be part of the conversation about just what dialogue is.

DIALOGUE AND PHILOSOPHY

The two trials of Lucian are preceded by a lengthy exchange between Zeus and Justice (Dike) that sets the scene for the trials. Infuriated by philosophers who claim the gods do not care about mortals, Zeus asks Justice to go down and oversee the courts. She is naturally reluctant to do so because of the way she was treated the last time when injustice triumphed at the trial of Socrates. When her father argues that the son of Sophroniscus (Socrates) had convinced everyone to honor her more than injustice, she reminds him of the treatment Socrates met. She is finally persuaded when Zeus points out how popular philosophy is:

> But at present, do not you see how many short cloaks and staves and wallets there are? On all sides there are long beards, and books in the left hand, and everybody preaches in favour of you; the public walks are

> full of people assembling in companies and in battalions, and there is nobody who does not want to be thought a scion of Virtue. In fact, many, giving up the trades that they had before, rush after the wallet and the cloak, tan their bodies in the sun to Ethiopian hue, make themselves extemporaneous philosophers out of cobblers or carpenters, and go about praising you and your virtue. Consequently, in the words of the proverb, it would be easier for a man to fall in a boat without hitting a plank than for your eye to miss a philosopher wherever it looks.[20]

The visit of Justice accompanied by Hermes, which Zeus encourages, creates an excuse for the unusual trials of Lucian and others. This prelude, with its asides on philosophy, is too long to be merely a device to set the scene for the trials that follow; its length suggests that the sorry state of philosophy is connected to the issue of Lucian's reuse of dialogue. The parody of the philosophical community that frames the issue of Lucian's rejection of Rhetoric has the effect of lessening our sympathy for the character Dialogue, who is after all the "son of philosophy." This in turn makes our judgment of Lucian's choice more likely to be favorable. If we laugh at the philosophy that laid claim on Dialogue we will be less upset with Lucian's reuse of the form associated with philosophy.

Lucian was writing at a time when literary innovation was not valued. While the Mediterranean world looked to Rome for political peace, writers tended to imitate the Greek forms and look back with nostalgia on classical Greek culture. Lucian stands out as one of the few literary innovators, and his innovation consisted in the repurposing of the classical forms. His educated audience would recognize the fact that he is using the philosophical dialogue to parody the very community that traditionally used the form. If the character that stands for Lucian defends himself against Rhetoric using Rhetoric's tools (the long discourse), Lucian the author is using philosophy's ways (the written dialogue) to defend himself against Dialogue, the scion of philosophy. The dialogue is an example of the reuse of dialogue that, while it may have offended literary purists, also addresses those offended, offering a defense of the innovation. The dialogues would not work if their audience were not acquainted with philosophical discourse and the importance of dialogue to philosophy. If dialogue is not related to philosophy then the parody doesn't work, and ironically, if the parody works, it distances dialogue and philosophy by perverting the form. (Would philosophy recognize her son after Lucian had combined him with comedy and dressed him up?)

The Double Indictment and Lucian's other works, because of their critical relationship to philosophy, are at the edge of the discipline. They discuss philosophical subjects and philosophers but are not serious enough to be considered philosophical. They draw attention to hypocrisy within philosophy, while remaining committed to the virtues that philosophers fail to attain. They create a parodic distance between the reader and philosophy, but in so doing, preserve the possibility of a purified discipline. By choosing to mock philosophy, Lucian shows a certain respect for it. In so doing he opens the question of form and philosophical content. If Lucian is successful you can't read a philosophical dialogue in the same naive way again, but that doesn't prevent you from returning to philosophy with pleasure.

Despite the distancing of philosophy and dialogue that takes place in threshold dialogues like Lucian's, I believe reopening an inquiry into dialogue is a perfect task for philosophy. First, dialogue has long been associated with philosophy. Despite the proliferation of nonphilosophical dialogues, the written dialogue is still associated with the discipline of philosophy. Even if the parent and child are estranged, they are still related by birth. Second, there is a rich, if ignored, tradition of written philosophical dialogues. This tradition is woven into today's renewed interest in dialogue. If there is a place to start an investigation of dialogue, it is with this written record. Third, explicit discussion of dialogue has already taken place in the history of the discipline, though the concerns then were different from ours today. We need to recover the discussion about dialogue that has taken place to better understand our present fascination with it. Fourth and finally, it has traditionally been the contribution (not the prerogative) of philosophy to define such subjects that cross disciplines.

Some might object that defining is an inappropriate move at this point, and that definitions tend to end discussion violently. While I doubt there is any real danger that an obscure book will silence anyone, let me assure the reader that this definition is intended to start discussion, not end it. I would like it said that this definition brought dialogue into focus so that it could be discussed, just as so many Socratic dialogues are launched with definition. For this to happen I will define dialogue in a manner becoming to the subject, through the reading of dialogues, so that they guide their definition.

DEFINITION THROUGH DIALOGUE

At the end of Rhetoric's accusation she asks the judge, Justice herself, to prevent Lucian from using her "weapons" (rhetorical discourses) against her in his defense. Instead, Rhetoric claims, Lucian should be forced to defend himself according to the ways of his new interest—Dialogue. Hermes, who is assisting Justice, comes to Lucian's aid, saying that it is impossible to defend oneself by dialogue.

The irony is that Lucian is doing just that. His dialogue is a defense of the choice of dialogue in dialogue form. Of course the defense by dialogue is not before Justice, but before us, the readers of the dialogue. In the dialogue the character Lucian is judged innocent on both counts, but it is left up to us readers to judge whether the author was justified in his abandonment of rhetorical discourse for dialogue, and whether he should be allowed his satiric repurposing of dry philosophical dialogue. If the reader is entertained by the dialogue and recognizes the appropriateness of the parody, then the author is acquitted.

One might ask, given my interest in dialogue, why this book is not in dialogue form. Why don't I investigate dialogue with its own weapons? Put abstractly, if this work is about the relationship between form and content, is the form of this work related to its content? The reason for which I have chosen to stick to the long-winded, traditional form of philosophical writing is that the written dialogue, as I will argue at the end of this text, works by carrying certain content in a less than explicit fashion. This content, to be discussed explicitly, needs another form—a form that in turn may hide another agenda. You might say that the hardest form to describe clearly is that in which one writes. Or you might write that dialogue cannot defend itself, only represent itself. Lucian does not defend dialogue in general, only his use of it. He does so by providing an example of his work. I am not interested in defending my use of dialogue, but in the investigation of dialogue that can inform the current fascination with it. Lucian would say that this work is philosophy getting the last word (though not the last laugh).

Even though this work is not in dialogue form, that does not mean that it will not be grounded in dialogue. In the redefinition of dialogue and his companions we are going to take a hint from Rhetoric and ask that dialogue defend itself by means of dialogue. We will stick to dialogues as evidence in our investigation. As we have done in this introduction we will cradle these long paragraphs of discourse with the short ones on particular dialogues. We are taking a step further the hermeneutical principle that works should be interpreted through their internal hermeneutical suggestions. We are trying to interpret a genre as it presents itself, and defends itself. Hermes, the god of hermeneuticians, would say it is impossible for writers of dialogue, or Dialogue itself, to define itself by dialogue; but Hermes is only one voice among many, in dialogue.

Despite the grounding in dialogues, this work is not a history of that vehicle. I will concentrate on particular dialogues appropriate to the line of the investigation, specifically those of Plato, Xenophon, Lucian, Cicero, Bruni, Hume, Valla, and Heidegger. The choice of dialogues is based on the needs of the investigation and the desire to cover a representative sample of works. I particularly want to show that there are interesting philosophical dialogues after Plato. While I do not presume to discuss these writers in as thorough a fashion as they deserve, I hope that the discussion of dialogue in general will prove interesting to those engaged in the discovery of any particular dialogue.

In Lucian we have the first sustained discussion of dialogue in a dialogue. This discussion is a defense against accusations that Lucian opened dialogue to unnatural uses, especially comical ones. *The Double Indictment* was both an example of the new dialogue and an answer to critics who were suspicious of this adaptation of a classical form. Today we find dialogue also adapted to new contexts, and we can expect charges to be brought that it is being misused. This book is neither a defense nor an accusation of the expanded use of dialogue. It is a working definition for those interested in thinking philosophically about dialogue and its possibilities.

NOTES

1. Lucian, *The Double Indictment*, in *Lucian; with an English Translation*, trans. Austin Morris Harmon, vol. 3 (New York: Macmillan, 1967), p. 139.

2. Giulio Ferroni, ed., *Il dialogo: scambi e passaggi della parola* (Palermo: Sellerio Editore, 1985), p. 11. This is my translation of the editor's introduction from the Italian.

3. As of July 1997, there were 19.54 million hosts on the Internet. The number of hosts grew an average of 15 percent a quarter in 1996. "How to Anticipate the Internet's Global Diffusion," *Communications of the ACM* 41, no. 10 (October 1998): 100.

4. In an article entitled "Goodbye, Gutenberg: Pixelating Peer Review Is Revolutionizing Scholarly Journals," Jacques Leslie discusses the growth in electronic academic publications. *Wired* (October 1994): 68–71. A good collection of papers on the subject is *Scholarly Publishing: The Electronic Frontier*, ed. Robin Peek and Gregory Newby (Cambridge, Mass.: MIT Press, 1996). For lists of these journals and essays on the subject there are a number of online sites including "NewJour" (http://gort.ucsd.edu/newjour/) and the "Journal of Electronic Publishing" (http://www.press.umich.edu/jep/).

5. The number of books dealing with the Internet has also exploded. Just go to your local bookstore and you will find an abundance of how-to books, directories of services, and so on. A readable history of the Internet is *Where Wizards Stay Up Late* by Kattie Haffner and Matthew Lyon (New York: Simon & Schuster, 1996). A good introduction to the Internet is still Ed Krol's *The Whole Internet: User's Guide and Catalog* (Sebastopol, Calif.: O'Reilly, 1992). For a more academic perspective there is *Global Networks: Computers and International Communication*, edited by Linda Harasim (Cambridge, Mass.: MIT Press, 1994). For an introduction to the field of computer-mediated communication, there is Starr Roxanne Hiltz and Murray Turoff's *The Network Nation: Human Communication via Computer* (Cambridge, Mass.: MIT Press, 1993). Finally, for those interested in a quick guide to the fuss over the convergence of media there is *Life After Television* by George Gilder (New York: W. W. Norton, 1994).

6. In an article called "Mass Communication and Para-Social Interaction: Observation on Intimacy at a Distance," Donald Horton and R. Richard Wohl comment on how television performers create an intimate atmosphere with the spectator. *Intermedia: Interpersonal Communication in a Media World*, ed. Gary Gumpert and Robert Cathcart (Oxford: Oxford University Press, 1979). We are invited to think of Johnny Carson as a friend who winks at us as he questions the characters that pass by.

7. Peter M. Senge, introduction to *The Fifth Discipline: The Art and Practice of the Learning Organization* (New York: Doubleday, 1990), p. xiii.

8. I published preliminary results of these results in "The Desire for Dialogue" in the *Toronto Semiotic Circle Bulletin* 1, no. 3 (November 1993): 2–6. More detailed results were presented by John Bradley and myself at the *ALLC-ACH '94* conference in a paper entitled "A Growing Fascination with Dialogue: Bibliographic Databases and the Recent History of Ideas."

9. Vatican II *Decree on Ecumenism* (Unitatis Redintegratio), 21 November 1964, chap. 1, sec. 4. "Then, 'dialogue' between competent experts from different Churches and communities; in their meetings, which are organized in a religious spirit, each explains the teaching of his communion in greater depth and brings out clearly its distinctive features. Through such dialogue everyone gains a truer knowledge and more just appreciation of the teaching and religious life of both communions."

10. Martin Buber, *I and Thou*, trans. Ronald Gregor Smith, 2d ed. (New York: Charles Scribner's Sons, 1958).

11. Michael Oakeshott, *The Voice of Poetry in the Conversation of Mankind* (London: Bowes & Bowes, 1959), p. 11.

12. An article in the 15 December 1994 issue of the *Chronicle of Higher Education* entitled "Humanities Endowment Steps Up Plans for a 'National Conversation'" reports that Sheldon Hackney, the then chairman, set up a "national conversation" to "bring citizens together to talk in intelligent ways about divisive issues" through grants that support "face-to-face meetings at the local level" (p. A22).

13. Michael Heim, "Grassi's Experiment: The Renaissance through Phenomenology," *Research in Phenomenology* 18 (1988): 234. He goes on to comment how dialogue became especially important in the English world of phenomenology after the Second World War: "The terms of 'existential phenomenology,' such as 'dialogue' and 'commitment,' became common coin and even intellectual clichés in postwar Anglo-European culture."

14. In his *Philosophical Apprenticeships* (Cambridge, Mass.: MIT Press, 1985) Gadamer writes, "My own nature was well suited to such a 'dialogical existence,' and I attempted to develop this into a teaching style" (p. 141). Likewise in an interview, Gadamer says, "I am a dialogical being." *Hans-Georg Gadamer on Education, Poetry, and History*, ed. Dieter Misgeld and Graeme Nicholson (Albany: State University of New York Press, 1992), p. 66.

15. In the editor's introduction to a collection of articles on "Argumentation in Dialogues," Douglas Walton writes, "Three main avenues of research are now converging towards a strong interest in analyzing the dialogue structure of argumentation." *Argumentation* 2, no. 4 (1988): 393. The three avenues named are the field of argumentation, the field of pragmatics in linguistics, and the field of artificial intelligence (along with associated areas of cognitive science). It is worth noting that in the field of artificial intelligence the most widely discussed test of machine intelligence, the Turing test, is a form of dialogue where the artificial system tries to convince a human judge that it is human by answering questions typed at a terminal.

16. Lucian, *The Double Indictment*, p. 149.

17. Ibid., p. 147.

18. This division of the important senses of dialogue was suggested to me by Eva Kushner, though she should not be held responsible for my wording.

19. There are two other technical senses of dialogue that I have omitted from this discussion. In music "dialogue" can refer to passages where the interaction of instruments is suggestive of oral dialogue. In theatre and film, "dialogue" can refer to the passages of conversation in the script.

20. Lucian, *The Double Indictment*, p. 95.

1 The DANGER of DIALOGUE

> I only know one thing: because reflection on language, and on Being, has determined my path of thinking from early on, therefore their discussion had stayed as far as possible in the background.[1]

The first use of dialogue that we will approach is that of ineffable dialogue where that which cannot be said is brought close. Plato is not the place to start a discussion about such dialogue, not because his dialogues are any less exquisite than others, but because the rich scholarly debate that surrounds them would distract us from the issue here: is there a sense of dialogue that cannot be defined? There are, fortunately, dialogues to turn to other than Plato's. Despite the impression that serious philosophical dialogue writing ceased with the death of Plato, there is a long tradition of this kind of writing from which to draw insight. One such work belongs to our time: Heidegger's excellent "A Dialogue on Language." In it the characters frequently pause to reflect on their dialogue and what can and cannot be said. This makes it a good place to start the discussion because it is a self-conscious work that reflects back on dialogue from a perspective not far from ours. It is also a good start because it opens the question of the limitations of definition. It suits as an introduction to thinking about the subject by warning us of the dangers of definition ahead. It approaches that about dialogue which cannot be said without forcing the issue.

Before looking for answers to our questions about dialogue, we need to ask how a particular written dialogue might answer our questions. It is unlikely we will find an authoritative definition of dialogue. For one thing, the words of a dialogue are addressed not to us, but from one character to another. We cannot, therefore, treat that which is said as unambiguously addressing our questions. Nor, to be honest, do we want definitive answers at this point; we want suggestions from the dialogue that will guide this discourse and frame it. How then will dialogues speak to our concerns?

In keeping with the hermeneutical principle mentioned in the Introduction (that we should try to interpret dialogue according to the interpretive suggestions of dialogues) we should listen to a suggestion in Heidegger's dialogue that what we can expect are hints. A hint is not an answer to a question. It only emerges when one comes bearing questions and then it encourages appropriate thought on the subject. This can be especially useful where there is no satisfactory statement that could answer a question, or where the appropriate response in the face of the ineffable is silence. Another feature of Heidegger's hints are that they come from the direction of the object of your seeking and beckon back toward it. So already we have our first hint from his dialogue: if we come bearing questions, we can expect hints, not answers. In other words, our approach to Heidegger's dialogue (and others) should be one of framing serious questions on which we wish to think, and remaining open to hints that guide our thought.[2]

BEGINNING WITH QUESTIONING

"A Dialogue on Language; Between a Japanese and an Inquirer" has a simple plot on the surface. As the subtitle tells us, there are two characters, an Inquirer who is clearly Heidegger, and a Japanese character who knew of Heidegger from his teacher Count Kuki and has translated some of Heidegger's work.[3] The German for "Inquirer," *Fragender*, comes from the word for question (*Frage*). That Heidegger names himself the "questioner" suggests the importance of the question to the character of the philosopher when he is in dialogue. Since Heidegger is not a questioner the way Socrates is, he does not expect only short answers, but he is still placing himself in a tradition of philosophers who work through questions that goes back to Socrates.

Confirming the importance of the question to dialogue, the Japanese talks (near the end) about the "movement of questioning that is called for here."[4] The characters agree that the type of speaking that is adequate to the issue of language cannot be found in expository writing like the scientific dissertation. The dissertation is for them a congealing of the movement of questioning.[5] Dialogue, on the other hand, can represent the movement. By that I presume they mean that a dissertation contains a single complex and consistent answer to a single complex question. In taking one moment in a larger movement of questions and answers, the dissertation freezes the movement for elaboration. In a frozen moment one can expect consistency; each part of the answer can be consistent with the others. By contrast, in a dialogue characters often change their minds as they are questioned; their later answers can be inconsistent with earlier ones.

The movement of questions can be said to provide the impetus to the dialogue and the plot. Heidegger's dialogue is driven by questions posed by the Inquirer and the Japanese; indeed, one could survey the dialogue by charting the questions asked. This movement of questions also suggests a movement in the questioner. Just how the Inquirer, or Heidegger the Questioner, moves through questions we will discuss later. Let us summarize the first hint we have drawn from the dialogue:

The approach to dialogue begins with questions.

DANGER

The two characters begin their dialogue remembering the deceased Count Kuki and his interest in aesthetics. This leads them gently to talk about language, hermeneutics, metaphysics, and the possibility of dialogue between people of different cultures and languages. There is no indication that this dialogue takes place before other people; it is the private communion of two thinkers that follows from earlier such informal conversations that Heidegger had with Count Kuki. Heidegger describes the earlier generation of dialogues in a way that applies to this dialogue, too:

> Our dialogues were not formal, scholarly discussions. Whenever that sort of thing seemed to be taking place, as in the seminars, Count Kuki remained silent. The dialogues of which I am thinking came about at my house, like a spontaneous game. Count Kuki occasionally brought his wife along who then wore festive Japanese garments. They made the Eastasian world more luminously present, and the danger of our dialogues became more clearly visible.[6]

One of the themes that stands out at the beginning of the dialogue is the danger of dialogue. Needless to say, if we are interested in dialogue, any suggestion of danger is worth listening to. The danger mentioned initially is the possibility that a dialogue taking place in a European language could fail to capture Japanese experience. In other words, the language of the dialogue might confine what can be said to distinctions and concepts of that language. Heidegger suggests that his earlier dialogues with Count Kuki may have failed because they tried to apply Western aesthetics to the Japanese experience of art. This is not necessarily a danger only to dialogue, but with multiple characters who come from different linguistic and ideological backgrounds this danger is often more apparent in dialogue.

The danger exists at a deeper level. Certain subjects, especially the nature of language, cannot be grasped in the usual philosophical ways. It is more than a question of the translation of experience in one language to another. Heidegger wants to discuss that from which all languages spring, if there is such a nature. There is a danger that such a discussion might be limited by the language of the discussion, in this case German. It might equally be limited by other limitations of Japanese. Discussing language in German, it is hard to avoid the Western metaphysical concepts that are part of the language even though they might not be adequate to the nature of language.

More specifically, Heidegger's characters agree that defining is a way of pursuing what is sought that can damage it for thought. Defining something fixes it as an object of study which may not correspond to its nature.[7] The danger is illustrated by the language used by the characters. They talk about defining as "grasping."[8] There is an implied violence to these ways of approaching that which one seeks to understand.

The language of questioning brings dangers to the investigation.

HESITATION

The two characters respond to this danger inherent in philosophical language and method with a number of interesting gestures. The most obvious reaction is a hesitation on the part of both characters to answer the questions posed. Both hold back their thoughts for fear that their answers be grasped as definitions. This gives the dialogue its tentative and teasing character. Heidegger asks, "What does the Japanese world understand by language?"[9] The Japanese "closes his eyes, lowers his head, and sinks into a long reflection."[10] Four pages later he can "hardly withhold" the word. Needless to say, this throws Heidegger into "a state of great agitation," which he deals with by exchanging roles, and then answering at great length an earlier, postponed question about hermeneutics. It isn't until page 45, near the end of the dialogue, that the Japanese responds to Heidegger's question, "after further hesitation."[11]

Not surprisingly Heidegger's characters explicitly discuss their hesitation: "We understand only too well that a thinker would prefer to hold back the word that is to be said, not in order to keep it for himself, but to bear it toward his encounter with what is to be thought."[12] Hesitation is the thinker's tactic; it leaves him/her time to reflect before speaking. The Inquirer goes on to say, "It (hesitation) is done truly when slowness rests on shy reverence."[13] The hesitation takes on a sacred character when one respects what one thinks and discusses. Given the respect for the truth this hesitation is understandable; both characters hold back, preparing the other, in order that their thoughts be taken in the right way.[14]

The hesitations give the dialogue its gentle wandering character. The dialogue can be described as a set of related themes starting with a question, and winding their way through each other to the end. Each theme surfaces a number of times throughout the dialogue, transformed each time by the intervening discussion. Each surfacing reminds us of the question and hints at answers. The hesitant character might not satisfy the contemporary philosopher expecting to find answers, but it is thought-provoking.

With hesitations dialogue wanders closer to the sought.

HINTS

Given the inadequacy of definition to thinking about language, the Inquirer proposes hints as an alternative.[15] Question and hint replace the definition as the way of this informal inquiry.[16] The key to understanding the hint is that its rhetorical purpose is not to answer a question, and thereby end discussion, but it is intended to promote thought and dialogue. A hint, if listened to, can change the question one had in mind, refining it or replacing it with a more appropriate one, hence the movement of questions.

Let us remind ourselves how a simple hint works, like the hints one gives a child who wants to know where a gift is hidden. The first thing to note is that a hint surfaces in response to a question or some desire to know. We don't provide hints when a child is uninterested in the question (or answer). Second, a hint is only heard when the person who wants to know stops to listen. The recipient of a hint has to open up to it for it to work. Third, the hint doesn't touch the target or answer the question. It points in the direction of the sought like a gesture. The gestures of the actor in the *No*-play are one of the images Heidegger leaves us with of how the hint works.[17] Fourth, a hint is generally designed to encourage the recipient to think along productive lines. A hint recognizes that the recipient may be lost or perplexed and encourages thought in a direction likely to bear fruit. A hint is not an answer that ends investigation. The recipient must still make his way once beckoned. Finally, a hint comes not from the inquirer, but from the sought, which is where this analogy breaks down. In Heidegger's view the hint comes from the sought, not some third party like the parent in this analogy. The philosophical hint is the way in which that which is sought reveals itself to the thinker so that the thinker can approach. It comes from the sought and beckons back.

In the dialogue we are given examples of hints. The phrase "house of Being" is a hint toward language which Heidegger feels became a "catchword."[18] It beckons us to think about language in the context of Being, and what it means to be at Home. It reminds us of the phrase "house of God." We are warned, however, that we should not build hints into a "guiding concept in which we then bundle up everything."[19] That is a danger we will risk for a moment.

What is striking about the language of hints, gestures, and bearing which Heidegger introduces to supersede names, definitions, and concepts, is that this language reverses the movement of understanding. Definition is a way of reaching out and grasping something. It is a willful act of the thinker to grasp the unknown. Unfortunately in reaching out to grasp, the thinker projects himself onto the target. By contrast, hints come from the sought toward the thinker who waits. The movement of understanding is reversed. The hints move toward the questioner, beckoning them in the direction of fruitful thought. The thinker is guided by that which he seeks to understand, not the other way around.

The discussion of hints as alternatives to definitions is a hint to the reader as to how to read the dialogue. Heidegger does not want his work read like an encyclopedia, full of "information in the form of theorems and cue words."[20] He wants us to enter into dialogue with him by bringing questions and listening to the appropriate hints—a dialogue through which the voice of the nature of language might be heard prompting us to think about what really matters.

Hints come from that which is questioned, beckoning us back to thought.

DEFINITION OF DIALOGUE

In the reversal of roles between the inquirer and that which is sought lies a hint that speaks to our question of definition:

> J: Thus we have indeed stayed on the path of the dialogue.
> I: Probably only because we, without quite knowing it, were obedient to what alone, according to your words, allows a dialogue to succeed.
> J: It is that undefined defining something . . .
> I: . . . which we leave in unimpaired possession of the voice of its promptings.
> J: At the risk that this voice, in our case, is silence itself.
> I: What are you thinking of now?
> J: Of the Same as you have in mind, of the nature of language.
> I: That is what is defining our dialogue. But even so we must not touch it. . . .

> J: For if it is necessary to leave the defining something in full possession of its voice, this does in no way mean that our thinking should not pursue the nature of language. Only the manner in which the attempt is made is decisive.[21]

Instead of the characters defining language, their dialogue is described as being defined by the nature of language. Heidegger's dialogue is an approach in which thinkers can let their discourse be defined by the sought rather than their defining it. There is a release of control on the part of characters that allows the voice of the sought to be heard.[22]

Heidegger doesn't tell us whether the release of his characters is paralleled by a release by the author. We would have to go outside the dialogue for definitive evidence, which would run counter to the spirit of this search. However, it would be difficult for Heidegger, as author, to maintain control of the subject when his characters agree that there is little difference between the written and spoken dialogue.[23] Heidegger, I suspect, felt the author should release control to the hints from the sought when writing dialogue just as his characters do when in dialogue. The release of the control by the author would include release of control over his characters so that they can speak "in character." For the moment let us take this as a hint that the release applies equally to the author of a dialogue.

The humanist, fascinated with the possibility of genius, will argue that it is the mastery of the author that gives the impression of absence of control, but does that match the hints we have from the authors themselves? Why not believe Heidegger when he talks about releasing control to the voice of language? The image of the author Heidegger presents is of the rhapsode, which he inherits from Plato's *Ion*. The rhapsode bears the "tidings of the poets' word,"[24] who in turn are the "interpreters of the gods."[25] Inspiration, or in this context, definition, flows from the gods through the poets to the interpreters. The author is a messenger for the defining power of the sought. What greater mastery is there than the ability to let another voice be heard through yours?

That which one seeks to understand defines dialogue in more than one way. First, it defines the scope of what is understood in the dialogue. The hints of the sought do not pinpoint answers but beckon us in one direction, not another. They narrow the scope of what is thought about. Second, the defining power of the sought promises that a work is a dialogue, not a conversation. Conversation is animated by the speakers, dialogue by that which the speakers wish to understand.

This hint is not a definition of dialogue in the traditional sense. The hint reverses the definition. The dialogue is not defined by its formal character, but by the authority animating it. It is a genre defined not by us the makers of dialogues, but by that spoken about in dialogue. The paradox is that, given the gripping character of definition, only when we are not defining dialogue can dialogue be defined (by that which should animate it). Nor is this definition a static thing; where there is dialogue there is defining constantly coming. The definition does not freeze dialogue but animates it. The defining power of the sought is the response to the movement of questions by the Inquirer.

Heidegger challenges us to abandon our search for a traditional definition and to think about what is important. The hints beckon us away from our initial concerns toward thinking and the nature of language. We need to be sensitive to the limitations of definition and find ways to let the sought speak through and do the defining.

When there is a release of control, the voice of the sought can be heard, defining dialogue.

DIALOGUE IN HISTORY

Abandoning a formal definition of dialogue means that we cannot easily say what is a dialogue or not. We cannot measure surface characteristics like the number of speakers or absence of plot. The Japanese interlocutor understandably asks whether "Plato's *Dialogues* would not be dialogues."[26] He is asking if they are dialogues in this ineffable sense, not the formal sense of being representations of conversations with two or more characters. If we redefine dialogue in this ineffable way, then what has been called dialogue in the traditional sense as belonging to a genre of writing may no longer be called so. Plato's dialogues, the paradigmatic philosophical dialogues, might have to be reevaluated. Heidegger doesn't pass judgment on Plato's work, but he does suggest that we are each in dialogue with those before and those who will follow.[27] It is typical of Heidegger to turn a concern about the interpretation of canonical works on its head and suggest that what is important is not whether Plato's dialogues are really dialogues, but whether we can enter into dialogue with Plato. If we apply Heidegger's definition of dialogue to such a conversation with Plato, the conversation would be redefined as dialogue by a voice other than ours or Plato's. In the dialogue with Plato would be heard the voice of that which we seek to think about, responding to questions we bring to Plato.

Heidegger is at pains to distinguish the dialogue with thinkers, past and present, and "mere busywork."[28] He wants to distinguish the "historical nature of every thinking" from "those enterprises which, in the manner of historiography, report things from the past about the thinkers and what they have thought."[29] There is a clear challenge in Heidegger to concentrate on what is important and avoid the tempting busywork.[30] What he means by the historical nature of thinking is beyond this study, but we are interested in some of the histories that run through the dialogue and the ways in which dialogue gathers histories.

First, the dialogue shows Heidegger in dialogue with a particular Japanese professor. I have noted how the foreignness of the Japanese character is important, but we should also note that Heidegger places this dialogue in the context of a larger one with a series of Japanese thinkers. These thinkers come from a different intellectual history. Our attention is drawn to the fact that the dialogue is between two markedly different traditions (histories). The dialogue is a story of the gathering together of these different histories. The difference between the histories is, on the one hand, a source of danger, and on the other hand, the source of the success of the dialogue.[31] The difference allows the two to escape their parochial problems, problems inherent in their respective traditions and not relevant to what is sought. Heidegger is trying to escape the tyranny of metaphysical thinking while the Japanese is trying to escape the fascination with Western thought that delegitimized his native thought. For each the otherness of the other is the lever with which to move beyond their intellectual history. The fact that the dialogue is successful is an answer to the question of whether different languages, like German and Japanese, have the same nature. The success of the dialogue is due to the other voice that comes through, the voice of the nature of language.

The second history worth noting is the intellectual autobiography that

Heidegger presents around the answer to the question about his use of "interpretation." Running through the dialogue is the story of the movement of Heidegger's thought on the nature of language up to the moment of the dialogue. The story begins with Heidegger's philosophical beginnings. The "quest of language and of Being" defined Heidegger's path, though discussion of the issues stayed in the background because of their importance. Heidegger admits that when he did "venture forth" in *Being and Time*, it was too early. On language he remained silent until 1934, when he gave a course on *Logic* that was really about *Logos*. As he describes it, he was then silent on the issue for another ten years. The story leads up to the dialogue itself. It is in this dialogue that he finds his voice, or that of the nature of language. The dialogue is a story that gathers within itself other stories, especially that of the way of Heidegger's thought on language.[32]

Third, there is the dialogue with past thinkers in the Western tradition like Plato. It is interesting how the dialogue form allows Heidegger to deal with such thinkers in a less formal fashion that keeps us focused on the sought rather than distracting us with historiographic completeness. Heidegger takes advantage of the fact that in conversation one can make passing references without there being the expectation of scholarly thoroughness. This does not mean the work is sloppy; it has a scholarly poetry. The references are gestures, like those of the *No*-play, which, with minimal movement, allow the other to appear and contribute to the dialogue. These gestures let the other shine through instead of freezing them with a critical comment. The reference to Plato's *Ion* is a good example, as the reference is an example of what it is a reference to. In the *Ion* Socrates presents us with an image of poetic inspiration as a magnetic power transmitted from the gods to the poets and then to the rhapsodes. That inspired image is itself transmitted from the poet Plato to the interpreter Heidegger through to us.

Heidegger's approach to the past and future history of thought is more than a de-emphasis of scholarship. Heidegger's vision of our relationship to this history is dialogical. As he describes it, we should not report about the past but prepare conversations with it. To paraphrase Heidegger, we stave off the danger of our work's degenerating into mere busywork as long as "we ourselves make an effort to think in dialogue."[33]

The thinking that wishes to listen to the sought must understand itself and that involves a dialogue with one's personal intellectual history, one's intellectual tradition, and with the other. The three types of history we have briefly described here are not gratuitous to that which is sought or to the dialogue. To hear the defining voice of language Heidegger needs to move through his history, and his tradition. An encounter with a foreign tradition provides the occasion. The dialogue at hand gathers these movements, which are themselves dialogues and brings them to the encounter with the reader who can enter into a dialogue with the text as history. Dialogue is recursive. There are dialogues within dialogues and so on.

Heidegger's dialogue gathers and carries within it reasons for its nature in the form of a story. The story of Heidegger's disenchantment with metaphysical concepts and scientific dissertation leads to the choice of the dialogue genre. The dialogue has a special relationship to its history, one of gathering and not just responding. The dialogue is not just a frozen picture of Heidegger's thought at a given time; it gathers his movement of questioning up to that point. Heidegger turns to dialogue to show the movement up to a decisive moment in his path of thinking about language and to point beyond.

Dialogue gathers its history so as to move beyond.

SAYING A DIALOGUE

So far we have concentrated on hints having to do with the dialogue form. This ignored Heidegger's hint that accompanies the reversal of definition; true dialogue is animated not by any subject of inquiry, but by the nature of language itself:

> Wherever the nature of language were to speak (say) to man as Saying, *it*, Saying, would bring about real dialogue.[34]

Heidegger is arguing that there is only real dialogue when the nature of language as Saying speaks to us. It seems peculiar to confine dialogue to one subject matter, ignoring all the dialogues, including Plato's, that are about other subjects. Either Heidegger had a very narrow view of what could animate a dialogue, and therefore, what was a dialogue, or he did not consider the nature of language to be a subject of inquiry like any other. Closer examination of Heidegger's thought on the nature of language is called for, though we can hardly match the artistry of an entire dialogue dedicated to this matter.

The word Heidegger proposes as the best hint as to the nature of language is *Saga*, translated "Saying" in the sense of "there is an ancient Saying that goes. . . ." A *Saga* is a story or legend that, while it may not be factually true, contains a deeper truth. The events in a *Saga* need not have happened—it is a speaking to questions that cannot be answered. It prompts thought on the undefinable. As with our word "Saying" there is also the suggestion that it is oral at its origin, although Heidegger deemphasizes the distinction between the oral and written dialogue.[35]

For our purposes a Saying is, first, not a neutral medium for any content. Inherent in the idea of a Saying is the suggestion that it contains a particular type of content and that this content is a truth (and not something false or trivial). Second, a Saying is a voice from the past with no definite author. Nobody owns Sayings. The anonymity of Sayings could be due to their antiquity, but I suspect Heidegger feels the anonymity is due to their coming from a source other than a particular person. Third, a Saying is an activity. The word "Saying" has the same ambiguity as the word "dialogue"; it can refer to the activity or the transcript of the activity. For Heidegger it is important that a Saying exists by virtue of the saying of such a Saying.

How can Saying understood in this threefold way be the nature of language? First, we should understand "nature" in its etymological sense of "birth." The nature of language is its source, not in the anthropological sense of the cause of humanoid speech, but in the sense of that which animates language. Heidegger is suggesting that language is animated by such Saying which comes from beyond our will.

A second suggestion also resonates through the dialogue. Without using religious terminology, Heidegger treats the nature of language with a reverence and awe that point to religious interpretations. While Heidegger avoids religious conclusions, his language and trajectory point to mystical interpretations. The hint for language, "house of Being," for example, suggests the phrase for a church, "house of God." The suggestion is that the source of language is a sacred space in which discourse takes place. When we are attuned to the silence of the space our discourse can bear the message of the gods.

What is important to this inquiry is that dialogue is not animated by any subject of inquiry, but by the source of language, Saying. Real dialogue, as opposed to idle gossip, need not have happened and yet it is an activity. It bears a truth to us from the nature of language.

Dialogue is animated by the saying of language.

FORM AND CONTENT

This in turn shows us the danger of relying on the traditional form/content distinction. Heidegger is hinting that the dialogue form has a special relationship with what would traditionally be called a particular content—the nature of language. As Heidegger shifts his approach to the nature of language such that it is no longer a content in the definable sense, he also shifts his view of the independence of form and content. The interdependence is held in the idea of voice. A voice has both a form and a content of its own. There can be more than one voice in a dialogue. A dialogue could be said to have many forms and contents. With the author's release of control there is a polyphony of voices, through which the voice of language can be heard, as Saying. When we return to the definition of dialogue we will look at a definition that avoids the distinction of form and content. Nonetheless, there will be times when it is convenient to use the distinction.

This hint as to the nature of dialogue also calls into question our understanding of the speakers. Traditionally dialogue is recognized by the presence of more than one speaker. If dialogue is that which is defined by the undefinable, does it matter if there is more than one speaker? This is the problem referred to above of whether works identified as dialogue on formal grounds are really dialogical. Indeed in Heidegger's dialogue the speech of one character often merges with that of the other. For example, in one place the Japanese interlocutor starts speaking, "It is that undefined defining something . . . ," and the thought is completed by the Inquirer, ". . . which we leave in unimpaired possession of the voice of its promptings."[36] As one reads the dialogue one frequently loses track of the distinction between characters as their thought runs in parallel. This communion creates a quickening to the reading. One doesn't have to track the differences as the characters merge into one voice.

This in turn has implications for our understanding of where the written dialogue fits in any scheme of literature. If dialogue has no form of its own, it can hardly be called a genre of literature. Dialogue has traditionally been placed among philosophical genres, or with comedy. For Heidegger dialogue is not a genre of writing; in fact it is closest to the oral *Saying*. It is inspired by poetry. Such dialogue would not necessarily have characters, but be distinguished from scholarly philosophy by virtue of the other logos that is heard through it.

Dialogue escapes the distinction of form and content;
through it speak voices.

THE LANGUAGE OF DIALOGUE

The last set of hints we will look at lie in how Heidegger uses language and the story behind this use.

One of the things that stands out in Heidegger's use of language is that it is relatively free of jargon, with the exception of a few words which are amply explained. That does not mean that Heidegger is limited by everyday language. He chooses words as a poet would, using the ones that will resonate, not the ones tied to the metaphysical tradition.[37] In the dialogue we see Heidegger moving toward words like "Saying," "hint," "bearing," and away from words from the metaphysical tradition like "language," "definition," and "Being." For example, in the beginning they talk about "interpretation," a technical term inherited from biblical scholarship. By the end of the dialogue they are talking about the "messenger's course." The metaphysical jargon that was unavoidable in the beginning gets shed as they move through hints.

To a degree this movement back to "poetic" words is called for by the project he has embarked on. Given the danger that the metaphysical tradition might not be adequate to discuss the nature of language, he has to release the terminology of that tradition and embrace a language that will not have the congealing character of terminology. He borrows such an inspiring language from the poets.

One unusual feature is the introduction of a few choice Japanese words—words that are entirely outside the metaphysical tradition. Though only a few are introduced they are amply discussed and play a fundamental role in breaking the grasp of metaphysical concepts. The Japanese contribution *Koto-ba*, as a word for language, is as important to the dialogue as Heidegger's Saying. The foreignness of the word is important. The word cannot be molded as easily into terminology as Saying could be.

Another facet of Heidegger's use of language is the imagery running through the dialogue. Heidegger replaces arguments with philosophical imagery. I have commented on the image of the rhapsode as bearer of the message of the gods. This image of the philosopher as messenger closes the dialogue. This image is not an argument about what it is to be a philosopher; it is a thought-provoking hint. I have also mentioned the violence of grasping, and the image of the gesture of the mountain, an image of an image-maker. Then there is the metaphor of movement, return and gathering. Running through the dialogue there are references to the path of thought, as if thinking were comparable to walking down a country path in the company of history.[38] The dialogue itself reads like a quickening river of questions and hints. It can be considered an image of authentic philosophical activity. The images of philosophy and philosophical work that Heidegger introduces would be interesting to follow through his later work, but that is beyond the scope of the present movement of questions. It is enough to note the importance of imagery in the dialogue.

The inevitability of the shift in language and use of imagery is paralleled on a larger scale by the inevitability of the dialogue form (if we can use the word "form" in this case). It is not enough to avoid the metaphysical terminology. Heidegger needs a form that discourages traditional ways of reading. The dialogue frustrates the reader who is looking for Heidegger's answer to the problem of language. All that can be found are hints of uncertain authority which, if one comes bearing questions, can direct thought. For this reason all we have done here is to use the dialogue as a foil for questions, listening for preliminary hints that will be pursued in the chapters to come.

ETYMOLOGY OF DIALOGUE

A final way in which Heidegger played with language will serve as a conclusion to this chapter. We will take a hint from Heidegger's playful derivation of "hermeneutics" and listen to the etymology of "dialogue."

When asked to explain "hermeneutics," the Inquirer suggests looking at the etymological derivation. He traces the word back to the ancient Greek, *hermeneuein*, and from there to the name of the divine messenger, *Hermes*. He ends up suggesting hermeneutics "is that exposition which brings tidings because it can listen to a message."[39] He calls his philosophical derivation "playful thinking that is more compelling than the rigor of science."[40] The Inquirer is not interested in the philologically correct derivation but in the playful one that provides thought-provoking hints.

This tactic of playful derivation is inherited from Plato.[41] In his playful interpretation by derivation the Inquirer refers back to a Socratic play on the etymology of "hermeneutics" in the *Ion*. Heidegger places his character in a tradition of playful philosophical derivation. Such derivation is an alternative to definition that attempts to listen to the Saying in the history of a word. Derivation is the counterpart to the poetic use of words such that their original senses resonate. In Heideggerian fashion we will conclude with a playful derivation of "dialogue."

Dialogue comes from the Greek noun *dialogos*, meaning conversation.

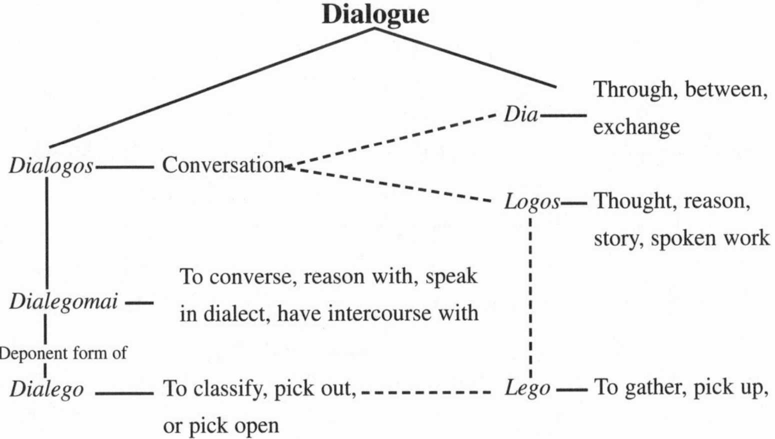

Dialogos can be broken into two parts, *dia* and *logos*. *Dia* means "through," "by means of," or "between," as in an exchange *between* people. *Logos* can be translated as "speech," "discourse," "story," or "thought." A *logos* is either the spoken word that expresses thought or the thought itself.[42] Combining the two parts, one can see how *dialogos* now means "the exchange of speech or thought."

If we play with the parts of the word we can generate some alternative derivations. The Greek word *logos*, is derived from the verb *lego*, which meant to arrange, gather, count, recount, and (eventually) any spoken communication. Likewise *dialogos* is derived from the deponent form (*dialegomai*) of the verb *dialego*. The deponent form *dialegomai* meant to converse, to reason with, to argue, to use a dialect or language, or to have intercourse. The verb *dialego* meant to pick out, classify, or to pick open a hole (escape).

Socrates is reported by Xenophon to have played with the connection between these senses, in particular *dialego* (having to do with classification) and *dialegomai* (having to do with conversation). Xenophon writes, "The very word 'discussion,' according to him (Socrates), owes its name to the practice of meeting together for common deliberation, *sorting, discussing* things after their kind: and therefore one should be ready and prepared for this and be zealous for it."[43] The italicized words are the translator's. He uses "*sorting, discussing*" where, in the Greek, there is only one word, *dialegontas*, a form of *dialego*.

From these etymological hints we can think of dialogue as a way of gathering and classifying through conversation. In Heidegger's dialogue we find a gathering of Heidegger's thought on the nature of language. We can also think of dialogue as a means of escape from the dangers of traditional ways of philosophical discourse. The history that Heidegger presents is one of an escape from the metaphysical structures built into German, back to a closer understanding of language. Dialogue is the path of escape or return. There is also a hint of intercourse in the etymology. While Heidegger's work does not play with the sexual dimensions of dialogue, other dialogue writers certainly do. Further, we can see a connection between the suggestion that dialogue is a use of language and the title of Heidegger's dialogue, "A Dialogue on Language; Between a Japanese and an Inquirer."[44]

We can also play with the senses of *dia*. Heidegger would be sympathetic with the idea of dialogue as that *through* which *logos* comes. Instead of understanding dialogue as an activity carried out *through* the spoken word, we can reverse the direction and suggest dialogue is that *through* which the Word flows. We do not reach out to grasp through dialogue; through dialogue we hear the voice of the nature of language. When it speaks through our conversation we have dialogue. This is the etymological derivation of dialogue that Peter Senge taught former U.S. vice president Al Gore.[45]

One of the most difficult suggestions of the derivation is the ambiguity in the *logos* of *dialogos*. *Logos*, as was mentioned above, can refer to either the thought or the audible expression of the thought. This ambiguity in *logos* is picked up by Plato. He has Socrates in the *Theaetetus* comment that thinking is an internal dialogue. "When the mind is thinking, it is simply talking (dialoguing) to itself, asking questions and answering them, and saying yes or no."[46] The word used is *dialegesthai*. Socrates frequently presents his thoughts as conversations, for example in the *Crito* when Socrates presents a conversation between himself and the laws of Athens. The ambiguity of *logos* may have suggested the analogy between thought and conversation. This analogy may have then led to the choice of the written dialogue as the obvious form in which to put down one's thought. Socrates' presenting his thoughts as a conversation with the Athenian laws leads to Plato's recording his thoughts in the form of a Socratic conversation, which led to the ambiguity today between dialogue as an activity and as a written form.

What is clear is that the Greeks did not speak of dialogue except as audible conversation. They did not even have a word for the written dialogue. Aristotle writes in the *Poetics*:

> There is further an art which imitates by language alone, without harmony, in prose or in verse, and if in verse, either in some one or in a plurality of metres. This form of imitation is to this day without a name. We have no common name for a mime of Sophron or Xenarchus and a Socratic Conversation; and we should still be without one if the imitation in the two instances were in trimeters or elegiacs or some other kind of verse.[47]

That Aristotle doesn't have a name for the Socratic Conversation is worth noting for two reasons. First, he does not use "dialogue" because that refers to oral conversation, not the written art. Dialogue as a form of written work is a later use of the word. Aristotle may see some similarity among works we would now call dialogues, but he is unwilling to formalize the genre. By the time of Lucian we find the word being used about an accepted form of discourse. Once there was a body of works, Lucian of Samostata could make dialogue a character.

Second, it is interesting that Aristotle refers to dialogues as Socratic conversations. Today we are more likely to call them Platonic dialogues or the "dialogues of Xenophon."[48] We emphasize the author not the spirit represented. From Aristotle's perspective these works were similar by virtue of the voice that speaks through them, that of Socrates the philosopher. This spirit was for Aristotle and his contemporaries a philosophical hero about whom they recounted stories for inspiration and possibly for legitimacy as philosophers.[49] The identification of dialogues with Socrates suggests we have to look back at Socrates and dialogue, which is the subject of the next chapter.

The word "dialogue" began by meaning simply conversation, was applied to thought, and then to the written representation. In modern times it has been applied to just about any positive exchange. The medium of dialogue is no longer the spoken (and heard) word, nor is the exchange exclusively between individual people. The boundaries of what can be called a dialogue have expanded to include any welcome intercourse. Buber talks about dialogue with trees, animals, and god. He believes that we are defined by the *I-Thou* dialogue, not the other way around. Heidegger's redefinition of dialogue likewise directs us to that which comes through dialogue as the defining. Heidegger and Buber have inverted the definition of dialogue in a way that has trickled through to common usage now, making it difficult to ask just what dialogue is. That which makes a dialogue a dialogue cannot be described, or one would not enter into dialogue; it is either something that comes through or it is dialogue itself that is defining us (such that we could define at all).

This elusive sense of dialogue should not prevent us from the more mundane task of asking about other senses of dialogue. In this chapter we have dealt with the ineffable dialogue and seen how it cannot, by definition, help us define dialogue; next it is time to look closely at the oral and written dialogue. The importance of the ineffable should warn us not to expect a definition that will grasp all aspects of dialogue, though I hope the definition proposed at the end of this book will not exclude reflection on the ineffable. In fact, I believe one can define dialogue in a way that helps us approach that which cannot be said.

To return to Heidegger's dialogue, we can imagine one answer to the question: Why have so many turned recently to dialogue? For Heidegger, dialogue is suited to the thinking that releases control to the nature of language so that its voice can be heard. One chooses dialogue when one wants to avoid the traditional lines of authority, by which I mean the traditional relationship between the author who owns what is read and the reader who does not. In dialogue that is confused by characters. That is the release of control. One chooses dialogue when one is concerned with the voices of Philosophy, especially the voice of that which is sought. In a dialogue one gathers these voices so as to allow through another voice. This is the gathering of histories wherein something other can be heard. To use the image inherited through Plato's *Ion*, in dialogue is gathered and transmitted the inspiration of the gods. Choosing dialogue is choosing to be a messenger instead of an authority. Perhaps we turn to dialogue and call for it because we hope to let something meaningful through that cannot be defined in a way that it could be sought through a method or technology.

NOTES

1. Martin Heidegger, "A Dialogue on Language; Between a Japanese and an Inquirer," in *On the Way to Language*, trans. Peter D. Hertz (New York: Harper & Row, 1982), p. 7.

2. There is a circularity to this approach, one which cannot be avoided when trying to interpret any work according to one's interpretation of its interpretative suggestion. In my defense, I believe this approach will be justified later when we examine the relationship between author and reader/interpreter of dialogue.

3. In an appendix to the collection of essays in which the dialogue appeared, Heidegger names the Japanese interlocutor: "The heretofore unpublished text originated in 1953/54, on the occasion of a visit by Professor Tezuka

of the Imperial University, Tokyo." *On the Way to Language*, p. 199. While Heidegger names the Japanese in this appendix, he does not in the dialogue, and the appendix is kept distinct from the dialogue. I believe Heidegger wants the reader to think of the Japanese as any intelligent, German-speaking, Japanese thinker. I would go further and say that what is important for Heidegger, in a dialogue on language, is the foreignness of the character, that he is from an East-Asian linguistic-philosophical background which shares little with German.

4. Heidegger, "A Dialogue on Language," p. 50.

5. Ibid.

6. Ibid., p. 4.

7. Right at the beginning the Japanese notes that Western aesthetics provided Japanese philosophers like Count Kuki with the concepts to grasp what concerned them. The Japanese language didn't have such concepts, which is why people like Kuki travelled to Germany to study. Western concepts met a lack in Japanese of "the delimiting power to represent objects related in an unequivocal order above and below each other." Heidegger, "A Dialogue on Language," p. 2. The Inquirer, needless to say, asks if this is a "deficiency." The suggestion is that the delimiting power of Western concepts is a limitation when discussing the nature of language. It is something peculiar to Western languages, not essentially part of the nature of language. The problem in a discussion in German is how to avoid falling into the metaphysical language of definitions and concepts.

8. Hints, on the other hand, are an alternative designed to be sensitive to the sought (from which they come). The Japanese talks about how Heidegger's hint for language, *house of Being*, "touches upon the nature of language without doing it injury." "A Dialogue on Language," p. 22. Compare this to page 45 where Heidegger says, "European science and its philosophy try to grasp the nature of language only by way of concepts." The tactile imagery is not unique to this dialogue. In "The Nature of Language" (in *On the Way to Language*, p. 60) Heidegger "converses" in an unscientific fashion with a poem by Stephan George entitled "The Word." In this poem we find naming, finding, and grasping are associated. Once the name of a wonder has been found then one can grasp it and bring it back, which would be defining it. Unfortunately this named wonder vanishes when so grasped and brought home. It is interesting that Heidegger appropriates from the poets a tactile, poetic language both to critique the metaphysical approach and then to replace the metaphysical language. He does not discuss definition by introducing further concepts, but by metaphorically associating it with violence.

9. Heidegger, "A Dialogue on Language," p. 23.

10. Ibid.

11. Ibid., p. 45.

12. Ibid., p. 26.

13. Ibid., p. 28.

14. It is tempting to draw a parallel between hesitation and Socratic ignorance. Both Heidegger, the hesitating Inquirer, and Socrates are reluctant to talk about that which they do not know or believe is too complex to be dealt with without a supporting context. Both have thought deeply on the subjects they are the most reticent on, and both recognize the need to avoid hasty opinions about these subjects. Socratic ignorance is the honest appraisal of the state of one's knowledge that is expressed by the admission of ignorance—knowing that you do not know. Heidegger's hesitation comes from the same knowledge of limitations, both his own, and that of the interlocutor with whom he might share his thoughts.

15. "They [hints] are enigmatic. They beckon to us. They beckon *away*. They beckon us *toward* that from which they unexpectedly bear themselves toward us." Heidegger, "A Dialogue on Language," p. 26. Hints are related to gestures and bearing. The image of the *No*-player conjuring up a mountain with a gesture on page 18 prepares us for hints. The irony is that the English word "hint" is derived from "hent" which meant to lay hold of, to grasp, or to seize. *Oxford English Dictionary*, s.v. "hint."

16. I am reluctant to call the hint a method, because Heidegger does not want to formalize the hint into a philosophical tactic. Heidegger instead talks repeatedly of the path or way of thought. Movement down this path is achieved through posing questions, thinking about the responding hints. At times on the path one might plod along methodically, but the way one moves is determined not by a predetermined method but by the beckoning hints of that which one seeks.

17. The image of the gesture of the actor of a *No*-play is itself a superbly crafted written gesture. We do not even see the actor gesturing up a mountain on page 18. We read about the gesture, which in turn conjures up the mountain. It is a gesture twice-removed from the signified, but it works nonetheless.

18. Heidegger, "A Dialogue on Language," p. 27.

19. Ibid., p. 25.

20. Ibid., p. 54.

21. Ibid., p. 22.

22. Release is one of the initial themes of Heidegger's other dialogue, "Conversation on a Country Path about Thinking." The dialogue starts with the three characters considering how one can understand thinking by looking away from thinking. This leads to a discussion of willing and the conclusion that, "so far as we can wean ourselves from willing, we contribute to the awakening of releasement." "Conversation on a Country Path about Thinking," in *Discourse*

on Thinking, trans. John M. Anderson and E. Hans Freund (New York: Harper Torchbooks, 1966), p. 60.

23. Heidegger, "A Dialogue on Language," p. 52.

24. Ibid., p. 29.

25. This is a quote from Plato's *Ion* (534e) lifted from Heidegger's "A Dialogue on Language," p. 29.

26. Heidegger, "A Dialogue on Language," p. 52.

27. Ibid., p. 31.

28. Ibid.

29. Ibid.

30. In Heidegger's other dialogue, "Conversation on a Country Path about Thinking," there is more of a treatment of the difference between the scholarly treatment of the past and the philosopher's. This can be seen in the names of the characters, Scientist, Scholar, and Teacher. On one level the three are representatives of three approaches to thinking. On another, the teacher, who is the closest to Heidegger, brings the other two into a dialogue on thinking where their respective inclinations have a limited place.

31. The Japanese makes a point of the value of otherness: "As far as I am able to follow what you are saying, I sense a deeply concealed kinship with our thinking, precisely because your path of thinking and its language are so wholly other." Heidegger, "A Dialogue on Language," p. 31. What is left unclear is whether Heidegger's otherness is in relation to his German contemporaries or his Japanese friends.

32. He does this for two reasons. On the one hand he wants to correct misinterpretations for which his early thought is responsible. On the other hand he is presenting the Japanese and his reader with a larger text on language by pointing out his development and works on the way that we should read. "A Dialogue on Language" is almost an annotated table of contents to a larger text made up of a selected history of works. Heidegger gathers and comments on his previous work (and that of others) providing a "hypertext" that encompasses and redefines the reading of the other works.

One could use the dialogue as the gathering point for a course on Heidegger's discussion of language, branching out to the indicated works. Or one could treat the dialogue as the story of Heidegger's thought on the nature of language, a story that concentrates on the path of his thinking. This saga leads up to "A Dialogue on Language" itself, and his reasons for choosing the form.

33. Heidegger, "A Dialogue on Language," p. 31.

34. Ibid., p. 52.

35. "[I]t would remain of minor importance whether the dialogue is before

us in writing, or whether it was spoken at some time and has now faded." Heidegger, "A Dialogue on Language," p. 52. Students of Heidegger like Derrida are less inclined to deemphasize the distinction between the oral and written. I think this passage in Heidegger's dialogue shows that Heidegger at least thought about the problem. His bias toward oral presence, if it exists, is not based on a lack of consideration of the problem.

36. Heidegger, "A Dialogue on Language," p. 22.

37. In "Conversation on a Country Path about Thinking" the scholar admits, "Of course I know that such (scholarly) terminology not only freezes thought, but at the same time also renders it ambiguous with just that ambiguity which unavoidably adheres to ordinary terminology" (p. 76).

38. This metaphor is taken further in "Conversation on a Country Path about Thinking." The course of the dialogue is metaphorically linked to the course of the characters' way on a country path. The rural metaphors in Heidegger's dialogues have not to my knowledge been adequately explored.

39. Heidegger, "A Dialogue on Language," p. 29.

40. Ibid.

41. In the *Cratylus* Plato portrays Socrates spinning out etymological derivations for a number of words, though *dialogos* is not one elaborated on.

42. Henry George Liddell and Robert Scott, *Greek-English Lexicon*, Abridged (Oxford: Clarendon Press, 1977). The lexicon suggests this connection between the thought and word.

43. Xenophon, *Memorabilia*, in *Xenophon in Seven Volumes*, trans. O. J. Todd and E. C. Marchant, vol. 4 (Cambridge, Mass.: Harvard University Press, 1968), 4.6.1.

44. The relationship between "dialogue" and "language" in the title is better seen in the German: *Aus Einem Gespräch Von Der Sprache*. *Gespräch*, the German for "conversation," is built on *Sprache*, for "speaking."

45. In the *The Fifth Discipline*, Peter Senge quotes Vice President Gore's recognition of Senge for this derivation: "Peter Senge gave us the distinction earlier today between discussion and dialogue, and in his presentation on the etymology of the word *dialogue*, he defined it as a process by which meaning comes through." *The Fifth Discipline: The Art and Practice of the Learning Organization* (New York: Doubleday, 1990), p. xiv. It is good to know that Heidegger is getting through to the former vice president.

46. Plato, *Theaetetus*, trans. F. M. Cornford, in *The Collected Dialogues of Plato*, ed. Edith Hamilton and Huntington Cairns (Princeton, N.J.: Princeton University Press, 1961), 189e–190a. This image of thinking as dialogue is left unchallenged among the images of thinking raised in the *Theaetetus*.

47. Aristotle, *Poetics*, in *The Basic Works of Aristotle*, ed. and trans. Richard McKean (New York: Random House, 1941), 1447a–b. For a discussion of this passage see W. K. C. Guthrie, *Socrates* (Cambridge: Cambridge University Press, 1971), pp. 11–12.

48. George Grote, *Plato and the Other Companions of Sokrates*, vol. 1 (London: John Murray, 1865), p. 134. Grote comments on how Plato's setting up a school provided a way for his writings to be transmitted accurately.

49. See Livio Rossetti's *Aspetti della letteratura socratica antica* (Chieti: 1977) for a thorough discussion of the explosion of written Socratic dialogues after the death of Socrates.

2 The ORALITY of DIALOGUE

> No, only the self-controlled have power to consider the things that matter most, and, sorting them out after their kind, by word and deed alike to prefer the good and reject the evil.
>
> And thus, he said, men become supremely good and happy and skilled in discussion. The very word "discussion," according to him, owes its name to the practice of meeting together for common deliberation, *sorting, discussing* things after their kind: and therefore one should be ready and prepared for this and be zealous for it; for it makes for excellence, leadership and skill in discussion.[1]

Xenophon thus ends one of his short dialogues intended to show how Socrates encouraged self-control (*sophrosyne*) as the key to good business. The Athenian gentleman who wanted to excel in affairs had first to learn self-control, which Socrates taught by example and by dialogue. Self-control in turn gave the gentleman the freedom from slavish desires that allowed him to sort things and select the best. In other words, self-control allowed the gentleman to prioritize issues.

It is notable that Socrates draws the attention of his listeners to the etymological connection between *dialego* (classify) and *dialegomai* (discuss). This etymological connection seems peculiar to us today. What does conversation have to do with classification? Why would Socrates or Xenophon deliberately draw our attention to the connection between classification and conversation held in the word "dialogue" as if it were obvious once mentioned? The answer lies in the centrality of dialogue in an oral philosophical community like the Socratic circle. When W. K. C. Guthrie discusses this passage in his work on Socrates, he notes the importance of classification to definition.[2] Classification was an important part of the Platonic strategy for defining terms. I will therefore use this anomaly to look at oral dialogue, the second sense of dialogue that this work looks at to define dialogue. This anomaly is a hint that we should try to make sense of the connection. To do so we will have to recover the character of philosophical practice in an oral environment. Once we understand the place of conversation in oral philosophical practice we can understand why this connection would make sense. To do that we have to concentrate on oral dialogue exclusively, being careful not to map aspects of written dialogue onto oral practice, something most discussions of dialogue have failed to do.[3] Rather than tackle the question of oral dialogue in all its manifestations I am going to concentrate on one oral philosophical community, the Socratic circle. The conclusions I draw from oral dialogue will then be carried forward and compared to the written dialogue to see if we can define the two as one thing.

The major problem we face when understanding an oral philosophical community, especially one that no longer exists, is the problem of evidence. How do we know about such communities? In the case of the Socratic circle we have written evidence. This evidence is, of course, problematic. Written evidence of an oral community would almost seem a contradiction. If there is contemporary written evidence the community can hardly have been entirely oral. Only with living oral communities can anthropologists collect the sort of evidence that would be entirely satisfactory. This inescapable problem of written evidence and oral communities is tied to the nature of the subject of study—orality. Until the invention of information technologies like the tape recorder we had no other way of gathering (and publishing) evidence of oral cultures. As a result the only oral cultures for which we have evidence (a demand that only makes sense to literate cultures) are those that are still living, or those which existed at the threshold of literacy like the Socratic circle. Our knowledge of oral cultures that are not still alive is perforce limited to those that could be written about.

There is a second problem with evidence that is specific to this project. The bulk of our evidence is written dialogues and plays, namely those of Aristophanes, Plato, and Xenophon. It would seem circular to look at an oral community through written dialogues in order to understand how oral dialogue is different from written dialogue. To escape this circularity I could have focused on oral philosophical cultures like those still alive in India, or communities for which there is evidence other than dialogues, like the circle of *philosophes* in eighteenth-century Paris. There is, however, a virtue to concentrating on the Socratic circle. We have to deal with the way that Socratic oral practice, as represented in Plato's and Xenophon's dialogues, has influenced oral practice in philosophy ever since, something that other oral communities have not done to the same degree. Whatever the real Socratics did, the perception that they dialogued in the fashion recorded has had an impact on the discipline: witness the Renaissance attempts to recreate the Academy and the practice of "symposiums" today. Whatever approach we take, we have to deal with the effect that written dialogues about the Socratic circle have had as records of oral practice. For this reason, I will reconstruct the practice of oral dialogue in the Socratic circle that a reader would notice who took these dialogues as reasonable windows on oral practice.

Recognizing the circularity, however virtuous, of this approach, I will digress to discuss orality in general, drawing heavily on Walter Ong's book *Orality and Literacy*. This digression is designed to reorient the subsequent discussion to those facets of the written dialogues that truly represent oral practice. I will borrow from Ong a scheme for understanding oral communities and apply it to the interpretation of written records. This will help us avoid the problem of reading written dialogue for evidence of the difference between oral and written dialogue. The scheme borrowed from Ong helps us escape the interpretative circle.

ORAL PHILOSOPHICAL CULTURE

We take literacy for granted when trying to understand orality.[4] To understand an oral philosophical culture we cannot simply take our literate philosophical culture, subtract books, and call oral what is left; we need to ask how philosophy was done without books to read, or paper to write out one's meditations. We need to ask what philosophy was like before it became conscious of its textual tradition. This involves a paradigm shift. Given the possibility that our way of thinking is based on literacy, it may be a shift of which we are not entirely capable.[5]

There are two issues that will drive this characterization of orality. The first is the self-perpetuation of oral communities (how an oral culture perpetuates itself without permanent records). For Ong, much of the intellectual effort of an oral culture is shaped by the need to maintain its knowledge. Not only is the practice of oral philosophy different, but the content of oral work is adapted to the exigencies of oral perpetuation. Asking how an oral culture can perpetuate itself without writing is one way to see the implications of the absence of literacy. The second issue is that of presence; how does the physical (and temporal) presence of the other that is characteristic of orality, affect the thought and words of oral communities? To understand orality, we need to ask about the spatial and temporal relationships between people. Who is present and how are they present? How does talking to someone, face to face and at the same time, affect the character of the exchange?[6] These two issues can help us understand our own culture in a way that allows us to shift to understanding a profoundly different one.

Research and Teaching

Knowledge is perpetuated today by means of published research and teaching. A distinction between research and teaching, which is fundamental to the way we organize our philosophical institutions, would have been alien to oral communities like the Socratic circle because the distinction is based on the availability of the technology of writing. Our community has expanded beyond the point where we can meet (be present to each other) in oral dialogue as the Socratics did; thus we depend on writing to communicate new ideas through time and space. It is not surprising that research is measured by publication; original thought that is not published has hardly any chance of surviving. Oral means of communication, on the other hand, are reserved for teaching where the demand for accuracy and communication with distant colleagues is not present.[7] This distinction between teaching and research, an organizational artifact that deserves more attention than I can give it here, would not make sense to an oral community—without writing, neither does research, measured in publication, make sense to an oral community. Without writing the distinction ceases to be useful for classifying philosophical activity. To do philosophy, for Socrates, meant to do it with others, in dialogue.[8]

We can now begin to understand the relationship between classification and dialogue that Xenophon reports. Classification, which would tend to be called a research skill today, and conversational ability, which is of use primarily in teaching, appear unrelated when research is presented mostly in writing. More importantly, today we tend to devise and represent classifications graphically with charts and tables that can be duplicated and circulated, not in dialogue.[9] By contrast, in dialogues like the *Statesman* and the *Sophist* we see how the two are connected in an oral community. The Eleatic Stranger, in both dialogues, presents his classifications in conversation. Socrates asks the Stranger if he would prefer to give a long speech or "to use the method of asking questions, as Parmenides himself did on one occasion in developing some magnificent arguments in my presence."[10] The Stranger remarks that it is easier to present through questions if the interlocutor is "tractable and gives no trouble."[11] The Stranger is offered Theaetetus as a tractable young man with whom to spin out his definition/classification.

The *Sophist* and the *Statesman* today seem dry and artless compared to other Platonic dialogues. It is assumed that Plato forced classifications into the garment of dialogue because he could not imagine writing in some other fashion. If he were writing today he might have presented the classification with a graphic or in point form. This ignores the possibility that he represented classifications this way because that was how they were done in the Socratic circle. Such classification makes for dull reading but did it make for uninteresting listening to those interested in complex ideas? Even if the listening were not entertaining, oral communities have no choice if they want to pursue such classifications. Did the Socratics have any other way of presenting such classifications?

Oral Events

For oral cultures, words are events or actions. We tend to think of words as information that sits passively in libraries waiting to be "looked up."

The activity around information today is its research, creation, and interpretation. In an oral culture, information can't be looked up; it has to be *re*-membered and *re*-articulated. Even the maintenance of information is an activity, that of retelling or rhapsodizing.[12] The distinction between original creation of information (research) and its maintenance (teaching) becomes blurred when both creation and maintenance are tellings.

Because oral stories have to be constantly retold to be maintained they are constantly being reworked in subtle ways. It is doubtful if there exists anything like static information in an oral culture.[13] (The word "information" is of limited use in describing the knowledge of an oral culture.) There is no canonically "correct" version of an oral tale in a book against which each telling can be compared. Each telling is both creation and maintenance, or research and teaching at the same time and in the same place. Philosophy in such a culture is not a body of ideas and arguments, assigned authors, subject headings, and dates for purposes of classification, but a gathering of characters and oral events, such as trials and memorable conversations.[14]

The trial of Socrates is not an anomaly from the perspective of oral culture; oral communities gather around such epic moments and their retelling. The trial made the conversations of Socrates memorable in two ways. First, the pathos of the event made not only the trial itself memorable, but also all the conversations around Socrates. Would Socrates have been remembered if he had not been put to death for his beliefs? Second, the judgment, attended as it was by a large number of adult male Athenians, and being controversial, provided grist for conversation for years. The community, as it continued to discuss the justice of the judgment, looked to those who could retell it to make the relevant events present. The demand for the relevant conversations may have led to their being written down.[15]

Orality and Thought

Another point Ong makes is that "in an oral culture, restriction of words to sound determines not only modes of expression but also thought processes."[16] Ong connects knowing with the ability to recall information. As he puts it, "you know what you can recall."[17] In literate societies we tend to recall information visually; we make use not only of written words (which are skimmed visually) but also of diagrams, pictures, and so on.[18] We also tend to devote less time to remembering information and more to learning information-retrieval skills such as library skills. The idea is that you do not need to remember something so much as to remember where to locate it. In an oral society, everything is built around gesture and speech, both of which are time-dependent media, which vanish as they happen. The demands of continuous retelling constrain the character of what is known. Anything that can only be remembered and retold with written or graphic aides is lost.[19] Thus the character of what is known, and can be thought about, is constrained by memory. For Ong, even the activity of thinking itself, as we perform it today, cannot be sustained without memory aids.

> How, in fact, could a lengthy, analytic solution ever be assembled in the first place? An interlocutor is virtually essential: it is hard to talk to yourself for hours on end. Sustained thought in an oral culture is tied to communication.[20]

The possibility that the character of thought in an oral culture is different from ours, and that the difference can be tied to dialogue, should remind us again of the problem of classification and dialogue. The Stranger in the *Sophist*, as mentioned above, feels more comfortable developing his "magnificent arguments" by posing questions to a tractable young man. The tractability is important—Theaetetus is chosen because he will help the Stranger deliver himself of his thoughts on the nature of the Sophist. Theaetetus's role is that of a convenient womb from which the Stranger can draw his child.[21] In the dialogue named after Theaetetus Socrates suggests that thinking is a dialogue the mind holds with itself.[22] It would make sense then that a dialogue with a tractable fellow would be a way to represent the original dialogue of the mind. (Where else can one find tractable characters?) It should also be noted that in both the dialogue within and that with the tractable fellow the intended audience of the thought is not the interlocutor but those who listen to the event.

Poetic Character of Oral Thought and Communication

The study of Greek orality grew out of attempts to understand the uniqueness of the Homeric epics.[23] In contrast to the romantic idea about the "genius" of Homer, Parry and subsequent scholars suggested that "virtually every distinctive feature of Homeric poetry is due to the economy enforced on it by oral methods of composition."[24] In order to think-know-recall, oral societies have to organize information into memorable patterns, formulae, and activities. Their information is sung rhythmically using various poetic devices to reinforce memorability. Sustained oral works use rhythm, rhyme, and meter to make them easier to recall. Such poetic characteristics restrict the possibilities of what can be sung in a verse, thereby making it easier to remember the next word, line, or phrase. Even the physical performance of the work, involving as it does the entire body, is harnessed to the task of remembering. By acting out the work, the student, who is learning the performance, adds physical clues to what is sung that can later assist in the recall of the work. The performance of a sustained oral work can thus involve the complete person, to the point where the person becomes the character portrayed in order to remember better. One can imagine feeling that something was speaking through you in a successful performance.

Another facet of oral memory is the way works are woven out of memorable sayings. Sustained oral works are modular, made out of standard themes, formulaic expressions, and epithets. The rhapsode does not memorize a work verbatim, but weaves each telling out of standard units to suit the occasion and the meter. Instead of remembering original material for each occasion, the rhapsode can reuse standard material, over and over.[25] This facet of oral performance is at odds with today's emphasis in philosophy on originality, avoidance of repetition, proper quotation, and clear references. In scholarly works, at least, we expect credit to be given where material is borrowed and encourage fresh expression over the formula.

The poetic character of oral work is to a degree functional; it assists the rhapsode in retelling the tale.[26] The poetic character is tied to the memorability of the work, and hence its age. The more "poetic" a work, the more memorable it is. The more memorable a work is, the better its chance of being remembered, and the longer it lasts. Thus we end up with a correlation between poetic character and age.

In a curious way this relationship between poetic character and persistence is also reversible. Oral work, or work designed to appear oral, is often given the character of "age-old wisdom." Such work presents itself as coming from a distant past, gods, or other cultures (of even older pedigree). Part of the poetic character of oral work (or work designed to sound like oral work) is this ageless, and authorless, quality. In certain cultures, not just oral ones, this quality gives the work authority, which in turn encourages the proliferation of works that appear to be ageless and authorless. Where original creations are not valued, and ageless wisdom is, the poets and philosophers are less concerned with scholarly questions of reference, often imitating the characteristics of oral epics.

In an oral community the issue of authorship does not appear as it does in ours. Where intellectual and poetic work are presented in oral events there is no doubt as to the identity of the author/performer. There is no need in an oral event, which by definition involves the authors of the event, to stamp the event with their signature. Performers might introduce themselves; they probably will say their performance is inspired by others (especially gods), but there is no call for keeping track of authors. Instead in an oral community a performer might attribute their words to other authorities to give it credibility.

Philosophical dialogue can inherit some of this dynamic. First, dialogue can have a modular character, inheriting common units like the banquet (symposium) or the battle (of minds). Another parallel to the modularity of the dialogue is the incorporation of stock ideas and definitions. Many of the Socratic dialogues play out the implications of stock formulaic definitions of the virtues like the definitions of piety produced in the *Euthyphro*.[27] One can even see in the characteristic "yes Socrates" an oral refrain or breather. Having a tractable interlocutor who could be counted on to answer appropriately might have given a rhythm to the performance of Socrates or the Stranger.[28]

Dialogues can also have an ageless and authorless character. Heidegger was hinting at this in his redefinition of dialogue. Heidegger asks us to see how a dialogue is defined by that which is sought and hence, in some sense, authored by the sought. The sought in turn should be the ageless truths that came from the gods, inspired the poets (the oral poets like Homer), and were passed down as "sayings." Writers such as Cicero and Hume distance themselves from their dialogues, trying to give them the character of authorless wisdom.

Additive Rather than Subordinative[29]

In oral works there is a tendency not to subordinate ideas but to concatenate them. Ong gives as an example the passage in Gen. 1:1–5 which can be translated, "In the beginning God created heaven and earth. And the earth was void and empty, and darkness was upon the face of the deep."[30] Today we would avoid introductory "ands," but in an oral culture there isn't the time or opportunity to reflect on the precise relationship between the ideas and subordinate them.

This tendency to addition can be seen on a larger scale in the earlier "Socratic" dialogues of Plato. In the *Euthyphro* there are four definitions of piety given by Euthyphro. Each discussion around a definition is relatively independent; the dialogue is, in effect, made up of the addition of four smaller modules (along with an introduction and conclusion). The *Symposium* also has a modular character, though it might not be considered an "early" dialogue. This is in contrast to longer Platonic dialogues like the *Republic* where individual parts are subordinate to the larger task of proving the superiority of the just life. In the *Republic* there is a nesting of issues, where, in order to understand justice in the individual it shifts to a discussion of justice writ large in the state.[31] If you think about it, in everyday conversations such subordination is difficult to achieve; one is far more likely to try to discuss first one thing *and* then another. Even when one returns to issues, the return cannot be as controlled as the deliberate nesting an author is capable of. Unless one writes down what was said before, it is difficult to return neatly to the original theme. Likewise it is more likely that written dialogues that have an additive structure are reports of what happened than the ones with more complex structures. Not surprisingly the Platonic dialogues that have an additive structure tend to be the ones considered earlier, and probably more representative of actual Socratic practice.[32]

Redundant and 'Copious'

When reading we can always turn back a page if we lose track of the argument—not so in an oral presentation. For this reason, in oral discourse, even today, we repeat ourselves to make sure that our listeners can follow.[33]

This problem of following an argument is made worse if the argument is an accurate philosophical one. For this reason we find in oral dialogue, and to an extent in written dialogue, a tendency for repetition. The difference in presence of the author/sayer leads to a difference in content.

An example of redundancy in oral dialogue is the way Socrates always has to explain more than once the type of definition he wants at the outset. In the *Euthyphro* Socrates begins by asking:

> State what you take piety and impiety to be with reference to murder and all other cases. Is not the holy always one and the same thing in every action, and, again, is not the unholy always opposite to the holy, and like itself? And as unholiness does it not always have its one essential form, which will be found in everything that is unholy?[34]

The question already includes unnecessary (from a written perspective) redundancy, and there is more repetition to come. Euthyphro, instead of stating what he thinks piety is, answers the final question affirmatively; so Socrates has to ask again, "Then tell me. How do you define the holy and the unholy?"[35] The first answer he gets is not really a definition, so he has to ask again (6c) and again (6d) and again (6e). It could be argued that Socrates has to put the question so many times because Euthyphro doesn't understand what is wanted, but that is exactly the point; the misunderstanding is oral and is therefore represented in dialogue. In oral dialogue there is redundancy that need not be represented in a written work unless the written work is designed to reflect oral practice. If Plato simply wanted to show the misunderstanding between Socrates and Euthyphro he could have summarized the discussion: "Euthyphro at first did not understand the question. . . . [E]ventually he defined piety in the following way. . . ." Instead Plato chooses to *show* the redundancy that is part of everyday orality, where we misunderstand each other repeatedly (or redundantly).

Conservative and Traditionalist

Oral cultures have to invest so much effort in maintaining information that there is little incentive to experiment with novelty. Instead novelty is introduced in the reworking of the oral tradition that takes place in every telling. Oral cultures have to be conservative in the sense of conserving what has been learned. A culture that does not preserve its traditions has none and can lose its cultural identity. By contrast in a culture where there is writing, preservation and experimentation can coexist.

There is throughout the Socratic project a tension over the issue of preservation and experimentation. Since this is not the place to tackle such a large issue extensively, I will confine myself to a few comments: Socratic practice clearly de-emphasizes the preservation of poetic wisdom in favor of analytic wisdom. At the same time we see within the Socratic circle the tendency to want to preserve the words of the master Socrates in both oral and written form. Socratic practice was designed to emphasize the truth over preservation of truths, but that practice itself was preserved with a veneration that may have been out of character.

It is also worth noting that Socratic practice may have only been possible thanks to the introduction of writing. Socrates himself seemed unwilling to embrace writing, but the technology relieved Athenians of the need to preserve the oral tradition which in turn gave them the time to experiment with analytic approaches.[36] In the *Phaedrus* Socrates is critical of the value of writing as a memory aide, but, if Ong is right, his praxis was made possible by writing. To add to the irony, our knowledge of his oral practice is also due to Platonic writing.

Finally, the Socratic project has a conservative dimension itself. Socrates was reacting against the excesses of the Sophists who in their experimentation lost sight of fundamental (aristocratic) virtues. Classicist Eric Alfred Havelock places the Socratic and Platonic projects in a continuum with the "pre-Socratics"; what distinguishes them is their invention of a philosophical language and method for dealing with abstract ideas. I would add that what distinguishes Socrates is his return to the epic virtues. He innovates in order to recover the traditional aristocratic virtues. He is adapting the aristocratic virtues in order to preserve them in the face of the new sophistic technology which has been released by the introduction of writing.[37]

Close to the Human Lifeworld

Havelock and Ong argue that oral cultures do not think in abstractions. An oral community relates everything to everyday experience, or as Ong puts it, to the "human lifeworld." Where we would use abstractions (or possible worlds) oral cultures have myths and characters that can be applied by analogy to other situations. Their stories embed the wisdom in a memorable and human context.

This is one of the more obvious oral characteristics of dialogue. The connection between the theoretical and the human lifeworld is twofold in a dialogue. First, dialogue as conversation is itself a human, everyday event. In philosophical dialogues the content is packaged in a pedestrian context—that of a conversation that takes place in a space and time that is accessible and "human." Second, the characters and their lives are often connected to the philosophical issues discussed. In the better-written dialogues, we see the philosophical issues tied to the dramatic context of the speakers. To adapt the phrase "think globally, act locally," such dialogues show characters thinking philosophically and acting locally. For example, in the *Euthyphro* the discussion of piety is occasioned by, and thematically connected to, Euthyphro's prosecution of his father (and the prosecution of Socrates). Socrates and Euthyphro run into each other in the royal porch right before Euthyphro has to prosecute his father and Socrates is to be charged. The context (the meeting of two people who have business with the courts) at first glance is a chance event with little relation to the content of the dialogue. When we look closely, the reasons for both characters' being there are related to the philosophical theme. The theme of piety is tied to domestic issues (Euthyphro's relationship with his father), and the tribulations of trials in Athens. The prosecution of Euthyphro's father by his son is comparable to the prosecution of the wise father of Athens, Socrates, by the young child of Athens, Meletus. The prosecution of elders (or betters) is, of course, a perversion of one of the basic forms of piety: respect for one's elders and betters.

In Xenophon's dialogues we see another facet of the pedestrian concerns of Socrates, namely his concern for everyday morality. He rebukes friends for not helping each other, he rebukes gluttons for eating too much rich food. Socrates' thinking is linked to everyday morality and illustrated by it. No doubt Xenophon emphasized the pedestrian morality of Socrates to counteract the claim that he corrupted his companions; nevertheless, the method Xenophon illustrates of teaching morality through shaming rings true.

One would think that works limited to a "human" context would be philosophically impoverished, but the opposite seems to be true. The closeness to the human allows for a correspondence between context and content that makes such works more accessible. Few Platonic scholars would argue that the everyday settings and characters of Plato's dialogues detract from the dialogues' value. Quite the contrary; most interpreters today argue that the context of the dialogues is part of the fabric of meaning. It is, if you will, the warp of the rhapsody of meaning. As pointed out above, Euthyphro's prosecution of his father can be compared to the prosecution of Socrates by younger men like Meletus, and to the mock education of Socrates by Euthyphro. The prosecution/education of older "father" figures by a younger generation is a secondary theme of the dialogue that enriches it and is connected to the primary theme of piety. I have put the theme abstractly. In the dialogue the theme is largely carried by the context of the dialogue—a context that adds to the meaning, instead of limiting it.[38]

The closeness to the human can be seen not only in the form of the dialogue, and as in the case of Xenophon, in the content of Socratic dialogues, but also by the nesting of dialogues within Socratic dialogues. While Socrates often insists on abstract definitions for the virtues that he is interested in, he also uses myths and stories. Stories are more accessible and more memorable than abstract definitions. They also personalize issues. A fascinating example, discussed in depth in a following chapter, is the story of the invention of writing told by Socrates to Phaedrus in the *Phaedrus*. Socrates makes his point about writing by recounting a story that is itself a minidialogue. While the characters in the minidialogue are gods, the atmosphere is still human and intimate. The gods sound like colleagues discussing administrative issues. The content is carried by a conversation that one can imagine having (if one were a god in the position to introduce technology to humanity). Such storytelling is a characteristic of oral cultures, where even technological issues are couched in human terms. Ong points out that oral cultures can reapply such stories to other situations without having to resort to abstractions.

The interesting question in this regard is about the nature of the life-world in which dialogues take place. Can we generalize about the context of dialogue beyond pointing out its everyday humanity? Since dialogue depends on the presence (or a mode of presence) of the interlocutors, does that have implications for the context of the dialogue? Does it have implications for the content? I will later, in chapters four and five, try to answer these questions by looking at the time and space (chronotope) deployed in the dialogue. The chronotope will help to differentiate types of dialogue and help show the constraints placed on content.

Agonistically Toned

To maintain interest and make oral stories memorable they are frequently presented as contests. As Ong puts it, oral work often has an agonistic tone. It is easier to remember something if it involved a struggle or battle between opposing forces. This is less true of abstract works, though writing manuals still suggest that presenting ideas agonistically improves readability. The agonistic tone of oral work carries through to dialogue. A dialogue, because it involves more than one character, offers an opportunity for competition in a way that a monologue does not. The copresence of the interlocutors (their being in a space and time that allows them to face each other and talk) affords the opportunity for wrestling. Dialogues that do not present differences in competition, like the one on truth by Anselm that reads like a catechism, tend to be the least interesting. By contrast the typical Socratic dialogue often pits Socrates against a pompous antagonist in competition for the minds of those around. Occasionally the contest/battle is even mentioned explicitly, as in the *Phaedo*. Socrates comments to Phaedo that like the Argives he should make a vow not to let his hair grow until he has "defeated the argument of Simmias and Cebes in a return battle" (*Phaedo* 89c). It is also interesting, in this regard, to consider the similarities between oral dialogue and the contests in the courts before a jury. Oral philosophical contest is even today considered a preparation for law school and the courts.

In the dialogues of Xenophon we can see that there were real stakes in the intellectual contests of the sophists and philosophers. Xenophon prefaces a dialogue with, "Antiphon came to Socrates with the intention of drawing his companions away from him."[39] Socrates and the sophists were battling over aristocratic students who could both pay for instruction, and bring prestige to the winner. Socrates got the handsomest prize of them all, Alcibiades—at least for a while. If today we measure philosophical might in terms of publications, in those days it was in terms of friends, students, and companions.

These battles also had a legitimate philosophical dimension; the major characters, including Socrates, represented important and different philosophical positions. Their contest of words was a peaceful method of resolving these issues. It is tempting to say that the philosophical reputation of Socrates (as compared to that of the sophists) is due to his conversational skills (or the artistry of his student Plato) not the depth of his thought. I suspect that such cynicism misses the philosophical dimension of his conversational skills. Socrates is reported to have won his arguments because he was committed to the truth, not financial success. The contest was not just a game for a living; Socrates was willing to die for what he believed. In the *Theaetetus* (165d–e), Socrates compares the sophist to a mercenary who captivates his audience with a show of arms/words and then holds them for ransom. The captives in the war of words are not the combatants; they are the bystanders, the children. Socrates may have seen himself as a citizen-soldier (guardian) whose job was to defend Athenian youths from the sophist-mercenaries, with his life.[40]

Empathetic and Participatory Rather than Objectively Distanced

The retelling of oral knowledge is not necessarily a simple matter of reciting things in a dry and matter-of-fact fashion. We should think of the retelling as closer to a dramatic monologue where the rhapsode imitates that of which he speaks. It is more accurate to describe the performance of a rhapsode as an act, complete with movement and gesture, than as a strictly auditory event. He is not merely reporting what was said but bringing the other before us—making the character portrayed present. This has interesting repercussions. Havelock and Ong argue that in oral cultures the performers of oral works empathize with their characters and beliefs when performing. Performers of an oral work would, in acting out the work, imagine themselves to be the characters being imitated so as to better remember their words (act). In modern terms, they enter the role so as to act it out better and the line between their personality and that of the character blurs. Empathy with the target character is the ultimate memory aide. Everything, including their personality, is sacrificed to the perpetuation of the oral work.

This is what Havelock believes Plato was objecting to in the *Republic* when he objected to the poets. The poetic educational tradition taught the epics through such acted empathy with the subject. One learned to become the characters of the oral tradition in order to preserve the oral tradition.[41] Plato, according to Havelock, objected to such education by empathy because of the effect that imitating disreputable characters would have. The alternative was education by dialogue where classification, not imitation, was emphasized.

Whether or not one agrees with Havelock, it is nonetheless important to understand how in oral performance the performer is not clearly detached from the character portrayed. This problem in various forms haunts dialogue in general.[42] In everyday conversation, especially gossip, as Bakhtin points out, we are always taking on characters as we speak. When we tell stories and report conversations (a large part of oral speech) we subtly wear the characters we present. When we are ironic we speak in the voice of another in a fashion that mocks that other, but nevertheless involves portraying the other. If we take Socrates' image of thought as a conversation, our speech, when it reflects such thought, resembles a conversation orchestrated from various characters within. One of the things that sets Socrates apart is his ability to orchestrate conversations among those around him (and from within). He may object to being possessed by distasteful people but he certainly had a host of interesting people within, at his disposal.

This returns us once more to dialogue and classification. The classification of which Socrates speaks, and of which we have an example in the *Sophist*, is but one of two skills that Socrates identifies with the dialectician in the *Phaedrus* (265d–266b). Classification is the ability to "divide into forms, following the objective articulation" (265d). Combined with the second skill (that of bringing things together under a form) the dialectician can define things, as the Stranger does. In an oral culture the process of definition is best carried out in dialogue. We should not be surprised at how many Socratic dialogues are driven by the attempt to define something as this reflects oral practice. That is not to say that definition is a characteristic of oral communities. Definition through dialectical dialogue is the Socratic alternative to the oral educational system that promotes empathy with the traditional heroes/heroines (and even antiheroes). Socrates is at the threshold of a change in philosophical education. Unlike his oracular predecessors he encourages his students to dialogue and classification. It allows them to sort out what is right and wrong without getting possessed by ignoble characters.

> Believe me, Phaedrus, I am myself a lover of these divisions and collections, that I may gain the power to speak and to think, and whenever I deem another man able to discern an objective unity and plurality, I follow "in his footsteps where he leadeth as a god" (*Odyssey* 5.193). Furthermore—whether I am right or wrong in doing so, God alone knows—it is those that have this ability whom for the present I call dialecticians. (266b)

Summary of Orality

To conclude this reorientation to orality we should, when trying to understand oral philosophical dialogue, remind ourselves that oral dialogue is an activity; that the character of the thought of oral communities can differ from ours; that there is a poetic dimension to dialogue; that oral dialogue is additive rather than subordinative; that it is redundant; that it is conservative; that it is close to the human lifeworld; agonistic; and empathetic. The following table will serve as a chart through Socratic oral dialogue:

Oral	**Written**
Event	Information
Dialogical Thought	Contemplation and Meditation
Poetic	Expository
Ageless	Dated
Authorless	Created
Additive	Subordinative
Redundant	Explicit
Conservative	Original
Situational	Abstracted
Agonistic	Balanced
Empathetic	Objective

ORAL SOCRATIC DIALOGUE

Having reoriented ourselves to the nature of oral thought and oral communities, it is time to look at oral dialogue in the Socratic circle. The general question before us is: What is the nature of philosophical oral dialogue? The specific question is: What was the nature of Socratic oral dialogue? Before answering these questions, there are two problems we have to address. First, was the Socratic circle an *oral* community such that we can learn about oral dialogue from it? Second, was the Socratic circle a community at all?

The secondary literature is weak on the subject of the Socratic circle. Writers like George Grote, author of *Plato, and the Other Companions of Sokrates,* are interested primarily in the philosophy of Socrates or that of individual followers of Socrates, especially Plato. The same is true of H. D. Rankin in *Sophists, Socratics and Cynics*. Neither treats the circle as something more than the sum of the companions. The same can also be said for W. K. C. Guthrie, author of *Socrates*, who has an interesting section on the effect of Socrates on others, but does not consider this effect within the social context of a community. G. B. Kerferd, in *The Sophistic Movement*, has a chapter entitled "The Sophists as a Social Phenomenon" that discusses the importance of patronage to the sophistical circles. He does not, unfortunately, ask about the social dimension of the Socratic circle and how it might have been different from the sophistical circles. Micheline Sauvage, in *Socrate et la conscience de l'homme,* reproduces some interesting Greek images of dialogue, but does not discuss them. In the imaginative reconstruction of the life of a fictional Socratic follower, *The Last of the Wine*, Mary Renault provides a picture of what it would have been like to be associated with Socrates; but she is more interested in the love of her character for Lysis, and the history of Athens through the eyes of a citizen, than in the daily life of the circle around Socrates.

This absence of discussion is more than offset by an excellent contribution by Livio Rossetti. In an essay entitled "Il momento conviviale dell'eteria socratica e il suo significato pedagogico," Rossetti discusses the evidence for a loose philosophical club around Socrates that gathered regularly, sharing food and ideas.[43] He is particularly interesting on the pedagogical dimension of this club; much of my discussion here is based on his.

The Orality of the Socratic Circle

Most of the points above about the nature of orality draw from Ong's discussion of entirely oral communities, which the Socratic circle was not.

The Socratic circle was not a "primary oral community," in Ong's sense of a community untouched by literacy. The Socratic circle formed in a time of transition; many members of the circle could read and write, but they did not conduct their business that way. The Socratic circle was a philosophical community at the threshold between oral wisdom and literate philosophy. They were freed to do philosophy by the increase in literacy, which reduced the need for the educational system to focus exclusively on maintaining the received wisdom and culture. Nevertheless, they philosophized orally, passing stories down—until they were written.[44] In so far as there was a large oral component to the business of the Socratic circle while Socrates was alive, I think it is fair to look at it for an understanding of oral dialogue in general.

The Character of the Circle

As for the existence of something that can be called the Socratic circle, we are better off asking, What is the nature of the collection of friends that Plato, Xenophon, and Aristophanes describe?[45] Obviously this circle did not have a formal, institutional existence unless we take seriously Aristophanes' depiction in the *Clouds* of the Socratic "think-tank"; instead what emerges from both Xenophon and Plato is that there was a group of men who had the leisure to spend lots of their time with Socrates and consequently were associated with him. Livio Rossetti finds in Xenophon evidence that they regularly ate together as a club, sharing their food at Socrates' house. Such clubs were common in Athens at the time, though they tended to be political organizations rather than philosophical. There does not seem to have been any formal mechanism for joining the circle or leaving it; Socrates was readily available to those who enjoyed his company.[46] Membership in the circle of acquaintances, like membership in any set of friends, depended on presence and participation. Alcibiades, for example, presents himself in the *Symposium* as a lapsed associate. What does emerge, however, is that the experience of joining the circle was similar for many of Socrates' followers. A number of commentators have noted the traumatic experience of being turned inside out by Socrates before becoming one of the companions. I will deal with this initiation later.

A revealing passage is the opening of Plato's *Symposium*, where Apollodorus, the character who narrates the bulk of the dialogue, describes how he recently had a chance to refresh his memory about the original event, "this party at Agathon's" (172a). Apollodorus was not at the original party, but learned about it from Aristodemus, and confirmed details with Socrates. Apollodorus's memory was refreshed by telling the story to Glaucon and he reports a brief exchange with Glaucon that framed that particular retelling. To Glaucon he reports having said:

> And don't you know it's only two or three years since I started spending so much of my time with Socrates, and making it my business to follow everything he says and does from day to day? Because, you know, before that I used to go dashing about all over the place, firmly convinced that I was leading a full and interesting life, when I was really as wretched as could be—much the same as you, for instance, for I know philosophy's the last thing *you'd* spend your time on. (172c–173a)

If we ignore for a moment the intricacies of the way the *Symposium* reaches us, we can use this passage, and the opening to the dialogue in general, to help us understand the character of the Socratic circle:

1. The passage quoted provides us with a description of an admirer of Socrates in his own words. The admirer describes himself as one who is trying to spend all his leisure time with Socrates. The Socratic circle was made up of such men who chose to spend their time discussing philosophy. This description should be compared to that at the end of the *Symposium* by Alcibiades who was a lapsed member of the circle. The opening of the *Symposium* (not just the part quoted) nicely sets out the differences between those within the circle and those outside. Apollodorus loves to talk philosophy, and finds financial discussion "tiresome." Apollodorus is thought of as a "poor unfortunate" but he *knows* that the others are really unfortunate. Apollodorus is crazy, in a philosophically correct fashion no doubt, while others are crazy from the point of view of the philosopher. Apollodorus is in love, again in a philosophically correct fashion, while others are victims of their desires, which they call love. (Apollodorus is also a parody of Socrates, barefoot and enthusiastic, but not necessarily as wise.)

2. To return to the intricate frame of the *Symposium*: the elaborate care with which Plato shows us how the story came to be told alerts us to the importance of the retelling of such stories. In the opening we see how members of the circle would pass down and memorize conversations of the master. Apollodorus is not simply telling of something he heard; he went to the trouble to learn the story and check details with Socrates, who, one might add, did not discourage such oral hagiography. The ability to retell such stories was probably one of the signs of serious interest and participation in the circle. People outside the circle turned to those identified with Socrates to hear such stories; they were expected to know such stories. These stories were the currency of the Socratic circle and the Socratic myth. It is not surprising that Plato, Xenophon, and others would start writing them down while they could still be checked, and when the character of Socrates was still at issue. The writing down was a reasonable extension of the oral practice of handing down such stories.[47] The writing down may have also been the death of the circle, as it would have devalued the memories of those like Apollodorus. The writing down established a new type of authority, that of the author Plato, around whom a new Academic circle formed.

The question of the nature of the Socratic circle resolves itself into questions around the nature of Socratic orality. The Socratic circle, if it existed, was an oral circle, bound by dialogue not membership rules. To fully understand the nature (and hence existence) of the circle we have to understand Socratic orality. We need to understand how and what was discussed to understand how those discussing were bound and circumscribed. We need to understand the political organization of their dialogue, which involves understanding how the activity of dialogue can set those in discussion off, circumscribing them such that they become identified as a circle. In other words the full answer to the question of the existence of the Socratic circle lies in the character of Socratic dialogue.

Joining the Circle

To understand the character of the circle and its dialogue one has to find a beginning from which to start. That start is the beginning of the trajectory of involvement in the Socratic circle that an Athenian youth might have traversed. We can start by asking, How would someone have heard about the Socratic circle? and What would they have heard?

The interesting thing about this question is the number of dialogues we have which depict first encounters with Socrates and his circle of friends. A number of Plato's and Xenophon's dialogues (not to mention the *Clouds* of Aristophanes) paint a picture of what it was like first to meet Socrates and then to become a member of the Socratic circle. I suspect the repeated treatment of the first encounter reflects the interest outside the circle in the potential for encounter. It could also be that these works were designed to act as an advertisement for Socratic philosophy—drawing readers to their first encounter. Who since then has not wondered how they would respond to such a commanding presence as Socrates? Within the Socratic dialogues there are many different reactions, and who does not wonder whether they would be like Theaetetus or Polus?

Hearing about Socrates

As Socrates points out in the *Apology* most Athenians would probably have heard stories about him before they ever met him. What most would have heard was a mixture of opinions, short reported dialogues (stories), and plays with Socrates as a character. Opinions about Socrates abound in the dialogues, and I suspect everyone in Athens who cared had one, though one wonders if they were as positive as that of Laches (181a–b). Plays like Aristophanes' *Clouds* would have been the most public source of hearsay, but stories, embedded with scraps of conversation, would have been a staple of what was heard about Socrates.[48] This is an important point, since today most of our first encounters with philosophers are by means of written works or, for a few, lectures. Stories about philosophers are not as important to the reputation and encounter as they were in the time of Socrates. The philosophically inclined youth would not have read about Socrates; he would have heard reports of Socrates' unique abilities.

Xenophon's memories are an example of what was probably in circulation, though many such stories were probably not as sympathetic. It is interesting to note the structure of most of Xenophon's dialogues. Unlike Plato's dialogues, Xenophon's are framed by comments by the author. Most of the dialogues are reported to make a point, that Socrates did not corrupt the youth, or that he was respectful of the gods. These stories of Xenophon's are designed to address the reader unsure what to make of the memory of Socrates or the justice of his execution. Likewise, while Socrates was alive, we can imagine stories circulating about this amazing character told and retold with embedded dialogues. No doubt the circulating stories provided fodder for the dramatists and dialogue writers later on.

A common feature to such stories would have been the way Socrates was portrayed as an unrelenting questioner. Most stories that report the words of another take the form of "and he said . . . ," followed by a statement. Socrates would have stood out as one who asked questions, not one who lectured. Storytellers would have been forced to embed dialogue in order to capture the character of the questioner. Tales of Socrates take the form of "and he asked. . . ." The stories would have stood out as reported dialogues compared to most stories that report actions or opinions. Some might even have heard of his extraordinary claim that he was charged to question people by Apollo.[49]

I commented above on the importance of these reported dialogues to those within the Socratic circle; here my point is that there were many such stories in circulation, both favorable and not. These stories would have fascinated young argumentative men eager to succeed and excel. The possibility that Socrates was the wisest man in Athens, the possibility that he could make the worst argument appear the best,[50] the way he humiliated the great men of the day not to mention the other sophists, and his peculiarities of character would have all contributed to his fascination in certain circles. Especially fascinating would have been his claim to be ignorant about everything except love. For the young men who were just discovering themselves this *silenus* would have been fascinating if not attractive in a perverse way. Who would not want to meet this daimon? Some may have joined the circle for the wrong reasons.

Overhearing Socrates

The next step in the trajectory of encounter would have been to eavesdrop or overhear a Socratic exchange. It is unlikely that many youths would have been questioned by Socrates without having had a chance to listen to Socrates perform with others. Plato especially goes to great lengths to show us how many would listen in to the conversations of the master, but the best example of the importance of overhearing Socrates comes from Xenophon's *Memorabilia* (4.2). In that dialogue, which Xenophon says is to "show his [Socrates'] method of dealing with those who thought they had received the best education,"[51] Socrates deliberately creates situations where Euthydemus, the proud boy in question, can overhear exchanges designed to bring him into the circle, even if by a humiliating route. The steps of the seduction are as follows:

1. Within earshot of Euthydemus one of Socrates' companions asks, "Was it by constant intercourse with some wise man or by natural ability that Themistocles stood out among his fellow-citizens?" (4.2.2) This gives Socrates a chance to answer in a way that pointedly criticizes Euthydemus's reliance on books for wisdom, thereby creating a situation where, if Euthydemus does not enter the dialogue to defend his book learning, he has to swallow his pride. It is, in essence, an ironic situation. There is a surface discussion between Socrates and a companion; on another level there is second communication between Socrates and Euthydemus.
2. As Euthydemus is not tempted to enter the conversation when obliquely mocked, Socrates creates a second overhearing where Euthydemus is explicitly mentioned. Socrates makes fun of how Euthydemus has no teachers (only books) by imagining an exordium he might give, "Men of Athens, I have never yet learnt anything from anyone" (4.2.4). Xenophon tells us that the mock exordium "set all the company laughing" (4.2.5). We can imagine how humiliated Euthydemus felt.
3. Socrates continued this treatment of ironic and explicit criticism until he found Euthydemus "more tolerant of his conversation and more attentive" (4.2.8). Then he went alone to the spot where Euthydemus used to hang out (a saddler's shop—which suggests the Socratic interest in the crafts may have had something to do with those who frequented the shops). There Socrates engaged Euthydemus directly, humbling him, as he did others, proud of their wisdom. By the end Euthydemus admits he knows little, "I am inclined to think I had better hold my tongue, or I shall know nothing at all presently" (4.2.39).
4. The last step in the process is best described by Xenophon:

> Now many of those who were brought to this pass by Socrates, never went near him again and were regarded by him as mere blockheads. But Euthydemus guessed that he would never be of much account unless he spent as much time as possible with Socrates. Henceforward, unless obliged to absent himself, he never left him, and even began to adopt some of his practices. Socrates, for his part, seeing how it was with him, avoided worrying him, and began to expound very plainly and clearly the knowledge that he thought most needful and the practices that he held to be most excellent. (4.2.40)

A number of points can be made about this remarkable dialogue:

1. To execute this tactic, Socrates involved others. It is interesting how the opening move is not made by Socrates, but by a companion, who presumably knew what to do. Whether the companions were prompted by Socrates or grew to know what was expected of them we do not know, though in Plato's *Lysis* we have a case where Socrates and his companions agree on their agenda before engaging the intended target.
2. The complicity of others would have changed the odds in any discussion with Socrates. Socrates is traditionally seen as the *eiron*, the dissembling underdog who at first seems to be defending a hopeless position, and then against all odds, comes out on top in the debate. In this dialogue of Xenophon's it would appear that many of Socrates' encounters were not so innocent. Socrates had a sympathetic audience primed to feed him the right questions and to tease the interlocutor who refused to play the game. Socrates often chose the grounds for a conversation and arranged the contest to suit his purposes. Rather than a David who routinely faced the sophistic Goliaths, Socrates could be a spider who laid traps for young men. Entering into discussion with Socrates would certainly have been an intimidating and hostile situation to enter for a youth—a situation hardly conducive to fair dialogue, something we are not likely to notice when reading a dialogue because the complicity of the Socratic circle is de-emphasized. (As readers we do not see the rest of the circle—old friends of Socrates gathering around.)
3. If Socrates routinely mocked people within their hearing, it is not

surprising that he was martyred. An essential part of the initiation into the Socratic circle was a purifying humiliation in which everything you believe is exploded. This feature of the initiation has been noted by others; Laszlo Versény, in *Socratic Humanism*, compares the method to Dionysian ecstasy.[52] Rossetti goes further; he feels the evidence suggests that there was almost a formula to the initiation of youths.[53] If this tactic for improving the minds of others was commonly used, there must have been a number of Athenians who did not return to Socrates chastened and ready to learn, but waited, humiliated, for their revenge. Today, someone who taught this way (and we should remember that for Xenophon there is no question that Socrates taught) would be called a bully. This is the dark side of Socratic teaching.

4. For those who returned, the return must have been difficult and comparable to a conversion experience. To overcome the humiliation, and to prostrate oneself intellectually before Socrates so as to be remade out of ignorance, would have involved a complete reversal, from detesting Socrates to depending on him for a new philosophical existence. Let us not forget how Euthydemus and others, once they adopted Socrates, did so with a vengeance. Euthydemus, like Apollodorus in the *Symposium*, returned to spend "as much time as possible with Socrates." This would explain the devotion of many of the Socratic circle to Socrates. He had broken them down until they had admitted ignorance in public, and then offered to rebuild them in his image. The rebuilding was paid for in time, complicity in the humiliation of others, and love. The story of how Socrates rebuilt his companions has not been told, but it would sound more like a cult initiation than today's academic apprenticeship.
5. Above all, this story shows the importance to the Socratic project of overhearing. The first two steps, ironic and explicit criticism, are aimed not at the interlocutor, but at a designated eavesdropper—a member of the audience.

One might object that I am making too much of a single dialogue by Xenophon. However, that Socrates deliberately created situations where people would overhear his conversations is confirmed by both Plato and Aristophanes. In Aristophanes' *Clouds* we have the short dialogue between the better and worse *logoi*. The dialogue of the *logoi* is trotted out by Socrates in order to teach Pheidippides.[54]

In Plato we see listening-in being arranged in a less devious fashion in dialogues like the *Protagoras*. There Socrates enters into debate with Protagoras, not for his own betterment, but to discover what Hippocrates might learn if he studied with Protagoras. On one level the potential student Hippocrates is the intended audience. On another there is also the assembled intellectual community for whom the contest between Socrates and Protagoras would have been of major interest.

In the *Lysis* we see Socrates conversing with Lysis so as to show how one should treat one's beloved. In the *Symposium* we hear from Socrates a dialogue between himself and the priestess Diotima. Socrates by reporting allows us to eavesdrop on his (mythical) past. You can see how this thread will be developed in the next couple of chapters. The reader of dialogue is just such an invited eavesdropper. In the *Apology* we see listening-in being used in the court when Socrates interrogates Meletus before the jury. This could be a model of the role of the reader. We are the jury—we are set up to overhear in order to judge, but the judgment concerns our souls, not that of Socrates.[55]

If we survey the Socratic corpus, dialogues where overhearing is part of the dynamic appear to outnumber the dialogues like the *Phaedrus* where there is no audience. We cannot escape the conclusion that Socratic oral practice was designed as much for the eavesdroppers as it was for the interlocutors. This is what oral dialogue might have in common with written dialogue, its design as an event that can be overheard. In the next two chapters we will look at the written dialogue to see if the relationship between author and reader is comparable to that between the Socrates and his audience.

Socrates' Accomplices

One of things that we should notice about the way dialogues were set up to be overheard is that this required the complicity of the Socratic interlocutor. We tend to think of Socrates as the sole genius behind the Socratic effect, which fails to recognize the role of the faithful companions who knew how to respond to the questions so as to achieve the ironic goal. The importance of the other performers is made explicit in the

Statesman where the Athenian Stranger asks for an interlocutor who will answer appropriately. By contrast Socrates often has to fight with interlocutors who are not cooperative: witness how he negotiates with Protagoras over the expected responses. I am not suggesting that the friendly interlocutor was an equal in the creation of the performance, but that he had a role, and this is a feature of the orality of the event. Socratic dialogues depended to a certain extent on the skill of both the Socratic figure *and* the friendly other. The case of the Athenian Stranger suggests that some wise men could not deliver their teaching without a well-trained amanuensis, much as some today cannot write without a word processor.

Another way of looking at this is to recognize the importance of the political structure of the dialogical space. The Socratic dialogue could not take place just anywhere with any group of people as long as Socrates was there. Socratic dialogue in so far as it was an oral product was authored by a community (if authorship is relevant to the work of an oral community). If we take seriously the authorlessness of oral work we have to consider the political character of the Socratic circle (not Socrates) as the principle (not author) of Socratic dialogue. This is not to say that Socrates wasn't a unique, necessary, and central member of the community, but we should not be blinded by our fascination with individual authors to the community spirit behind Socratic dialogue. Although we will return later in this book to considering generally the politics, time, and space in which dialogue in general takes place (this is, for Bakhtin, the appropriate feature with which to distinguish dialogues), for the moment here are some observations about the political space and time of the Socratic dialogue.

Public Space

Oral dialogue needs two or more people to take place at all. This puts a constraint on the opportunities for dialogue. If one wants to engage in dialogue one has to make oneself available. One has to enter some sort of meeting space where others who wish to dialogue also converge. Public places like the market and the gymnasium are logical spots to loiter if one wants to engage others in conversation. Socrates, we are told, spent his whole day in the marketplace and other public spots. He was available for dialogue in a public space in a way few others were prepared to be. This alone would account for the quantity of dialogues reported about him.[56]

While public space was available to most men it was difficult for women. Cultural restrictions on access to the public spaces where dialogue takes place might account for the scarcity of women characters in dialogue. It is only with the courtly dialogue by authors like Castiglione that one has conversations taking place in spaces where women were at home.

Symposium Space

Not all Socratic dialogue took place in the public marketplace. A less accessible space also frequented by the Socratics was the private home of a patron of discourse. The evening dinner dialogue, because it is usually among a circle of friends, is less competitive and more prone to entertaining exchanges. The space is intimate and jocular, though we should not compare the space of a symposium with the typical dinner party today. It is not surprising that love is a theme of dialogue in such a space.

Leisure Time

Along with considerations of space we need to also be alert to the time available. As I mentioned above, Socrates made himself available all day. His companions like Apollodorus also made it their business to spend their day with him. It is interesting how few dialogues are interrupted by events or appointments that have to be kept. One gets the sense that the Socratics have unlimited time at their disposal. They can talk all day and then party until the morning if that is called for.

Needless to say, only people with substantial amounts of free time could participate in such constant daily dialogue. (This also gives us a sense of how much talking went on.) This may have further restricted participation to those who could afford the time (or those prepared to give up the material benefits of being employed). The leisurely time available for dialogue is difficult to find today, especially in academia.

The Varieties of Dialogue

To conclude this chapter we return to the original question about the nature of oral dialogue, specifically that of the Socratic circle. We have traced a trajectory from hearing stories about Socrates to becoming an accomplice. We have discussed some of the issues around the time and space of Socratic dialogue. It now remains for us to lay out the variety of Socratic oral dialogue. This will serve as a classification of oral dialogue in general.

This also brings us back to the problem of dialogue and classification. Oral dialogue in the time of Socrates was not what it is today, something we rarely have time for because of the evidence that has to be read and the research that has to be done. Oral dialogue was the medium of the Socratic discipline much as the essay and book are the medium of philosophy today. Classifying the types of dialogue that we find in the Socratic corpus is a way of surveying the variety of philosophical experience available in an oral philosophical culture. (It is also interesting to compare this list to the list in the Introduction of contexts in which dialogue has arisen in our culture.)

1. Reported dialogues. Stories with embedded dialogue were the way youths would first encounter Socratic philosophy. These stories (and their exchange) were the fabric of the Socratic circle after the death of Socrates. They were also a component in Socrates' oral practice: witness his story of his exchange with Diotima (*Symposium* 201d–212b).
2. Competitive dialogues. The more aggressive teachers would attract students (steal them) from other teachers by engaging others in dialogue. Xenophon reports dialogues where sophists try to attract Socrates' followers from him (*Memorabilia* 1.6.1). We could read the *Protagoras* and the *Gorgias* as examples of this sort.
3. Political dialogues. Dialogue was a political tool for Socrates. He used it in two ways:
   a. He would engage prominent figures in dialogue. Whatever noble motives this served, it definitely helped cement Socrates' reputation and entertained his followers. This type of dialogue is similar to the competitive dialogues though the stakes are different. When engaging politicians Socrates was not interested in stealing away students, so much as acting as a political critic, contributing in his stinging way to the well-being of the *polis*.
   b. Socrates describes spending time questioning the craftspeople (*Apology* 22c–d). Systematically engaging the craftspeople

would have had some interesting implications. For example he would have been in a position to recommend teachers (for the crafts) as he is reported to have done in the *Laches* (180c–d). Dialogue with the craftspeople would have been a good way to understand where they saw the crafts fitting into the state and a good way to make connections with the various experts of which Socrates so often talks. One might call this a form of networking in preparation for a political career. Socrates may have engaged the craftspeople before his circle as an alternative to the sophistic political preparation.

4. Conversion dialogues. Related to the competitive dialogue is the type where Socrates and an interlocutor set out to be overheard in order to convert an eavesdropper. A subset of these would be the more intimate dialogues immediately around the moment of conversion.
5. Morality dialogues. In Xenophon we see how Socrates would use dialogue to shame his followers into ethical behavior (*Memorabilia* 1.2.8). This sort of shaming through questions is a surprisingly resilient type of dialogue. How many of us have heard such tactics used to teach today? (How often do such tactics work? More often than not, the embarrassment of the other results not in moral improvement, but in self-satisfaction on the part of the would-be Socrates.)
6. Dialectical dialogues. The *Sophist* and the *Statesman* show us how dialogue was used for research. Dialogue with a tractable interlocutor was the preferred way of presenting definitions and perhaps also for developing such definitions. Such dialogue was also a way of developing the skill of asking questions that elicit definitions. Presumably one would start by learning to be a tractable answerer and then move on to learning to ask questions. This type of dialectical dialogue should not be confused with Aristotle's version which is aimed at convincing people away from what they believe, though it would be interesting to consider the similarities.

To conclude this section on oral dialogue, we have seen how important overhearing is to oral dialogue. Socratic dialogue, unlike casual conversation, was not aimed at the interlocutor, but at the eavesdropping audience for whom the dialogue was arranged. It was often a purifying event comparable to an initiation where the target is humiliated and then built back up into a member of the Socratic circle. We also began to look at the setting of dialogue: the types of space and time of dialogue. Having sketched the nature of oral philosophical dialogue we now turn to the written dialogue to see if it works the same way. The next couple of chapters will look at the written dialogue to see if there is a target comparable to the eavesdropper, and if there is a mode of persuasion comparable to the purification of oral dialogue.

NOTES

1. Xenophon, *Memorabilia*, in *Xenophon in Seven Volumes*, trans. O. J. Todd and E. C. Marchant, vol. 4 (Cambridge, Mass.: Harvard University Press, 1968), 4.5.11–12.

2. W. K. C. Guthrie, *Socrates* (Cambridge: Cambridge University Press, 1971), p. 120. Guthrie attributes this connection to an assumption that there are forms under which things can be classified.

3. The discussion of dialogue in general, and our understanding of Socratic dialogue in particular, is haunted by a failure to look at the nature of oral dialogue, and to distinguish between oral dialogue in a literate culture against dialogue in an oral community. While a number of writers have admitted the importance of oral practice to the character of written dialogues, few have looked exclusively at oral practice before asking about its relationship to written practice. Even fewer have taken into account the character of primarily oral philosophical cultures. There is a wealth of literature about written dialogues and their interpretation; everyone these days admits that one cannot read Plato's dialogues without taking their form into consideration, but few go the next step and ask about the relationship between the written form and the oral practices that influenced them. Fewer still have considered what it meant to do philosophy in an oral culture. This is understandable given the absence of evidence about such cultures other than what is written. With little independent evidence of oral practice, how do we dare go beyond the written?

4. "We—readers of books such as this—are so literate that it is very difficult for us to conceive of an oral universe of communication or thought except as a variant of a literate universe." Walter Ong, *Orality and Literacy: The Technologizing of the World* (New York: Routledge, 1982), p. 2.

5. One of the extraordinary things about the discussion around orality today is the variety of different disciplines that are interested in it. Anthropologists, communication scientists, information scientists, historians, classicists, linguists, and computer scientists are all interested in different aspects of orality and their discussions are driven by different concerns. I believe a common element to the interest is a perception that we are going through a shift in information technology comparable to the shift from orality to literacy. We are returning to a form of technologically mediated orality where the written text no longer dominates discourse. Orality itself (and to an extent dialogue) is one of the ways academia is coming to terms with the changes around it. Orality, if you will, is an issue driving the discussion of the relationship between changing media and messages.

6. Readers should not confuse my discussion of presence with that of Derrida, who has made it the crux of his problems with the metaphysical tradition and Heidegger.

7. One might argue that I am ignoring the conference where original positions are presented orally. If we look closely at this phenomenon we see that it has more to do with writing and publication than orality. Most conference presenters "read papers." They do so largely with a view to refining their ideas for publication.

8. Only with Descartes's story about a solitary meditation do we get a compelling alternative model for what it is to do philosophy, one which is built on the retreat from others. The Cartesian story shows philosophy being done in a scientific fashion, where one retreats from others to do research. Today's academic philosophy is built largely on this Enlightenment model of doing philosophy by research. This applies not only to those philosophical traditions that are fascinated with the model of science, but, also to those, like Gadamer, who attempt to return to dialogue as a model for philosophy. Gadamer's vision of philosophical dialogue is built on the solitary writings of Plato, not on a recovery of oral practice.

9. Ong, in *Ramus: Method, and the Decay of Dialogue* (Cambridge, Mass.: Harvard University Press, 1958), argues that with the advent of printing it became possible to reproduce charts and tables accurately. This led to a change in teaching practice where graphic schemas were used to show students information rather than teaching by dialogue. Schematization became a method by which any subject could be appropriated quickly. Ong speculates that this technological/educational shift prepared the ground for the scientific advances of the eighteenth century. In effect, the Enlightenment was based on new visual methods for representing knowledge and a technology that allowed these views to be published. The light of the Enlightenment was seen in tables like those at the beginning of the *Encyclopedie* which show schematically the totality of human knowledge.

10. Plato, *Sophist*, trans. F. M. Cornford, in *The Collected Dialogues of Plato*, ed. Edith Hamilton and Huntington Cairns (Princeton, N.J.: Princeton University Press, 1961), 217c.

11. Ibid., 217d.

12. Ong points out in *Orality and Literacy* that the word *rhapsoidein* means 'to stitch songs together' in Greek (p. 13). The rhapsode would weave a new song at each telling to suit the context.

13. Havelock describes the knowledge carried in the Homeric epics as an encyclopedia.

14. It is interesting to speculate on the relationship of an oral philosophical community with its past. I suspect there is less call for the maintenance and classification of all ideas, thinkers, and subjects. Instead every philosophical event is, at the same time, supposed to come from a distant past (in the sense that it embodies age-old wisdom), and is a fresh weaving suited to the context.

15. Xenophon's *Memorabilia* begins with an introduction where he wonders "by what arguments those who drew up the indictment against Socrates could persuade the Athenians that his life was forfeit to the state" (1.1.1). Many of the conversations reported by Xenophon are explicitly designed to prove that he was innocent of the charge of impiety or corruption of the youth. The *Memorabilia* seems designed to set the record straight in a continuing discussion. One wonders what effect written reports like those of Xenophon and Plato had on the discussion.

16. Ong, *Orality and Literacy*, p. 33.

17. Ibid.

18. Ong is interesting on this in *Ramus: Method, and the Decay of Dialogue*. As the title suggests the introduction of graphic schemes that could be reliably reproduced led to the decay of dialogue in education.

19. In the *Timaeus* Critias describes the short memory of cultures without writing. "Whereas just when you and other nations are beginning to be provided with letters and the other requisites of civilized life, after the usual interval, the stream from heaven, like pestilence, comes pouring down and leaves only those of you who are destitute of letters and education, and so you have to begin all over again like children, and know nothing of what happened in ancient times, either among us, or among yourselves." *Timaeus*, trans. Benjamin Jowett, in *The Collected Dialogues of Plato*, 23a–c.

20. Ong, *Orality and Literacy*, p. 34.

21. In the *Theaetetus* Socrates suggests that his role is that of the midwife who delivers people of their ideas and then judges the value of the ideas (*Theaetetus* 149–50). This is a slightly different midwife role than that of the Stranger who has a tractable interlocutor. The Socratic midwife is not just there

to assist with the birth, but acts as a doctor and judge after the birth, examining the child and judging it. Theaetetus is a tractable womb, at the service of the father of all ideas, unlike the mothers that Socrates deals with, so there is less need for postpartum judgment. Socrates works with people who should not be pregnant; he takes control of the birthing, inducing babies where there may not have even been anything, and then critically offering them up for public examination. The Stranger places his seed in a carefully selected mind and draws out his children confident they will be healthy. Plato, *Theaetetus*, trans. F. M. Cornford, in Hamilton and Cairns, *The Collected Dialogues of Plato*.

22. Ibid., 189e.

23. See the chapter entitled, "The Modern Discovery of Primary Oral Cultures," in Ong, *Orality and Literacy*.

24. Ong, *Orality and Literacy*, p. 21. This extreme position has since been challenged by scholars. Hugh Lloyd-Jones provides a useful survey of the debate in "Becoming Homer," *New York Review of Books*, 5 March 1992, pp. 52–57. The debate, if one considers the exchanges that followed this survey (14 May 1992; 25 June 1992), is a civilized example of the sort of written dialogue that can traverse journals and reviews. Considering the sophistication of the discussion among classicists around orality it is surprising that few classical philosophers have risen to the challenge of Havelock's *Preface to Plato*. Why are we not interested in the character of oral philosophy the way the classicists are in the issues of orality and the epic?

25. As Ong says, "The oral poet had an abundant repertoire of epithets diversified enough to provide an epithet for any metrical exigency that might arise as he stitched his story together—differently at each telling, for, as will be seen, oral poets do not normally work from verbatim memorization of their verse." *Orality and Literacy*, p. 21.

What is interesting is that, "Moreover, the standardized formulas were grouped around equally standardized themes, such as the council, the gathering of the army, the challenge . . ." (ibid., p. 23). To what extent were Greek dialogues built around standard themes? Certainly over time certain themes emerge, like the symposium, and the dialogue of the dead.

26. This does not belittle the beauty and artistry of the Homeric epics. While there may be a functional aspect to their poetic structure there is still the room for genius in how that is played out.

27. Aristotle argues that this is the point of dialectics—to know what the common opinions are and to know how to use them to lead people to the truth. In so far as dialogues are representations of dialectical practice they are by definition built on common opinions or stock philosophical formulae. A variation on this principle is found in Cicero who argues that oratory has to be couched in

everyday language. While philosophy understandably has to develop a jargon, oratory, whose purpose is moving people, has to work with the common language and that includes the philosophical expressions and clichés in circulation. Most dialogues, in fact, are refreshingly free of jargon.

28. This comparison should not be pushed too far. The Socratic circle was, as far as we can tell, committed to truth and would not have subsumed the content to poetic constraints. The dialogue as an oral event and later written form is at the threshold of oral wisdom and literate philosophy; the poetic constraints are largely abandoned, in part because writing can handle the problem of perpetuation.

29. Many of the subsequent headings are borrowed from Ong.

30. Ong, *Orality and Literacy,* p. 37. Ong quotes the same passage from two translations of the Bible. In the Douay version of 1610 (quoted above) the additive character is preserved. In the *New American Bible* of 1970, the "ands" have been replaced by "when," "while," and "then."

31. It is interesting that Socrates, when he proposes to examine justice in the state as an alternative procedure, gives as an analogy the example of trying to read small letters: "We should employ the method of search that we should use if we, with not very keen vision, were bidden to read small letters from a distance, and then someone had observed that these same letters exist elsewhere larger and on a larger surface." *Republic*, trans. Paul Shorey, in *The Collected Dialogues of Plato*, 368d.

32. I suspect one could use the characteristics of oral dialogue to distinguish the "Socratic" and "Platonic" dialogues. Given that Socrates did not write his dialogues, and that we can clearly distinguish oral from written dialogue, it would follow that written dialogues that were inspired by oral practice (or report it) would be distinguishable from the ones that were invented in writing. This also assumes that Plato did not draw on other oral sources like conversations within the Academy for the later dialogues. Nevertheless such a method of categorization would have the virtue that the criteria used to distinguish the dialogues would be independent of the dialogues themselves and would not depend on a theory about what Socrates thought. Such a distinction between orally inspired (or reported) dialogues and written (invented) dialogues also gets at one interesting difference between Socrates and Plato. One of the few things we can be certain of is that Socrates was a conversationalist who entered into dialogue, while Plato wrote his dialogues.

If I am right, in the transition from the reported to the invented dialogues we can see the dialogue form being explored by Plato. Initially he sticks to what could have happened and draws from experience. By the end when we get to a work like the *Laws* he feels entirely free to invent characters and situations to suit didactic purposes different from those that drove Socratic practice. One might argue that the distinction between reported and invented dialogues might not map cleanly onto the distinction between earlier and later dialogues.

In *Socrates, Ironist and Moral Philosopher* (Ithaca, N.Y.: Cornell Univeristy Press, 1991), Gregory Vlastos lists the earliest Platonic dialogues as: *Apology*, *Charmides*, *Crito*, *Euthyphro*, *Gorgias*, *Hippias Minor*, *Ion*, *Laches*, *Protagoras*, and *Republic* book 1 (p. 46). His division is based on the content of the dialogues, not the oral or written character.

33. In a similar fashion data communications systems use redundancy to ensure reliable communication. As we design new communication systems for everyday environments we are beginning to appreciate the characteristics of existing ways of communicating, especially oral communication.

34. Plato, *Euthyphro*, trans. Lane Cooper, in *The Collected Dialogues of Plato*, 5c–d.

35. Ibid., 5d.

36. According to Professor of Greek History Rosalind Thomas, *Oral Tradition and Written Record in Classical Athens* (Cambridge: Cambridge University Press, 1989), the *Metroön* or city archives were established around 405 B.C.E. It should be mentioned that Thomas differs from the technological determinists, like Ong and Havelock, who believe technological changes, like the introduction of writing, lead to rationality, objective thought, logic, and individuality. I do not want to suggest that the introduction of writing was the only factor in the philosophical changes of the fifth century B.C.E.; nor do I believe that such technological changes inevitably lead to intellectual changes. I am only suggesting that the spread of writing made it possible to shift intellectual resources away from the preservation of the oral culture.

37. In a similar fashion we may be experiencing a technological shift as dramatic as the introduction of writing. There is some of the same enthusiasm in information science and computing today that one senses among the sophists of Socrates' time. Computer vendors advertise their technology as "empowering" and "liberating." Philosophers need to challenge these claims and participate in the debate around the ethical implications of the new technologies.

38. One might also argue that this connectedness of content and context is only a feature of composed works and not oral dialogue as it takes place. In other words, the closeness to the human is a character of the reported or written dialogue, not the live oral one. I suspect that a composed dialogue (be it composed for oral recital or written) can maximize the fit between context and content, but that it is a natural inclination in living dialogue to relate what is being said to one's context. It is a characteristic of oral exchanges that abstract issues are related to the moment and the people around. It is frequently the case that the

issues that are raised are those relevant to the living concerns of the interlocutors. The author of a composed dialogue has time to make the connection more artistic though he is less likely to have the reflex to connect the two, given that the context of writing is not that of the dialogue.

39. Xenophon *Memorabilia* 1.6.1. One wonders if Socrates also drew students away by challenging their teachers? Could that be one of the dramas in the *Protagoras*?

40. The agonistic character of dialogue may be one reason why women are so rarely found in dialogues or author them. The aggressive combativeness that characterizes Socrates and his line has been questioned (with good reason) by feminist philosophers. As a character in C. D. Reeve's dialogue "The Naked Old Women in the Palestra" puts it, "I worry still, though, that philosophy is so agonal and competitive, so much like fighting, so—if you'll forgive me—*male*" (p. 35).

41. Eric A. Havelock, *Preface to Plato* (Cambridge, Mass.: Belknap Press, 1963).

42. It is never clear in a written dialogue who, if anyone, speaks for the author. At times we can only say that the author empathizes with all the characters, finding something of each within himself/herself. Another way of putting it is that each character carries something of the author. The same might be true of the reader.

43. This essay appeared in *Ancient Society* 7 (1976): 29–77. Rossetti also notes the absence of research on the social role of Socrates (p. 31). I suspect one reason for the absence of discussion of the Socratic circle is because most of the evidence is to be found in Xenophon and Aristophanes, neither of whom are as interesting philosophically as Plato. Because Plato is far more interesting for us to read we tend to take him as the better historian of Socrates. Plato brings us into the circle of Socratics, while Xenophon describes a cranky Socrates who was concerned with the personal problems of people long dead. As for the picture of Socrates proposed by Aristophanes, it has been soundly discredited by essays like Kenneth J. Dover's "Socrates in the Clouds," in *The Philosophy of Socrates: A Collection of Critical Essays*, ed. Gregory Vlastos (New York: Anchor Books, 1971).

44. Livio Rossetti, in *Aspetti della letteratura socratica antica* (Chieti: 1977) goes into depth about the exceptional literary production of dialogues by the Socratics after his death. He points out that for half a century the Socratics published around three dialogues a year of which at least one dealt with Socrates. This production of dialogues came after the death of Socrates; his death was the turning point between oral and written dialogue. Havelock in "The Orality of Socrates and the Literacy of Plato" makes a similar point regarding the shift from an oral community to a literate one. See Eric A. Havelock, "The Orality of Socrates and the Literacy of Plato: With Some Reflections on the Historical Ori-

gins of Moral Philosophy in Europe," in *New Essays on Socrates*, ed. Eugene Kelly (New York: University Press of America, 1984).

45. All three write as if there were people who spent much of their time with Socrates and were therefore associated with him. I call this collection of stalwarts the Socratic circle. See for example: Plato, *Apology*, trans. Hugh Tredennick, 33b–34b; Plato, *Phaedo*, trans. Hugh Tredennick, 58c–59b; Xenophon *Memorabilia* 1.1.4; and Aristophanes *Clouds* 94.

46. A couple of Plato's dialogues take place when Socrates returns after a prolonged absence and is greeted enthusiastically by his friends.

47. See Havelock, "The Orality of Socrates and the Literacy of Plato," and Rossetti, *Aspetti della letteratura socratica antica.* Rossetti describes how the Socratic circle used written dialogue to defend themselves and Socrates after his trial. The trial of Socrates, which could have eliminated the Socratics as a philosophical movement, caused the young men whom he was supposed to have corrupted to band together to present a positive picture. Defending Socrates was, for those that he was supposed to have corrupted, a defense of their character. Rehabilitating Socrates was a way of washing away the stain of corruption associated with the circle.

48. I distinguish a story from an opinion in the following fashion. An opinion simply states what the opinionated believes about the other—it tells us something. A story shows us someone in a light that encourages us to draw an opinion. Often what is said is a combination of both, for example, Alcibiades' description of Socrates at the end of the *Symposium.*

49. Socrates was not the only one who asked questions. According to George Grote on the authority of Aristotle, it is Zeno who invented dialectic examination. See *Plato, and the Companions of Sokrates*, vol. 1 (London: John Murray, 1865), p. 96.

50. Plato *Apology* 18b.

51. Xenophon *Memorabilia* 4.2.1.

52. "Thus Socrates' erotic *periagoge,* this turning of man inside out, or rather turning him away from the unessential pursuits toward himself, has as we have seen a great deal in common with Dionysian ecstasy." Laszlo Versény, *Socratic Humanism* (Westport, Conn.: Greenwood Press, 1979), p. 146.

53. Rossetti, "Il momento conviviale dell'eteria socratica e il suo significato pedagogico," p. 60.

54. Aristophanes *Clouds* 889–1104.

55. See Rossetti, "Il momento conviviale dell'eteria socratica e il suo significato pedagogico," for more examples.

56. The American School of Classical Studies at Athens has produced a charming pamphlet called *Socrates in the Agora* (1978) which discusses, with illustrations, the Athenian Agora that was Socrates' stamping ground.

3 The READER of DIALOGUE

> Much more is this the case in dialogue. For here the author is annihilated, and the reader, being no way applied to, stands for nobody. The self-interesting parties both vanish at once. The scene presents itself as by chance and un-designed. You are not only left to judge coolly and with indifference of the sense delivered, but of the character, genius, elocution, and manner of the persons who deliver it.[1]

INTRODUCTION

Having looked at oral dialogue, we turn to the written dialogue to see if they can be defined as one thing. In the oral dialogue we found that one of the most important characters was the eavesdropper who says little, but for whom the dialogue is arranged. We must look, in the same vein, at the stakeholders in the written dialogue, especially the reader. Who are you when you read a philosophical dialogue? In a written dialogue the author does not address you, having vanished before the characters or become a character that addresses others.[2] What role is there left for the reader? We will find the reader is like the eavesdropper of the oral dialogue—the written dialogue is arranged for you.

This chapter is divided into two parts. In the first I will examine a tempting misunderstanding of the place of the reader in Socratic dialogues. In the second part this chapter will move to an answer suggested by two Socratic dialogues of the Renaissance author Lorenzo Valla. In short, I will try to show that the reader of a Socratic dialogue is not to be confused, however tempting that may be, with the Socratic interlocutor. The reader is an eavesdropper, who may sympathize with the interlocutor, but does not go down in embarrassment with that interlocutor when he is humiliated by the Socratic figure. This chapter is not a sociological study of the types of people likely to read Socratic dialogues at a particular time; it is about the characters the author arranges for the reader. As such it is about the relationship between author and reader, though the author's choices will be discussed in the next chapter.

I should begin by stating that I am concerned primarily with dialectical dialogues, otherwise called "Socratic" dialogues. I am not going to discuss the place of the reader in the tradition of convivial dialogues like the later dialogues of Plato (*Republic* and *Laws*) and those of Cicero or Hume. Nor am I going to comment on the place of the reader in the tradition of dialogues of the dead such as those of Lucian. Perhaps the best examples of the sort of dialogues I am looking at are Plato's early dialogues like the *Gorgias, Meno*, and *Protagoras*, and those of Valla that will be treated in the second part of this chapter. (One reason I have chosen to focus on Valla's dialogues is to move the discussion beyond Plato.) A Socratic dialogue is one where an interlocutor—traditionally, but not necessarily, Socrates—through cross-examination of another, convinces him that the other does not know what he thought he knew. The Socratic character convinces the other by asking a series of questions, the answers leading inexorably to conclusions the other did not hold at the beginning. The other is led to, not told of, these conclusions.[3] By contrast, in convivial dialogues, the characters are more evenly matched, the conclusion is less a victory for any one side, you do not have one interlocutor always questioning and one answering (instead you have longer set speeches by the characters), and the dialogue usually takes place in a private location rather than a public one.[4]

The Socratic Interlocutor

To answer the question about the reader in Socratic dialogues, let us look at what Socrates has to say about how he convinces his interlocutors. Can the relationship between Socrates and his interlocutors be a model for the relationship between the author and reader? In the *Gorgias*, Socrates explains what he is trying to do in conversation by contrasting his style with that of court orators:

> My dear sir, you are trying to refute me orator-fashion, like those who fancy they are refuting in the law courts. For there one group imagines it is refuting the other when it produces many reputable witnesses to support its statements whereas the opposing party produces but one or none. . . . Yet I, who am but one, do not agree with you, for you cannot compel me to; you are merely producing many false witnesses against me in your endeavor to drive me out of my property, the truth. But if I cannot produce in you yourself a single witness in agreement with my views, I consider that I have accomplished nothing worth speaking of in the matter under debate.[5]

For Socrates a successful dialogue is one where he convinces only his interlocutor of the truth, and does so without appealing to the authority of others. Because he cannot appeal to others, this conviction is obtained step by step, the other assenting to one proposition after another, until he is forced to agree with the conclusion. Socrates never tells the other explicitly what to think, or produces authoritative witnesses; he draws the desired conclusion, and therefore its approval, from the other. Socrates describes himself, in the *Theaetetus*, as a midwife of ideas.[6] His delivery method is dialectical cross-examination. There is some question as to whether this is what Socrates actually did; nonetheless, this is the canonical Socratic method that critics take as a paradigm for the relationship between author and reader, or teacher and pupil.[7]

The Reader as Interlocutor

What is the role of the reader of such a dialogue? One answer is that he sympathizes with the Socratic figure; that the reader becomes friends with Socrates. I will deal with this possibility at the end of this chapter. A second suggestion is that we enter into dialogue with the text. It is difficult to pin down just what that would mean; dialogues do not address us, ask us questions, or answer our questions. One possible way in which we enter into dialogue with the text is the method I took in the first chapter on Heidegger's redefinition of dialogue. In that case we brought questions to the dialogue and mined it like an encyclopedia for answers. This is only a dialogue in the vague sense of an interaction through which something meaningful comes. The work of both questioning and answering that takes place is done by the reader. The dialogue forces us to create answers; it does not provide them as a living interlocutor would. Such an interaction with the text if it is a dialogue is better described as a dialogue within the reader, between the characters let loose by reading the text. This is not to demean the experience. I noted then that in reading there can be a quickening sense that something ineffable is being communicated though the text. We bring to life that which comes through the text when we read with an open mind.

A third answer, which I will concentrate on, is that the reader is to the author as the interlocutor is to the Socratic figure. Just as the Socratic figure delivers the interlocutor of his ideas and misconceptions through dialectical cross-examination, so we, the readers, are delivered vicariously of the same ideas and misconceptions by the same cross-examination. It is assumed that, in our vanity, we are tempted to wear the cloak of those who profess to know (the interlocutor), and as that character is humiliated we learn about our ignorance and are purified of our pretensions. The skill of the author, in this model, lies in creating an atmosphere where we will identify with the interlocutor. The dialogue achieves its effect by first entrapping us in the professing character and then cross-examining this profession.

This view is rarely stated explicitly; it is often presupposed in the interpretation of Socratic dialogues. When critics talk about entering into dialogue with the text they sometimes mean entering into dialogue with Socrates as if we were the interlocutor. Or, when critics talk of Socrates' position as if it were the author's position, it follows that there is a similar equivalence between the author's addressee (the reader) and that of Socrates (the interlocutor). Because the question has not been raised in quite this way, we find this view in asides, like this passage from Michael Walzer, "A Critique of Philosophical Conversation":

> Affirmations of this sort (the "Yes, Socrates" type) add to the force of a philosophical argument or, at least, they make the argument seem more

> forceful (why else would philosophers write dialogues?) because the acquiescent interlocutor speaks not only for himself but for the reader as well. Plato has built our agreement into his discourse, and while we can always refuse to agree, we feel a certain pressure to go along, to join the chorus.[8]

Hans-Georg Gadamer, the later German philosopher and student of Heidegger, can be read this way when he proposes:

> A knowledge of our own ignorance is what human wisdom is. The other person with whom Socrates carries on his conversation is convicted of his own ignorance by means of his "knowledge."[9]

I believe Gadamer's position is actually more sophisticated, but he can be sufficiently ambiguous about exactly who is being questioned by Socrates that some readers might be tempted to assume that he believes that it is the reader.[10] Another example of this view is quoted (without question) by Chaim Perelman in *The Idea of Justice and the Problem of Argument*:

> Dialectic proceeds by way of questions and answers so that one never passes from one assertion to the next without first having gained the approval of the interlocutor. The dialectical art consists in never failing to secure this approval. This method of dialogue is essentially oral and requires the participation of at least two persons. Why does Plato think nevertheless that it could be applied to a written work, where the same person, the author, presents the questions as well as the answers? Plato takes it for granted that no interlocutor could answer differently from the one whom he lets speak.[11]

For Perelman and Edmond Goblot the issue of the reader vanishes before the fate of the interlocutor in a dialectical exchange with Socrates. It is assumed that the only role for the reader is that of a possible interlocutor, and that all interlocutors would answer in the same fashion. Goblot is so fascinated by the struggle of the interlocutor with the Socratic juggernaut that he fails to ask if the reader, himself included, actually reads as if he were an interlocutor.

There is some evidence to support the view that we vicariously read as the interlocutor. As I will show later, authors like Valla deliberately make the Socratic character unappealing at the beginning in case we are tempted to immediately sympathize with him. In addition, authors like Plato will put widely held opinions in the mouth of the interlocutor. The contemporary reader recognizes opinions that he has voiced and is drawn to the interlocutor. The combination of a bizarre or antagonistic Socratic figure, along with a superficially reasonable interlocutor, tempts the naive reader to sympathize with the interlocutor. Obviously anyone who has read a number of Socratic dialogues is less likely to be so tempted, but such a well-read reader is another matter.

Part of the attraction of this answer, as to the reader's identity, is its simplicity and symmetry. It is the simplest answer because then we only have one philosophical relationship to contend with: that of Socratic figure and interlocutor. We do not need a different relationship for the author and reader. It is symmetrical in that it suggests a symmetry between Socrates' project and Plato's. What Socrates did orally, Plato did through writing. This allows us to scale everything we know about the Socratic relationship up to the Platonic one about which we have few explicit statements. The answer is also tempting because of the respect for Socrates within the discipline of Philosophy. We admire Socrates, one of our few philosophical heroes, and would like to think that what he could achieve in oral cross-examination can also be achieved by Plato in the written dialogue, even today. Dialectical cross-examination has been the paradigmatic method of philosophical conviction; it is tempting to ascribe it to a corpus of written works to which we are all attached. If Plato's works can have that effect on the reader, then we can in some sense extend the dialectical grasp of Socrates beyond his martyrdom to our students.

Problems with the Interlocutor

There are a number of problems with the identification of the reader and the interlocutor. First, we should look carefully at the dialectical model put forward by Socrates to see if it can be applied to the reader according to its own terms. I believe, if one takes seriously Socrates' pronouncements about what his method achieves, that it cannot be applied or scaled out to the relationship between reader and author. Let us remind ourselves of the argument.

The dialectical method, which is supposed to guarantee conviction, has a definite target. Socrates, as was said above, claims to be concerned only with the conviction of the person being questioned. He ignores the authority of others when it comes to his own beliefs, and he convinces others without recourse to authority. For this reason only those cross-examined can actually be said to be convinced dialectically.[12] We, and others who witness the exchange, are not participants in the dialectical conviction, nor should we let ourselves be convinced along with the unfortunate interlocutor in the same way that the interlocutor is convinced. At most, we should be open to the possibility that, if questioned directly, we might come to similar conclusions, though from different grounds—our own presuppositions. The conclusions the interlocutor arrives at with Socrates' help are his, and to believe them without going through the process ourselves would be to be convinced by a doubtful witness. In other words, if we are convinced by Socrates while identifying with his interlocutor, this conviction is not dialectical since we were not answering the questions.[13] The conviction would be an example of exactly what Socrates objects to, a form of intellectual laziness where we form opinions without going through the rigorous questioning ourselves.

That we should not read as interlocutors is shown in other ways by Plato. In the *Gorgias*, quoted above, Socrates questions three different interlocutors: first Gorgias himself, then his disciple Polus, and finally Callicles. In each case he covers similar ground, even though they are witnesses to each other's conviction. At no point does Socrates say, "Well, we can take for granted the point shown in the previous conversation." Each interlocutor has to be convinced independently just as Socrates expects to be convinced without appeal to the opinion of others. Perelman draws our attention to the personal character of the dialectical method. He argues, in contrast to Goblot, that the method does not depend on there being no alternative answers. For Perelman the method is used where demonstration fails—where there are too many different ways to answer. The dialectical method therefore starts from the interlocutor and adapts itself to his beliefs, and the way he answers. It is a rhetorical device to secure conviction where demonstration is not possible. The rhetorical force of the method lies in the questioning and the customized character of each exchange. It can convince where there is no demonstrable truth.

The Eavesdroppers

Another way of looking at the issue of the reader of Socratic dialogues is to look at the models he gives us of the Socratic audience. Look at the extent to which Plato describes a public setting for the Socratic dialogues. Plato includes descriptions of the audience for the Socratic exchange. He creates a framework into which we can fit our reading by describing the listening in of others. Take the *Lysis*, which starts in the following fashion:

> I was walking straight from the Academy to the Lyceum, by the road which skirts the outside of the walls, and had reached the little gate where is the source of the Panops, when I fell in with Hippothales, the son of Hieronymus, Ctesippus the Paenian, and some more young men, standing together in a group.[14]

Socrates is invited to join a group conversing in a newly erected palestra. He inevitably asks who is the prime beauty and discovers that Hippothales has a crush on a youth, Lysis. Socrates, discovering that Hippothales is head over heels in love, offers to engage Lysis in conversation so as to show Hippothales how he should talk to his beloved. The result is an exchange between Lysis and Socrates about friendship with Hippothales "writhing with agitation" at the proximity of his loved one.

> I turned my eyes on Hippothales, and was on the point of making a great blunder. For it came into my head to say, This is the way, Hippothales, that you should talk to your favorite, humbling and checking, instead of puffing him up and pampering him, as you now do. However, on seeing him writhing with agitation at the turn the conversation was taking, I recollected that though standing so near, he didn't wish to be seen by Lysis. So I recovered myself in time, and forbore to address him.[15]

Socrates clearly views his relationship with Hippothales to be different from the humbling of Lysis. The care Plato puts into creating this atmosphere indicates where we the reader might fit in. Perhaps like Hippothales we are listening and writhing with agitation as we watch our loved ones being humbled. This is different from being humbled and checked ourselves. We sympathize with the interlocutor, but we would feel uncomfortable if included in the conversation. As readers we have a security that not even Hippothales had; we know readers as readers can't be included. We can take this observation a step further. Sometimes we read because we do not want to be included. When one chooses to read about something rather than to participate in a discussion about it, one chooses the security of being an untouchable spectator, gazing on the participants in dialogue without risk. It is easy today to think that we have no choice but to read and to forget that choosing to read involves choosing a distance from which to engage in a subject, a distance that has its advantages and disadvantages.[16]

One might reply that it would do the reader good to identify with the interlocutor, that we might still learn that way. We may not be the interlocutor, but could we not profit by imaginatively playing the role? If the Socratic dialogues are any example of such an educational tactic, it does not work.[17] Most of Socrates' interlocutors in the early Platonic dialogues leave, not purified, but antagonized. They leave like Euthyphro, polite but impatient to leave,[18] or grind to a halt like Meno stunned as if by a sting ray.[19] Some leave furious like Antyus who will later return the insult when he joins forces with others to accuse Socrates of corrupting the young and so on.[20] Few leave convinced despite what they say. Few interlocutors (Crito in the *Crito* and the slave boy in the *Meno*) take the learning gracefully in the Socratic dialogues. Only in the later dialogues, like the *Republic* and *Laws*, do we see characters who enjoy learning, but these dialogues are beyond the scope of this chapter. Considering the number of characters in Plato's early works who reject the learning, why would Plato risk our identifying with them? If Plato intended us to identify with the interlocutor, wouldn't he have taken more care not to present such violent reactions on their part? Why would he want us to leave furious? He should want us to distance ourselves from the bigots Socrates has to contend with, not from Socrates. We, like those listening to the exchange, should be progressively embarrassed by their blindness.

Sacrificial Characters

Now we are closer to the character of the reader. Perhaps the interlocutor is being sacrificed for the sake of the audience including those who read.

Perhaps Socrates engaged people publicly in the hope that the youth who gathered around would learn from the humiliation of the great.[21] Plato likewise might want to offer a larger audience the chance to profit from the humiliation.

The point is that we profit because we can reject the interlocutor instead of identifying with him. The pernicious opinions of the interlocutor, to which we might be attracted, are sacrificed for and in us. If we identify too closely with the interlocutor we would not be able to reject his pernicious opinions once he is humbled. We would probably choose, like Callicles in the *Gorgias*, to refuse to learn.[22]

It is nonetheless important that we can imagine ourselves as the interlocutor. The sacrifice of the interlocutor within us can only take place if we sympathize initially with him. The rejection of the opinions of the interlocutor will only take place if we are at first fascinated by them. For this reason Socrates often appears to be an innocent, ignorant questioner and the other the mature authority to side with. For example in the *Protagoras* Socrates sets himself up as the simple representative of Hippocrates who wants to study with the great Protagoras. The sympathetic character of the other along with the promise of conflict with Socrates captivates us. Captivated by the exchange and fascinated by the other, we lose sight of ourselves, and this is why interpreters do not distinguish between reader and interlocutor. Perelman loses sight of the distinction because the work is successful at getting his attention. When the reader stands for nobody, as Shaftesbury suggests, it is understandable that the unfortunate interlocutor stands out as a tempting character with which to confuse oneself.

It is no coincidence that critics have confused the reader with the interlocutor, because, I believe, the author of Socratic dialogues wants us to become invisible to ourselves. He wants us to be captivated by the interlocutor's fate, and in rejecting him to reject that side of ourselves. To become captivated we must be invisible and hence tempted to confuse ourselves. To judge and reject we have to be other than the interlocutor. We have to leave the interlocutor's anger behind with him. The author does not, however, want us to think about the mechanism of sympathy and rejection, because that would undermine its effectiveness.

VALLA AND JUDGMENT

So far I have made my point negatively by discussing problems with the common view of the reader's role as the interlocutor. What remains is to look positively at the reader's judgment, a term I use to cover the entire process of sympathy, rejection, and purification. It also remains to show that the mechanism is not limited to Plato's early "Socratic" dialogues, but has been imitated by others. For this reason I am going to look closely at two dialogues by Lorenzo Valla, "De libero arbitrio" (On Free Will) and *De professione religiosorum* (On the Profession of the Religious), which nicely illustrate the call for judgment. This discussion will also, I hope, encourage readers who are not familiar with Valla to read his works.[23]

The Frames of Valla's Dialogues

"On Free Will" and *On the Profession of the Religious* are relevant to our project of discovering the reader, because both employ an outer frame that explicitly places the reader in the chair of judgment. How does Valla do this? Both dialogues begin with an address to a powerful contemporary dignitary, in other words an authority. Both end with a character other than Valla suggesting the discussion was so excellent it should be sent to the very dignitary it is addressed to, thereby explaining within the dialogue the eventual dedication at the beginning. This authority, and by implication the reader, is asked to judge the value of the work. The dedication and final call for judgment are a frame designed to orient the reader. The author attempts to restrict the role of the reader to that of a judge (and then to make sure that the case of the Socratic character is the best by the end). The explicitness of this process makes these two dialogues ideal texts to illustrate the place reserved for the reader by the author.

In both dialogues there is a Socratic character Lorenzo (Laurentius) who engages, in a combative fashion, another character. The character Lorenzo is clearly the author. Part of Valla's genius is the way he goes to great lengths to make Lorenzo (the character) unpalatable at the beginning of the dialogue. In both dialogues the initial address goes hand in hand with a provocation. In "On Free Will" the opening passage goes:

> I would prefer, O Garsia, most learned and best of bishops, that other Christians and, indeed, those who are called theologians would not depend so much on philosophy or devote so much energy to it.[24]

The dialogue is addressed in a flattering manner to a powerful bishop. In the same breath Valla launches into an attack on those who use philosophy to defend religion. He is attacking the orthodox religious scholars who looked back to Aristotle for a philosophical defense of Christianity, a position that many of his readers, including philosophers today, find attractive. Not far down the page Valla slips into addressing us directly, "You have likewise reached such a degree of insolence that you believe no one can become a theologian unless he knows the precepts of philosophy."[25] The rhetorical effect is to make the reader feel he is being accused of insolence. We are tempted to take the philosophical side (as opposed to Lorenzo the Socratic's side) simply because Valla is so provocative. The polemical beginning is a rhetorical device for getting our attention and tempting us to sympathize with the other interlocutor.

The provocation is nicely handled in the opening of the second dialogue under consideration here, "Baptista, your honour, many persons commonly marvel at me and some even reproach me personally, partly because I tackle subjects that are too lofty and difficult and, partly, because I never fail to select someone to chastise."[26] Here, once more, we see Valla addressing a powerful figure, and launching into the polemical issue that frames the dialogue. The dialogue turns out to be an example of Lorenzo chastising someone much as Socrates humbled public figures. The rhetorical effect of this opening is similar to that of "On Free Will," for the reader is engaged and challenged. We expect Valla to be controversial and to a certain extent to enter into controversy with us. What is interesting here is that Valla's reputation for polemicizing is the very issue that he raises polemically here.

The polemical character of Valla's work in general has been noted by most of his commentators. This is not the place to discuss his uses of the rhetoric of praise and blame; however, it is worth noting that Valla seems to be encouraging this myth about himself in *On the Profession of the Religious*. Why? Because his project is one that feeds on controversy. Invective, as Nancy Struever points out, is part of his "redefinition of the role of the author/speaker"[27] and consequently also of the reader/listener.

She argues that the use of invective and the use of the letter form (both these dialogues are framed in letters addressed to the ideal reader) respectively ensure the malevolence and benevolence of the reader. The polemical parts, especially the accusation of insolence, provoke the reader while the epistolary character of the work, addressed in a flattering manner, encourages the reader by the end to judge in a friendly fashion.

Why would Valla want to risk the friendly outcome by being polemical and insulting the reader? For the same reason that Plato would want the reader to sympathize initially with the unfortunate interlocutor who is humiliated. The reader must have a stake in the discussion if he is to profit from it. To be more specific, the opinions that are rejected in the Socratic dialogue are usually those the author's intended reader might be tempted to hold. The characters and opinions Socrates engaged were often the authoritative ones of his day. It is central to his project that he engage the public characters and popular opinions. A provocative opening makes sure that the reader is not lulled into thinking that he has nothing at stake here.

Likewise, when Valla talks of theologians who depend on philosophy, he is addressing a large segment of his contemporary readers who looked to Aristotle and Boethius for inspiration. If the reader connects the other interlocutor with opinions she has held, then the rejection of these popular notions is felt as a provocation.[28] But, just in case the reader does not realize he has something at stake, Valla accuses him of insolence or mentions what an ornery fellow he is. "By the way, did I tell you how controversial my opinions are?" Valla does not do this so that the reader stays connected to the interlocutor. As I mentioned above, this connection between reader and interlocutor is not one of identity. The reader can reject the opinions of the interlocutor, letting the unfortunate interlocutor leave with them in anger.

We can now understand why Socrates is not a likely role model for the reader, at least the first-time reader. First, authors like Valla go out of their way to make the Socratic character unpalatable. Plato does this with Socratic ignorance, irony, and paradoxes. Who, after all, would side with someone who insists that it is better to be wronged than to wrong another? Try to remember, if you can, your first encounter with Socrates. Look at how students buck and fight with Socrates when they first encounter him in Plato. The Socratic paradoxes serve nicely to alienate the average "sensible" reader.

A second reason why Socrates is not likely to be the intended role for the reader is the logic of judgment. If I am right that the intended rhetorical effect of a Socratic dialogue is to get the reader to distance himself from popular opinions, and if to do so one has to awaken the sympathy of the reader for those opinions (so that the opinions are at stake) then it follows that the reader who sympathizes with the Socratic character has either already been converted, or will not be affected by the dialogue in the desired fashion. A reader who finds the Socratic character the most attractive from the beginning is either free of the opinions that Socrates critiques, or has not connected the opinions he holds in other contexts with those at stake in the dialogue. It is unfortunately all too easy to read about ethical issues without considering one's own beliefs and actions.

To a certain degree it does not make a difference to my argument if the reader does sympathize with the Socratic character. Even if you like Socrates, that does not necessarily mean that you cannot also sympathize with the common opinions carried by the interlocutor. The reader who likes Socrates can still find the experience of reading a Socratic dialogue purges him of his latent affection for other opinions. This does not alter the fact that as readers we are not participants in the dialogue, but among the extended audience who hear about it. It is important to note that just as sympathy with the interlocutor is not the same as being the interlocutor, so sympathy for the Socratic character is not the same as being him. Whichever character we sympathize with, the experience of reading is that of overhearing, then judging, and purging.

This is not to dismiss the intense identification with Socrates which some feel; though I believe this is a later phase in the development of the reader. Identification with Socrates is comparable to the third step in the treatment of Euthydemus described in the previous chapter. Readers, like Euthydemus, first listen in and are purified of their conceits. Only when they are ready does Socrates approach alone in a friendly fashion, offering to rebuild us in his image. Just as this happened in the oral Socratic circle, it can happen to readers who, as they become familiar with the Socratic corpus, are able to bring Socrates close by reconstructing his character within themselves. They can then enter into friendly dialogue with this reconstruction. It is a testimony to Plato's skill as an author that he has infected so many over the years with this character. The internal dialogue with Socrates is not really with the text, but with an imaginary friend that reading the text brings to life. When the reader talks with Socrates it is more of a soliloquy with that of Socrates within, and as such, we are not readers so much as recreators of dialogue. While reading we are catching the infection of Socrates, but we are not, as readers, talking to him.

The Call to Judgment

We have looked so far at the opening of Valla's framed orientation of the reader. The initial engagement in both dialogues is combined with a final situation where we are called to judge whether Valla was right in the first place. We are called at the end to forgive the Socratic character who gradually becomes the more attractive one, and to reject the superficially reasonable interlocutor. "On Free Will" ends with a call from Antonio, the other interlocutor, to involve others, like ourselves:

> *Ant.* . . . Will you not commit this debate which we have had between us to writing and make a report of it so that you may have others share this good?
>
> *Lorenzo.* . . . That is good advice. Let us make others judges in this matter, and, if it is good, sharers. Above all, let us send this argument, written and, as you say, made into a report, to the Bishop of Lerida, whose judgment I would place before all I know, and if he alone approves, I would not fear the disapproval of others.[29]

It is as if the characters of the dialogue created the written work. With no author we have two characters in search of an audience. They create the context for the reading of the dialogue. This tidy circularity, which is also found in *On the Profession of the Religious*, is a rhetorical effect that is hard to miss as a reader. The obviousness of it draws attention to the ideal reader of the work, the excellent bishop whose judgment is worth so much. This bishop, who is now a character whose judgment has been praised, is the ideal against which the reader compares himself. The reader begins the work accused of the insolence of philosophy and finishes the dialogue being given the chance to live up to the example of the bishop, judging the dialogue as the bishop would.

The judgment that Valla calls for from his ideal, and hopefully benevolent, reader involves choosing to reject one side for the other. The judgment is between two characters who hold two sets of beliefs that by the end of a Socratic dialogue cannot be reconciled. As I have suggested above, the judgment has all the more force if the reader has been engaged. The judgment called for is not the same as the dispassionate judgment between propositions. The opinions in dialogue have character. When the reader judges which character he prefers he rejects one. The rejection can be seen as a purification of that of the character within him. The reader decides who he wants to be, or, to be more accurate, who he does not want to be. That is the rhetorical power of the written dialogue, its ability to change our very character. There is always the risk that the reader will refuse to judge, in which case the dialogue has failed to move him.

There is also the danger that the reader will still judge in favor of the unfortunate other. Most Socratic dialogues, however, do not leave much room for judgment. By the end the other has shown himself to be a thoroughly unlikable character whatever his opinions. Both Plato and Valla make sure of this by using the very fact of the other's refusal to continue the pursuit of truth as a sign of insincerity.

> Then I said: . . . "And if a week from today, at the same time and in the same place, our Friar does not present himself and keep the appointment, so to speak, not only shall I make it public, but I shall bring the work to the attention of some very learned and wise person and have it examined by him. . . ." As he did not turn up on the appointed day, we were enabled to have the work brought for examination to the designated authority.[30]

Thus ends *On the Profession of the Religious*. How could we sympathize at the end with a Friar who hasn't the courage to come back and argue the point any further? The unfortunate Friar, as is the case in so many Socratic dialogues, leaves convicted in our eyes. We are invited to judge where the case is clear.[31]

Refusing to continue the discussion and hence the pursuit of truth is the ultimate sin of dialogue. It is a rejection of the very ground of the event. It is a rejection of the reader who is willing to listen. We the readers naturally end up preferring the interlocutor who is committed to knowledge. The other, by quitting, leaves us with only one possible hero, the Socratic fool who provoked us in the first place (and also has the time to stick around).

More on Judgment

Why doesn't the author invite us outright to judge between positions? "Here are two positions, choose the best please." If he did, the work would not be a dialogue and we would not be judging character. It would be either a survey of opinions or a work of one character, the author, whom we are asked to judge. In the traditional philosophical work, which Collingwood calls the confession, the reader is addressed directly by the author. He is invited into dialogue with the author. The author confesses his belief about the subject and the reader attends silently under the illusion he can respond. As Shaftesbury suggests, the author tries to seduce the reader with this confession, not to put him in the position to judge for himself. In this sort of work there are no other characters from which to judge. For us to judge between characters, not opinions, we have to be given characters, at which point the author loses his privileged status; his call for judgment is just the act of one of the characters. The logic of character is unforgiving. Once the author presents the reader with more than one character he loses his authoritative voice; the author as authority becomes nobody. The author has to resort to subtler tactics to convict and convince.

Another reason we are not asked to judge is because the choice to judge should come from us. To be rhetorically effective, not only how we judge, but that we judge, should appear to be our decision. The author does not want us feeling frustrated the way the unfortunate interlocutor does. The author wants the opposite effect, the illusion of freedom of choice. The author wants us to feel that we chose to stay and listen, that we chose to judge between the positions, and that we chose the position of the Socratic character. The author does this by creating a situation that calls for a decision, without explicitly asking for decision. The illusion of our listening-in is necessary to give us the space to decide. It is for that reason that we are incidentally tempted to think the place of the reader is that of the interlocutor. The author does not want us to realize we are being encouraged to judge—he just wants us to judge transparently and leave with that judgment on our lips.

This also explains the absence of the author. There would be no call for decision if the author told us explicitly what he believed. Then we would be judging the author and work, not the characters set up within. We might take the author as an authority and believe him without deciding for him. In so doing we would hardly be convinced. The rhetorical effect of being talked at is negligible. As in so many circumstances there are times when it is best to be silent and let the other make up her mind. So the author vanishes, creating the space for an informed decision, and forcing us to take responsibility for a character, our own.

CONCLUSION

In this chapter I have raised the question of the relationship between author and reader of Socratic dialogues. The astute reader will notice that I did not discuss the author much—that is left for the next chapter; instead, I drew attention to the temptation to confuse the reader with the Socratic interlocutor and show how that answer is unsatisfactory. I then argued that authors of Socratic dialogues want the reader to sympathize initially with the interlocutor, but, by the end, to judge between the Socratic and the interlocutor (and to judge for the Socratic character). The reader is provoked into listening in to the conflict and, by the end, is called to judge. In judging the reader purifies himself of the often popular opinions held by the interlocutor. This purification is similar to the effect described in the previous chapter that the staged discussions of the Socratic circle had for possible converts like Euthydemus. The reader, like Euthydemus listens in, and is purified that way, not through direct dialogue. (This is the way in which the oral and written dialogue are the same, and this similarity to those outside is what we will later try to define.)

Does this rhetorical mechanism throw any light on dialogues that are not "Socratic?" Although this is not the place for an extended discussion of the types of philosophical dialogue, it is worth mentioning a major type of dialogue that can be traced to Plato's *Phaedrus*, the rural conversations between friends. These dialogues, taking place outside the polis, are often without the surrounding of eavesdroppers that help us fit in as readers. Only the cicadas listen in to Socrates' dialogue with Phaedrus. Certain dialogues of Cicero, the dialogues of Cicero's Renaissance imitators like

Bruni, and those of the English eighteenth-century authors like Berkeley and David Hume, all fit loosely into this pattern. These dialogues take place in secluded country locations (often aristocratic estates). The characters are friends and their speeches are longer. There is not the systematic questioning that leads one character to contradict himself. Since the characters are often friends they are less likely to humiliate each other. The outcome, without one character's being forced to admit he contradicted himself, is not as decisive as a Socratic dialogue. Instead, you often have one character who shows off his oratorical skills by arguing first one side of the issue and then the other. This character, like Socrates in the *Phaedrus*, first convinces the others of one position and then appears to reverse himself, thereby displaying his ability to argue both sides, a skill that an orator like Cicero appreciated.

The reversal, a feature of a number of philosophical dialogues in the Ciceronian vein, provides a clue to how such dialogues might work rhetorically. The reader is first convinced one way and then surprised by an argument the other way from the same character. This works on the reader in a fashion similar to the provocation of Socratic dialogues. The reader is sucked into one position, only then to have it undermined. The reversal calls into question the first position forcing the reader to judge between positions (though not always characters).

There are, however, some differences between the Ciceronian and Socratic dialogues. The Ciceronian dialogue often ends up emphasizing the importance of rhetoric and discourse over one or the other position. Often the author's concern seems to be the culture of discourse around an issue rather than the individual positions on the issue. Hume leaves us with a picture of how civilized people can coexist who disagree over something like the nature of god.

A second difference lies in the absence of a clear victor at the end. The reversal provokes the reader to judge between the positions rather than merely acknowledging the difference, but the choice is harder. In the case of Hume's *Dialogues* and the dialogue by Cicero which inspired it (*The Nature of the Gods*), the reversal provokes judgment, but the reader is more likely to judge in favor of what might be called the first position rather than the second. The absence of a clear choice in the Ciceronian dialogue, or the fact that often both positions are presented by the same person, means that the reader is not so much purified of any position, as left skeptical of any claims to certainty on either side. It is no coincidence that both Cicero and Hume were skeptics of one kind or another. One can also see the connection between the skeptical result—no one position is a clear victor—and the focus on discourse. On issues where certainty is unlikely, the health of the culture of discourse becomes important. In these dialogues the character of the dialogue itself is the issue.

While I believe the analysis above of the Socratic reader can be modified to explain the relationship in Ciceronian dialogues, that does not mean that we can perfectly fit this model to all philosophical dialogues. It is a testimony to the wealth of rhetorical possibilities of the dialogue that no one relationship can capture all of our experience of the works and their authors. I leave it to the reader to imagine how one might deal with the reader's place in Plato's *Symposium*, or Diderot's dialogue-novels.

NOTES

1. Anthony Ashley Cooper, Earl of Shaftesbury, *Characteristics of Men, Manners, Opinions, Times, etc.*, vol. 1 (Gloucester, Mass.: Peter Smith, 1963), p. 132.

2. I am not going to argue this point about the author. I am interested in the reader. Suffice it to say that the author does not in dialogue address his reader as if he were there. As David Hume puts it, "The dialogue writer desires, by departing from the direct style of composition, to give a freer air to his performance, and avoid the appearance of *author* and *reader*." Hume, *Dialogues Concerning Natural Religion* (New York: Bobbs-Merrill, 1970), p. 3. Often the writer might address the reader outside the dialogue, thereby entering into a different sort of dialogue, but that is a different story.

3. A good discussion of the Socratic method that characterizes the early Platonic dialogues can be found in Richard Robinson's *Plato's Earlier Dialectic*. "The outstanding method in Plato's earlier dialogues is the Socratic elenchus. 'Elenchus' in the wider sense means examining a person with regard to a statement he has made, by putting to him questions calling for further statements, in the hope that they will determine the meaning and truth-value of his first statement. Most often the truth-value expected is falsehood; and so 'elenchus' in the narrower sense is a form of cross-examination or refutation." *Plato's Earlier Dialectic* (Ithaca, N.Y.: Cornell University Press, 1941), p. 7. It is worth reading the first chapter of Robinson's book simply for the way he criticizes this all too often worshipped method. He does not hesitate to question our heroic Socrates.

4. As for dialogues of the dead they achieve their effect largely through the interesting combinations of characters from across time and including the gods. This otherworldly combination can only be achieved among the dead. One of the things one can do when combining characters that could never have met in this world is bring Socrates together with thinkers of another era, in effect producing a "Socratic" dialogue. It is worth noting, however, that often Socrates is brought into play to mock him as the father of philosophy, not to use him.

5. Plato, *Gorgias*, trans. W. D. Woodhead, in *The Collected Dialogues of Plato*, ed. Edith Hamilton and Huntington Cairns (Princeton, N.J.: Princeton University Press, 1961), 472b.

6. Plato, *Theaetetus*, trans. F. M. Cornford, in *The Collected Dialogues of Plato*, 150b. It is a pity he delivered so many stillborn children, i.e., that so many of the beliefs he drew out of his interlocutors were phantoms.

7. A close reading of Xenophon's dialogues suggests that Socrates was concerned with the opinions of those who listened inasmuch as those of his interlocutor. I suspect Socrates often sacrificed the interlocutor for the sake of the audience, not the other way around.

8. Michael Walzer, "A Critique of Philosophical Conversation," *Philosophical Forum* 21, nos. 1–2 (fall–winter 1989–1990): 183.

9. Hans-Georg Gadamer, *Philosophical Apprenticeships*, trans. Robert R. Sullivan (Cambridge, Mass.: MIT Press, 1985), p. 185.

10. Gadamer's view, as he fleshes it out in *Truth and Method,* is that through careful interpretation we can bring the conversation to life and then learn from it. Our learning through it involves an openness to the question the text is an answer to. See the section entitled "The Model of the Platonic Dialectic," pp. 325–41, in *Truth and Method*, 2d ed., trans. W. Glen Doepel (New York: Crossroad, 1985).

11. This quote is taken from Chaim Perelman, *The Idea of Justice and the Problem of Argument*, trans. John Petrie (London: Routledge & Kegan Paul, 1963), p. 162. Perelman quotes Edmond Goblot (*La logique des jugements de valeur; théorie et applications* [Paris: A. Colin, 1927]) as offering an answer to the question he wants to answer, "What would be the value of the dialectical method, not only for the readers but for Plato himself as well?" It is worth noting that Perelman does not agree with this answer. However, he falls for the identical temptation of seeing the reader and interlocutor as identically affected by the dialogue. He forgets the issue of the reader, not mentioning it again. Like Goblot, he is concerned with the effect of dialectic on the interlocutor, not a third party.

12. Richard Robinson, in an essay entitled "Elenchus," expresses something similar: "The Socratic elenchus is a very personal affair, in spite of Socrates'

ironical declarations that it is an impersonal search for the truth. If the ulterior end of the elenchus is to be attained, it is essential the answerer himself be convinced, and quite indifferent whether anyone else is." "Elenchus," in *The Philosophy of Socrates: A Collection of Essays*, ed. Gregory Vlastos (New York: Anchor Books, 1971), p. 88.

13. One might argue that if we can imagine no different answers than those offered by the interlocutor then we are dialectically convinced. But experience tells us that this is hardly the case. We do, while reading the dialogue, imagine different answers. Like Polus and then Callicles in the *Gorgias*, we will disagree with a tack taken by the interlocutor and want to pick up that thread with Socrates. We may even disagree with the initial question from which the discussion stems. I think the burden of proof lies with those who want to argue that the interlocutor and reader are convinced in an identical fashion. The experience of hearing someone being questioned and being questioned oneself is obviously different. Even if the audience is convinced, they are not convinced in the same fashion. This chapter is trying to show how the reader might be convinced.

14. Plato, *Lysis*, trans. J. Wright, in *The Collected Dialogues of Plato*, 203a.

15. Ibid., 210e.

16. Socrates in Xenophon's *Memorabilia* (4.2) makes fun of Euthydemus's reliance on book learning. One of his points is that one needs to get involved in a community of discourse to become wise—books are not enough.

17. Robinson in *Plato's Earlier Dialectic* criticizes the educational and purgatory effects of Socratic cross-examination: "The irony seems to be a main cause of the anger which, as Socrates declares (*Apology* 21E etc.), often results from the elenchus; and if elenchus really makes people hate you, surely it is bad teaching and a bad form of intercourse in general. We can hardly suppose that after the victim's anger has cooled they admit their ignorance and start to reform their lives" (p. 18).

18. "Another time, then, Socrates, for I am in a hurry, and must be off this minute." Plato, *Euthyphro*, trans. Lane Cooper, in *The Collected Dialogues of Plato*, 15e.

19. Meno says, "Socrates, even before I met you they told me that in plain truth you are a perplexed man yourself and reduce others to perplexity. . . . Not only in outward appearance but in other respects as well you are exactly like the flat sting ray that one meets in the sea. Whenever anyone comes into contact with it, it numbs him, and that is the sort of thing that you seem to be doing to me now." Plato, *Meno*, trans. W. K. C. Guthrie, in *The Collected Dialogues of Plato*, 79e–80a.

20. Antyus prophetically warns Socrates, "You seem to me, Socrates, to be too ready to run people down. My advice to you, if you will listen to it, is to be

careful. I dare say that in all cities it is easier to do a man harm than good, and it is certainly so here, as I expect you know yourself." Antyus leaves and Socrates says, "Antyus seems angry, Meno, and I am not surprised." Plato *Meno* 94e–95a. Neither are we.

21. It is worth remembering that Socrates was martyred for corrupting the youth of Athens through his teaching. In the *Apology* he denies that he ever taught anything. One can imagine how the citizens, many of whose sons were impressed by the Socratic habit of humiliation and tried to imitate it, greeted this argument. It is amazing how close the decision of the jury was.

22. Callicles complains about having to continue the dialogue once it is clear that it is not going his way: "How importunate you are, Socrates; if you will listen to me, you will bid good-by to this argument, or else debate with somebody else." Plato, *Gorgias*, 505d. Socrates recognizes the irritation of Callicles: "If you refute me, I shall not be vexed with you as you are with me" (506c).

23. Lorenzo Valla was born in Rome in 1407 and died there in 1457. He was the secretary to Alfonso V of Aragon from 1437 to 1448 during which time he wrote works critical of papal power and traditional Aristotelian philosophy. It was during this time that he finished both "On Free Will" and *On the Profession of the Religious*. Despite his criticism of papal power he then went to Rome to work as a papal secretary and professor of rhetoric and lived there until his death. One of Valla's lasting contributions was his use of careful philological analysis. In *On the Profession* his character repeatedly comments on the origin of the words he is using, accusing "you friars" of corrupting the words they use. His interest in philological analysis was not mere pedantry; he used it philosophically and for rhetorical advantage. Another aspect of Valla, to which he himself draws attention, is the polemical character of most of his work. Rarely satisfied to make a point, he has to insult those before him. That makes his work engaging but it also led to his appearing before the Inquisition.

24. Lorenzo Valla, "On Free Will," in *The Renaissance Philosophy of Man*, ed. Eugenio Garin (Milan and Naples: Ricciardi, 1952), p. 155.

25. Ibid., p. 156.

26. Valla, *On the Profession of the Religious and the Principal Arguments from The Falsely-Believed and Forged Donation of Constantine*, trans. Olga Zorzi Pugliese (Toronto: Centre for Reformation and Renaissance Studies, 1985), p. 17.

27. Nancy Struever, "Lorenzo Valla: Humanist Rhetoric and the Critique of the Classical Languages of Morality," in *Renaissance Eloquence: Studies in the Theory and Practice of Renaissance Rhetoric*, ed. James J. Murphy (Berkeley: University of California Press, 1993), p. 199.

28. Carol Sherman argues something similar to my point: "The dialogue form can force him (the reader) to uneasiness and responsibility. The author, for his part, gives up his position as intermediary between the public and fictional world. The reader in immediate contact with the latter world, is constantly summoned, and may feel himself encouraged to weigh opinions, adopt resolutions, and make judgments." Sherman, *Diderot and the Art of Dialogue* (Geneva: Librairie Droz, 1976), p. 19.

29. Valla, "On Free Will," p. 182.

30. Valla, *On the Profession of the Religious*, p. 55.

31. It is worth noting that later dialogues, like those of Hume and Diderot, are far less clear at the end. Both authors have dialogues where there is no clear victor. But these are not really Socratic dialogues; they resemble Ciceronian ones without a clear Socratic character and without the careful cross-examination. Nonetheless I think this discussion of the role of the reader still applies. We are still tempted to sympathize with interlocutors. We still find our beliefs questioned and ultimately are put in the position of having to decide what we really believe after the dialogue.

4 The WRITING of DIALOGUE

In the last chapter we looked at the role of the reader. To use Umberto Eco's term we looked at the model reader as he is manipulated by the text.[1] We now turn to the other stakeholder in the written dialogue, that is, the model author. This character has such a small part in philosophical dialogues we have to turn to the prefaces of reported dialogues for hints.[2] Recovery of the model author will lead to the central problem of the writing of philosophical dialogues which in turn will close the discussion on oral and written dialogue. In the last chapter we found that the model reader finds himself in a role similar to those who overhear oral dialogue; in this we found a point of continuity of oral and written dialogue. In this chapter we will look for further points of continuity.

HINTS TO THE CHARACTER OF THE AUTHOR

We should be specific about the author we are looking for. We do not want information about the empirical author who actually wrote the work. Rather we are looking for the model author—that character that emerges from the text itself as the creator of the text. The model author is a creation of the empirical author as much as any other character, though this does not mean that the model author is a conscious creation. The model author is the face or voice that emerges for the reader in the reading as the apparent author of the text.[3] It is the character of the writer presented in the writing for those who are interested. Here we use the concept of the model author, partly to avoid questions, impossible to answer in many cases, about the intentions of the "real" or empirical author. More importantly, I am interested in the model author because one should begin by respecting the way the text chooses to present itself. Often dialogues are prefaced by the words of a fictional reporter like Pamphilus, who is the model author of David Hume's *Dialogues*; we should take seriously such characters set up by the empirical authors for us to read about. They are the hint left within the text as to the nature of the author.

Absence

The first thing that stands out about written dialogue is the inaccessibility of the author. As Anthony, Earl of Shaftesbury puts it, "For here (in dialogue) the author is annihilated, and the reader, being no way applied to, stands for nobody. The self-interesting parties both vanish at once."[4] The author is annihilated as the various characters become accessible. In a dialogue they are allowed to speak for themselves and are not merely summarized by the author. There is no author telling us what the characters really thought. There is rarely the overt intrusion of the author as there is, for example, in the treatise or essay. The author, if he or she appears within a dialogue, is simply one more character; their special authority on the issue at hand is annihilated by the act of letting others through. Even reported dialogues, which are ostensibly in the voice of the first person, tend to devolve into a direct report of what everyone said with the authorial voice left for the preface and epilogue (and a few moments in between).[5] It is in the nature of dialogue, where most of the words are those of characters, that the author retreats or becomes another character.

Why would authors surrender their authority? The cynical view is that they do so to better manipulate the reader while giving the impression of freedom of judgment. This assumes that all acts of writing are acts of willful intellectual colonization. A simpler explanation for the silence is that the author does not want, in dialogue, to appear. When Shaftesbury points out that in the disappearance of the reader and author the self-interested parties vanish, he identifies what about the two is absent—their interests, or more precisely their self-interest. The authors' interest lies in submerging their other interests.[6] We can say only that they do not want the reader to know what they believe or what their intentions were. We do not know why they do not want to appear. The cynical view ascribes them an intention where there is no evidence. We can speculate about the reasons for this: Authors may not have a single opinion of which they are trying to convince the reader. The author may want us to pay attention, seriously, to the voices orchestrated, or to some other voice that comes through, as our reading of Heidegger's dialogue suggested. In Cicero we find the suggestion that the author might actually be interested in what the characters he lets loose have to say, as if even he were surprised by their words![7]

Why, then, are we still tempted to attribute to the missing author a hidden agenda? More generally, why are we so fascinated with authors? Could it be our self-interest? Are we so used to suspecting texts of having authors and authors of having an agenda (why else would they bother to write?) that we cannot imagine a philosophical work without some thesis belonging to someone it wishes to promote? Must all works have only one position embedded within? Must we be so suspicious? The cynical view is built on an unexamined politic of suspicion which is not the only possibility that fits the character.[8]

Chapter 1, on Heidegger's dialogue, hinted that the author's vanishing is due to a redefinition of authority. Oral dialogue participates in and evolves from the authority of a community or tradition. Sayings of an oral community have no individual author. The authority of oral sayings lies not with their performer. Rather, an oral saying in an oral community would be perceived as being without authority if believed to have been invented by the performer. The authority of such oral sayings is the community and its perception of its history. The written dialogue emulates, in the vanishing of the author, this type of authority. The fact that most written dialogues have empirical authors, who put pen to paper, does not mean that the authority of these works has to be the empirical author. An interviewer is not treated as the sole source of the content of an interview, and likewise we recognize that the simple "one text = one author" formula does not describe all documents. The authority for Plato's dialogues lies partly with Socrates, whatever Plato's artistry. In sum, we should open our mind to the possibility that dialogues are paths through to sources of authority other than the empirical author.

Apology

Given his or her absence, can we learn anything more about the model author? The intentions of the model author in most dialogues are inaccessible because there is no literal text by the author—everything is in another voice. In a few dialogues there are interventions by the model author which provide other hints as to his or her character. An easy way to categorize dialogues is to divide them into those that are reported by a narrator, and those that are direct transcripts of a conversation. While those that are reported eventually settle into something similar to direct dialogue, the reporting allows the narrator an opportunity to comment on the dialogue outside the context of the conversation reported. Reported dialogues often have outer frames composed of prefaces and epilogues that give a broader context to the conversation, justify the work, and create an audience for it. Such dialogues are often epistolary; the letter encloses the direct dialogue with words addressed to another. The best examples of such prefaces are Cicero and his many imitators like Hume. We will use the Ciceronian tradition of epistolary dialogues to gather further hints.

A familiar dialogue to start with is Hume's *Dialogues Concerning Natural Religion* where the narrator Pamphilus prefaces the conversation he observed with comments about the virtues of the dialogue form and its particular suitability to the subject at hand. The preface and concluding remarks of Pamphilus frame the direct recital, making the whole appear to be a letter to Hermippus, a friend who is also interested in these subjects and personalities. Pamphilus begins the reporting with:

> It has been remarked, my Hermippus, that, though the ancient philosophers conveyed most of their instruction in the form of dialogue, this method of composition has been little practiced in later ages, and has seldom succeeded in the hands of those who have attempted it. . . . To deliver a system in conversation scarcely appears natural. . . . [The dialogue writer] is apt to run into a worse inconvenience and convey the image of *pedagogue* and *pupil*. Or if he carries on the dispute in the nat-

> ural spirit of good company . . . he often loses so much time in preparations and transitions that the reader will scarcely think himself compensated, by all the graces of dialogue, for the order, brevity, and precision, which are sacrificed to them.[9]

Let me begin by noting that Pamphilus, who is writing a letter, not a dialogue, is apologizing for the dialogue form of the work. Pamphilus, a clearly fictional character, as his Greek name suggests, defends the form when all he is doing is writing to a fictional friend Hermippus in which he reports a conversation of his elders. That should alert us that the model author is coming through. This opening from the author acknowledges that the dialogue form is rarely used in philosophy, has been frequently misused, and has certain disadvantages, like long preparatory passages, of which the preface might be an example. The opening is surprisingly apologetic, conscious of the difference in form of the work, and careful to justify it when it does not need justification (at least not to Hermippus). None of Hume's other works are as self-conscious. We will find that the model author, when he or she speaks through, is often uncertain about his or her choice of the dialogue form. They regularly apologize for their work. The author who wants to disappear often expresses uncertainty about the writing, an uncertainty that is often in contrast to the certainty of the characters.

This apologetic quality can be found in the very form itself. Dialogues in a curious way call into question all philosophical writing. They point in a unique way to an unwritten activity (oral dialogue) and, by representing it, dignify it over the written. Other written philosophical forms do not undermine themselves this way, or undermine their written quality. In the writing of dialogue one is not engaging in oral dialogue, which the written dialogue tends to glorify by imitation. Writing a dialogue is an admission of absence of oral dialogue in the act of representing it. The author of dialogue opens himself to the accusation of hypocrisy. (How could Plato write dialogues after what he reports in the *Republic* and the *Phaedrus*? Why was Cicero writing dialogues when he should have been exercising his legendary rhetorical skills to save the Republic?) Even without an apologetic authorial intervention, the written dialogue has an apologetic character.

Leisure

This preface of Hume's should remind us of the prefaces of Cicero's dialogues, such as *The Making of an Orator* or *The Nature of the Gods*. (For one thing, the work is obviously related in content and structure to *The Nature of the Gods*.) In *The Making of an Orator*, the work presents itself as a prolonged letter by Cicero to his brother Quintus in which he introduces and then recounts a conversation on oratory. Cicero the empirical author creates an authorial character, Cicero the narrator/author, who uses his brother to justify writing at such great length:

> But none the less, though events are thus harassing and my time so restricted, I will hearken to the call of our studies, and every moment of leisure allowed me by the perfidy of my enemies, the advocacy of my friends and my political duties, I will dedicate first and foremost to writing. And when you, brother, exhort and request me, I will not fail you, for no man's authority or wish can have greater weight with me than yours.[10]

Cicero, the model author, places his writing in the context of a busy political life. He writes when he has the leisure—leisure which is at a premium for a busy man like Cicero. In *The Nature of the Gods* he returns to this lament, blaming that work in part on "The state of the nation [which] was such that the government had of necessity been confided to the care and wisdom of a single man."[11] In a dictatorship there is no place for orators like Cicero, forcing him to withdraw from politics and turn to writing. This writing, to which he turns in a moment of enforced leisure, is by his own admission less important an activity than his work as an orator-statesman. Only when circumstances force Cicero to abandon the oral dialogue of the courts and politics does he have leisure to pen a written dialogue. Enforced leisure is connected to the apologetic uncertainty of the author. When one is uncertain about writing one does not turn to it unless all other avenues of expression are restricted. Leisure is that time when one is not doing more important things. The produce of leisure is "just for fun," and therefore not to be judged as the real duty of a person. Leisure is when one can experiment and play; you will be excused if the result is frivolous as you have done your duty elsewhere. This is all the more true if one is writing dialogues. They represent the types of activity Cicero would be involved in rather than writing.

Culture

Cicero's dialogues are not only the result of enforced leisure but a response to the state of the nation. The dialogue form by its nature presents material as the opinions of many in communion; in Cicero's case this is a response to a state of government by one. The form is justified by the political circumstances (dictatorship) and hark back to the day when the characters of the dialogue conducted politics as they did philosophy, at their leisure and in conversation. Cicero's dialogue is the product of the absence of oral dialogue and a response to the state of the culture. An author who values the existence of discussion over the outcome of any discourse would have reason to disappear before a lively set of characters. She or he would also have a reason for writing other than the putting forward of a particular opinion. Only in a culture where there is freedom of expression do we suspect all authors of opinions. Even where there is a certain freedom, model authors are concerned with the character of discourse in the culture at large. One reading of Hume's *Dialogues* is that his final concern is not with the nature of god so much as with the character of the discussion around religious issues which could, and still does, get heated.

The reallocation of authority from the model author back to the culture also illustrates the importance of culture to writers of dialogue. Authors like Heidegger want to let something common to us all speak through their language. Renaissance dialogue writers like Bruni wanted to glorify and encourage the emerging philosophical culture of Florence. Bruni was adapting the example of Cicero, whose dialogues were an attempt to model a native Latin philosophy. I use the word model in both the sculptural sense, that dialogues attempt to shape culture, and in the sense that they are modeled on what is already there. In effect, dialogue shapes by pretending that it is imitating what is already there; when in fact what is there is being reinterpreted in a utopian fashion. We might say that dialogue inaugurates culture, showing what could be.

Character

Underneath all the previous characteristic concerns of the model is a general concern for character. Character can be provisionally defined as a unity of action and speech in a person. The way someone acts and speaks is their character. Important to character is the congruence between action and speech. One of the most obvious differences between dialogues and other philosophical works is the way ideas are presented in character. One does not have the cold itemization of positions in a dialogue; one has a dressing up of positions into characters whose actions can be compared to their words.

The model author is absent because the author, if he does speak, has been reduced to being another character who need not have more authority than other characters. The apologetic quality of the model author, where he appears, is part of his character, as are his claims about leisure. What the author does with his leisure is an issue for a character who wants their words and actions (like writing) to be congruent. The author who values oral dialogue has to explain why he would waste time writing. ("Oh, I had a few spare hours, so I wrote a dialogue.") Finally showing how characters are cultivated and how they interact is the way dialogues model culture.

Central to Cicero's recreation of a philosophical culture are the characters he fashions. Like Plato he chose people who existed, and like Plato he took liberties with their character in order to fit them into the culture he imagines. Cicero embarks on a conscious project to create a Latin philosophical tradition as capable as the Greek. To do this he needs to distort the character of famous predecessors in order to line them up as his worthy predecessors.

Cicero portrays these people as friends of his and learned teachers, thereby also fashioning his reputation. This is one of the vain aspects of Cicero. He praises his characters in a fashion designed to reflect glory back on himself, their worthy student. This vanity is peculiar to Cicero and is explained by the circumstances of political life in Rome. An orator's reputation, which was based on his family's reputation, was a major component of his authority and ability to convince. Logical arguments were less convincing to the Romans than the speaker's reputation, which was largely a matter of family lineage. Cicero did not have an illustrious family; he was a self-made man and his dialogues were part of this making. The reflected vanity of his dialogues was part of a strategy to give himself and Rome an illustrious philosophical past.[12]

Obscurity

In *The Nature of the Gods* Cicero elaborates on the surrounding critical context which would call for a justification of dialogue. This work followed the publication of other dialogues which irritated some of his contemporaries whose "malicious slanders" he reports:

> I see that there has been a great deal of talk about the several philosophical works which I have recently published within a short period. Some have wondered how I have acquired this sudden enthusiasm for philosophy, while others have been curious to know what conclusions I have reached on the problems I have tackled. I have felt too that many have been surprised that I have shown myself most inclined towards a philosophy which seems to them to put out the light and plunge everything into darkness.[13]

Cicero feels he has to first justify his interest in philosophy when he has been busy so long with politics—again an apologetic face to dialogue. He also has to explain how he could have time to write and publish so much on philosophy in such a short period. He does not help matters by giving the impression that he composed his works rapidly in a few moments of enforced leisure. (To admit that he had a lot of leisure would suggest he was not wanted as an orator.)

More interesting is the way Cicero feels obliged to raise, and answer, the charge that his philosophical inclinations have brought more darkness than light to the questions raised. By that his critics were referring to his academic skepticism and choice of the dialogue form which led him to give voice to more than one opinion on any subject. His academic inclinations lead him to present issues in reported dialogues where no single opinion is clearly master; this in turn causes his critics to accuse him of obfuscation. *The Nature of the Gods* is written as a dialogue in the face of this criticism that his academic dialogues obscure rather than clarify. To make things more interesting there is a resonance between the characterization of the subject of the dialogue and this question of obscurity. Cicero starts the dialogue by saying how "the question of the nature of the gods is the darkest and most difficult of all."[14] The subject is dark and Cicero has been accused of obscuring with dialogue; one can't help but see a connection, an obscure form for dark questions. (Hume in his revisiting of the issue explicitly makes the connection between the obscure form and the dark subject.) Cicero, in effect, admits that his critics are right—he does not give simple answers to philosophical questions, but he considers this reluctance a virtue. Some issues are so difficult that there are no clear answers; therefore to deal honestly with the issue you should choose a form that captures the uncertainty and obscurity. For Cicero "philosophy is the child of ignorance."[15] His skeptical conclusions lead to his choice of philosophical form. When we can only be sure of our ignorance then we need a way of discoursing that respects the absence of conviction. The ignorant author absents himself, apologizes for the work (and form), confines his writing to moments of leisure, models a philosophical culture that can deal with obscurity, and imagines characters as he would meet them in such a culture.

Beyond the Ciceronian Dialogue

This prefatory tendency found in Cicero and Hume to raise issues around the writing of a dialogue would be curious if it were an isolated phenomenon. However, digging deeper we can find many of the characteristics mentioned above in writers who do not write in a Ciceronian vein. Let us take the apologetic characteristic, because it is the least obvious: Lucian dedicated an entire dialogue to defending not only his choice of dialogue but his retooling of the form, as did his imitator Fontenelle. Valla in his characteristic fashion launches his dialogue on free will with a criticism of the philosophy of Boethius followed by a snipe at Cicero's dialogical style. He doesn't apologize for anything but tells us he is improving on these two classic dialogue writers, drawing our attention to his reuse of the form. His polemical protestations are a sign that he has something others might think he should apologize for, namely his unorthodox antiphilosophical use of the form. It is not exactly an apology, but admission. Boethius himself starts his consolation with verses inspired by the "Muses of Poetry." The character Philosophy upon seeing Boethius "driven by grief to shelter in sad songs"[16] says, "Who . . . has allowed these hysterical sluts to approach this sick man's bedside."[17] With these words the actual dialogue begins and Philosophy reconciles Boethius with his martyrdom displacing the initial sad verses with robust dialogue. The opening gives us a not-so-subtle indication that dialogue was chosen over poetry, which is the expected form for such moments of grief. It is a beautifully crafted apology for the form. We could go on with this list of opening justifications, but that would distract from our point that the hints that come through from authors of dialogue point to an apologetic self-consciousness in their use of the form that is different from the authors of essays, for example. We can tell that dialogue writers carefully choose their form because they go to the trouble to explain why.

It is not only at the edges of reported dialogues that one finds apologetic uncertainty about the appropriateness of dialogue. In direct dialogues like the *Phaedrus* the question of writing comes up, framing the second part of the dialogue. The discussion doesn't preface the dialogue but arises within it. There is an explicit discussion of what constitutes good and bad writing and when writing is appropriate as an activity. The writing in question is the writing of speeches, but the critical results of the discussion call into question all writing including that of the dialogue itself. In a similar fashion the critique of imitation in the *Republic* raises the question of the suitability of an imitative work like the *Republic* in the ideal Republic. These two discussions of writing leave the impression that if the author does not have ambiguous feelings about the writing of the very works in which they appear he hasn't taken Socrates' arguments seriously. Only through elaborate rationalizations can one explain how Plato could have confidently written in the face of the Socratic voice he bears. There are also other points about writing in the *Phaedrus*, but that is what the next part of this chapter is about.

What, then, are the hints we have gathered about the identity of model authors?

Absence: Authors, in choosing to write a dialogue, have chosen to withdraw. This is the only solid clue to their character—they do not want readers to pay attention to them. Authors of dialogue are shy. When they appear, it is as a character with no special status compared to the other characters.

Apology: This withdrawal is connected to an unease with writing which manifests itself in an apologetic attitude toward the writing of the dialogue itself. Authors of dialogues often justify writing in general, and the choice of dialogue in particular. They are curiously self-conscious about a form that doesn't portray them, but others for us to overhear. The apologetic attitude toward writing is tied to a concern with the appropriateness of writing as a philosophical event.

Leisure: The authors of dialogues tell us they only write when they have the leisure to do so. Leisure is that time which cannot be used more usefully, for example, in real dialogue with others. It is the time left over for playful diversions that imagine a better time. This leisure is not always welcome; it can be the enforced leisure of prison or exile.

Culture: The leisurely writing of dialogue is tied to the state of the political and philosophical culture. The author at his leisure responds to the state of the culture of discourse and imagines ideal possibilities. The author's unease with writing is tied to the oral culture of discourse he imagines.

Character: Creating the culture of discourse involves imagining ideal characters in interaction. Authors who withdraw want us to focus on other characters as the authorities of the work. The characters become the vehicles for content(s). In the disappearance of the author and the domination of characters there is a problematization of traditional notions of authority.

Obscurity: Finally the writing of dialogue can bring the darkness of difference forward. Dialogue is often chosen when what is at stake is not an answer but the preservation of the difference of discussion, something tied closely to the skeptical agenda.

THE PASTIME OF DIALOGUE

Cicero's dialogues used to be more influential than even Plato's. The dialogue writers of the Italian Renaissance turned to Cicero as their literary paradigm. But he in turn had read his Plato and the themes that we isolated in his prefaces find their first expression in Plato's dialogues and letters.[18] Plato, being the first writer of mature philosophical dialogues, and having left posterity with a large corpus of dialogues that were rediscovered in the Renaissance, has had a disproportionate effect on the written dialogue. Plato's discussion of writing has been influential despite the absence, except in his few letters, of his explicit thoughts. We have no prefaces, epilogues, or even Plato as a character; so where does Plato's influence come from? This influence comes primarily through the extended discussion of writing in the *Phaedrus* and thus "is grounded in the authority" of Socrates, to paraphrase Cicero. For this reason we will now turn to Plato's discussion of writing in the *Phaedrus*. The previous section catalogued the characteristics of the elusive author of dialogue; now I want to recapture the logic of the reluctant choice to write. By understanding why Socrates felt writing should be confined to moments of leisure, "when other men resort to other pastimes, regaling themselves with drinking parties and suchlike,"[19] we can understand those influenced by him.

The *Phaedrus* divides into two parts, the first composed of three speeches around the relationship between the lover and beloved, and the second a discussion of those speeches and the writing of speeches. The first speech of the *Phaedrus* is the only one that is written down, carried under the cloak of Phaedrus when he encounters Socrates. We are told this first speech took Lysias, who is not otherwise present, "weeks to compose at his leisure."[20] Phaedrus, as Socrates correctly surmises, is taken by the speech and has decided to take a walk in the countryside to practice declaiming it, presumably so that he can return to the city having learned the speech by heart, thereby making it his own. On his way out Phaedrus falls in with Socrates, who describes himself as a lover of discourses, and they set out together to find a quiet spot where they can go over the speech. The writing of Lysias is thus the occasion for the encounter of these two friends and their subsequent dialogue. Socrates on hearing the speech first betters it with one of his own on the same theme, then reverses his position arguing even more forcefully against the position of Lysias's speech and his second. The set of three speeches is then followed by a conversation on speech writing and rhetoric.

Love and Character

The subject of the three speeches is the relationship between lover and beloved, nonlover and (non)beloved; I will digress for a moment to discuss the subject and its relevance to the relationships between the characters.

Lysias's speech is intended to convince the reader that the beloved should bestow his attentions on the nonlover instead of the lover. Socrates' speech, the second of the three, argues that the beloved should avoid the lover who is driven by lust and then in the final speech he argues that the beloved should respond to the authentic lover who has his good in mind. Much of the tension between lovers and nonlovers is found on a dramatic level between Socrates and Phaedrus, though it is not clear who is the lover, nonlover, or beloved. Like many of the best dialogues hints as to what is to follow can be found retrospectively in the prefatory exchanges. Here are Socrates' comments on Phaedrus's feigned unwillingness to recite Lysias's speech:

> Then he [Phaedrus] fell in with one who has a passion for listening to discourses [Socrates], and when he saw him he was delighted to think he would have someone to share his frenzied enthusiasm; so he asked him to join him on his way. But when the lover of discourses begged him to discourse, he became difficult, pretending he didn't want to, though he meant to do so ultimately, even if he had to force himself on a reluctant listener.[21]

On the one hand Phaedrus would appear to be the beloved while Lysias and Socrates are competing for his attention with speeches. Phaedrus, attracted to the thesis of Lysias that he should avoid a passionate lover like Socrates, gets difficult. But there are other angles to the erotic tension. Phaedrus is not erotic the way Socrates is; he isn't as fond of people—witness his abandonment of Lysias, who is left in the city—as he is of discourses, particularly speeches. Socrates, on the other hand, though he claims to love discourses, has a way of always turning up after long speeches are finished (*Gorgias*) or postponing them in favor of dialogue (*Protagoras*). Phaedrus the lover of speeches who is uninterested in people is going to force his love on Socrates the lover of people who is uninterested in speeches. Socrates is going to use Phaedrus's passion for speeches, like Lysias's up his sleeve, to plant the seeds of philosophy, thereby showing that he is the sort of lover described in the third speech, who has the good of his beloved in mind. Socrates is going to show that the type of discourse one should love is that implanted in the soul that can answer questions, not that written down and delivered as a set speech.

The second part of the dialogue is a discussion of rhetoric, the "art" of speech-giving, framed within a discussion of the place of writing. The second part of the dialogue on the one hand serves as a commentary on the set of three speeches, identifying the flaws and qualities of the speeches. On the other hand the second part is itself a fourth discourse, this time a dialogical alternative to set speeches, but a discourse nonetheless. This fourth discourse follows from the third by being an example of the love of a wise man whose concern is the improvement of the beloved. Socrates doesn't just say what should be; he exemplifies it. Because the beloved is a lover of speeches, the lover, who believes dialogue is better for the beloved than speeches, has to make speeches (and dialogue) an issue in his conversation. So much for our digression about lovers and love.

Talking about Writing

In the first part of *Phaedrus* we are shown the superiority of Socratic rhetoric, and in the second Socrates on the one hand explains his art and the deficiencies of Lysias's, and on the other hand shows a higher form of rhetoric—loving dialogue. Phaedrus is convinced Socrates is a better orator after the speeches but he doesn't know why. The second part is a critical discussion that returns to the three speeches for evidence. On a simple level one can imagine the first three speeches to be the text which Socrates, now the teacher of a different rhetoric, uses to illustrate his points. For the moment we will focus on the second part not as a fourth type of discourse on love, which it is, but as a discussion of writing.

It is useful to summarize the organization of the fourth part. The following is a schematic outline of the nested questions that Phaedrus and Socrates raise and deal with. The scheme is a representation—a paraphrase—of the flow of questions that will guide a closer replay. It is designed to show the structure of the questions and answers not their literal sequence.

Is Lysias to be reproached or praised for writing speeches?

Is the composition of discourse in general praiseworthy or shameful, or under what conditions is it shameful?

What is the nature of good and bad writing?

Is Rhetoric an art or a knack? What is the nature of Rhetoric?

Rhetoric is the art of (1) knowing souls, (2) knowing the types of discourse, and (3) knowing which discourse is suited to which soul. It is based on the dialectical knowledge of the truth (about souls and discourses).

Good writing and the art of Rhetoric are based on the dialectical knowledge of the truth. This involves (1) the ability to isolate the subject in definition and (2) the ability to divide it into kinds. Rhetoric is the residual art of matching souls to discourses.

Good writing can be recognized by (1) its use of definitions to clarify terms and (2) its organization of parts to suit the audience.

The composition of discourse is only praiseworthy where it displays an understanding of the truth (including the truth about writing-composition), the audience of the discourse, the types of discourse, and their applicability.

In particular this means (1) a recognition that writings do not deserve serious attention, (2) that they are only to be composed in times of leisure, (3) that they should be backed up by a willingness to defend themselves through the answering of questions, and (4) that they at best serve as a memory aide for those who have understood the truth (by other means).

Phaedrus should deliver a message to Lysias that he should not be reproached if he can show that (1) he composed with a knowledge of the truth, (2) he can defend his writings, and (3) he can orally demonstrate the inferiority of his writings.

Phaedrus opens the discussion by commenting that Lysias should be reproached as a speechwriter for his work. The term "speechwriter" was considered an insult and Phaedrus, after the display of Socrates, is willing to use this insult for Lysias. A little-noticed, but revealing, feature of the dialogue is how Socrates turns Phaedrus around so that his final attitude to Lysias is one congruent with the Socratic definition (and example) of rhetoric. Phaedrus at the end is going to deliver an oral message designed not to insult Lysias but to educate him. Rather than insult him in public Phaedrus is convinced to deliver a message directly. Phaedrus in delivering a message will put himself in a position so that Lysias can question him and he Lysias. The message, in effect, will be an opening for dialogue. Socrates turns Phaedrus around to love Lysias in the Socratic fashion where one gently corrects those one loves rather than insult them.

The way Socrates does this is to first place his discussion of Lysias's speech writing in a larger context. Phaedrus wants to tar Lysias with the brush of being a mere "speechwriter," an insult he has heard voiced by a politician. Socrates points out that the politician is also a speechwriter; his laws are speeches written for the people and approved by the people. His speeches even include the name of those addressed by the written work—the people. Socrates opens up the circle of people who could be mere speechwriters. He plans to leverage Phaedrus's new disrespect for speech writing into a critique of all composers. The group that Socrates gathers for his larger critique is put succinctly when wrapping up at the end:

> Do you now go and tell Lysias that we two went down to the stream where is the holy place of the nymphs, and there listened to words which charged us to deliver a message, first to Lysias and all other composers of discourses, secondly to Homer and all others who have written poetry whether to be read or sung, and thirdly to Solon and all such as are authors of political compositions under the name of laws.[22]

Gathered together are all composers of discourses, poetry, laws, or speeches. This collection will strike the modern reader as peculiar. The gathering principle for Socrates has to do with whether a discourse is composed or not, not whether it is delivered orally or not. Socrates is grouping together those who compose their works—speechwriters (whether they deliver their speeches or not), poets, and legislators—

whereas we have grouped by method of delivery, distinguishing those who deliver their work orally from those who publish writings. Socrates' composers are to be distinguished from those who organize their thoughts spontaneously in response to their audience's needs and questions.[23]

To Socrates the dialectical understanding of something depends on knowing what to gather and where to divide the subject. To gather by method of delivery for Socrates would be inappropriate. We should gather composed works, oral or not. Oral and written dialogues which are scripted have in common something other than the fact that one is the representation of the other. This is a crucial point for us. Our distinction, based on the method of delivery, or the medium of the message, is inappropriate. It leads to the view that one type of dialogue is a representation of the other. Socrates' distinction places composed dialogues, be they oral or not, in the same camp. The difference is what the dialogue is composed on, paper or souls, as we shall see later.

We began this series of chapters by asking what we should make of the oral/written ambiguity in dialogue and here is a hint that suggests the crucial distinction is another. To understand the written dialogue we are here beckoned in the direction of composition. In retrospect, an oral performance, including the sorts of oral dialogues described by Xenophon, could be scripted to be performed in a fashion similar to a written dialogue.

Once Phaedrus accepts the gathering of a larger context, that of composed discourse (be it spoken or written) the question becomes the "nature of good and bad speaking and writing."[24] In order to know what to say to the likes of Lysias they have to understand the nature of discourse; and to give an ethical spin to the discussion, they need to understand specifically what makes for good and bad discourse. Socrates and Phaedrus fortunately have the discourses of Socrates and Lysias from the first part of the dialogue to use as material for this examination, as do the readers. They work from the differences between Socrates' speeches and Lysias's. They discover that Socrates' speeches had two stylistic features that are indicative of their inner quality. First, Socrates' speeches worked from a definition (specifically a definition of love as madness). Second, they were organized into parts that fit the divisions of the subject matter—parts that could not be moved around. Lysias's contribution, by contrast, neither began with a definition that gathered the issue together, nor was it made up of parts that matched the division of the issue. Its parts were interchangeable; Lysias's speech was a collection of points, not an argument with organic unity.

The stylistic differences between Socrates' and Lysias's speeches reflect a deeper difference. Socrates early on asks: Does a good and "successful discourse presuppose a knowledge in the mind of the speaker of the truth about his subject?"[25] The discussion returns repeatedly to this typically Socratic hypothesis. It turns out that knowledge of the truth involves knowing how to gather the subject into an appropriate definition and knowledge of its parts should one want to divide it. The use of appropriate definitions and divisions are a sign of the knowledge of the composer. An unwillingness to define the subject under discussion could mean that the composer knows not of what he speaks. Likewise a crude butchery of the subject, one that does not follow the nice dotted lines that one finds on those butchering diagrams, is also an indication of ignorance.

This dialectical knowledge is useful to the rhetorician, even when you want to mislead. If you know the truth you know which ambiguities to exploit when, like Socrates, you want to give a speech which is not the whole truth in order to captivate someone like Phaedrus. Socrates' first speech is an example of how knowledge, and its manifestation in definition and division, make for a more convincing argument when one wants to distort the truth. Knowing the truth makes it easier to make the distortion sound close to the truth; Plato not only has Socrates prove this, he also has material in the form of the early speeches which demonstrates this.

The discussion around the nature of good discourse runs hand in hand with a question about the existence and nature of the art of rhetoric. Socrates and Phaedrus do not simply want to know whether there are good and bad discourses and how to distinguish them by superficial traits; they want to know whether one can learn to compose good discourse. Hence the interest in the art of rhetoric. Socrates is not convinced there even is such a thing as an art of rhetoric, a position he also takes in the *Gorgias*. It turns out that the art of rhetoric is built on the dialectical knowledge of the truth. The dialectical art of the philosophers turns out to be the crucial art, and rhetoric the supplementary art of when to say what to whom once you know the truth.

The discussion of the art of rhetoric is the heart of the discussion between Socrates and Phaedrus. Socrates has led Phaedrus to the point where he has an idea of the path he would have to take if he really wanted to speak well, as opposed to the shortcut he was taking when he ran into Socrates—that of memorizing a clever speech by Lysias. This path involves learning about the types of souls (psychology if you will), the types of discourses, and the correct application of discourse to soul. The dialogue does not provide a manual on souls and discourses, though there are plenty of hints to remind someone who has learned this art, like the image of the soul as a chariot. At the end of the hour, the dialogue points in the direction of the questions that would have to be pursued to learn the art of rhetoric. Unlike in the *Gorgias*, Socrates does not seem to really care if there is one art (dialectic) or two (dialectic and rhetoric as a supplementary art, perhaps). His point is that to speak well—even when one wants to distort the truth—one needs to be a dialectician with a dialectical knowledge of souls and discourses. This final extension of the dialectical art into souls and discourses can be called rhetoric.

It is worth pointing out that the discussion around the art of rhetoric is geared toward the ethical question of how one (specifically Phaedrus) can acquire the ability to speak and write well. Socrates is identifying a course of education, not a position. His message to Phaedrus and through him is that if one aspires to rhetorical excellence one needs to learn the truth and the philosopher's art.

The Story of Writing

Once they have identified the heart of the matter they return to the question of writing: "there remains the question of propriety and impropriety in writing."[26] The propriety of writing can be addressed now that they have understood the art of rhetoric or composed discourse in general. The general answer is that the good discourse is tailored specifically for the soul of the audience and hence is based on knowledge of souls and discourses. The question is now the use of written works as distinct from other compositions. There is an ethical dimension to the way the question is put. Socrates wants to know when and how it is proper (ethically acceptable) to write. To do that he needs to know what the written character adds or detracts from discourses. Of the various types of discourses, what is the proper place of written ones? This is related to our original question: What is the difference between written and oral dialogue?

To start, Socrates offers a tale that has come down from their forefathers.[27] The tale is about the invention of writing: Theuth, an Egyptian god, brought his inventions including writing before King Thamus who made it his business to evaluate the inventions before passing them on to the Egyptians. Theuth is excited about writing; it "will make the people of Egypt wiser and improve their memories; my discovery provides a recipe for memory and wisdom."[28] Thamus, like any good philosopher king, is not so enthusiastic. He first distinguishes the role of the god as inventor from his role as legislator. Theuth is enamored with his offspring writing so he can't see whether it will really profit or harm the citizens. Looking at the larger picture, Thamus argues that writing

> will implant forgetfulness in their souls; they [citizens] will cease to exercise memory because they rely on that which is written, calling things to remembrance no longer from within themselves, but by means of external marks. What you have discovered is a recipe not for memory, but for reminder. And it is no true wisdom that you offer your disciples, but only its semblance, for by telling them of many things without teaching them you will make them seem to know much, while for the most part they know nothing, and as men filled, not with wisdom, but with the conceit of wisdom, they will be a burden to their fellows.[29]

One of the first points to be made about the myth of writing presented by Socrates is that it is presented as a short dialogue between them. Socrates sets the scene and then reports a short exchange between Theuth and Thamus. The bulk of the tale is the response, quoted above, of Thamus to the claim that writing will provide a recipe for wisdom. It is interesting that Socrates at this juncture should introduce a myth to make his point, especially when at the beginning of the dialogue he tells us that he does not concern himself with such stories. To be more precise he says that he doesn't indulge in skeptical reinterpretations of myths preferring to "accept the current beliefs about them."[30] One would expect Socrates to avoid such stories entirely, but instead he peppers his discourse with them in an apparently uncritical manner. When Phaedrus accuses him of making this myth up, he responds by pointing out that their forefathers were "content in their simplicity to listen to trees or rocks, provided these told the truth."[31]

Socrates' position is that these stories should be taken at face value.

Their authority should not depend on their provenance but on the truth of their lesson. It doesn't matter if Socrates made the story up or if it was uttered by a tree; the story either offers a truth or not and the listener is in a position to evaluate the value of the lesson. If the story is implausible one should not waste time trying to redeem it through clever reinterpretation. Given the number of traditional stories of dubious value, any attempt at a reform of the oral tradition through reinterpretation is doomed to failure.

Rather than try to redeem old stories through interpretation, Socrates offers new stories designed to replace the inherited ones. Socrates' position against overinterpretation is connected to his practice of introducing new stories, including snatches of dialogue which, if they are to make their point, should also be taken at surface value.[32] It is worth noting that it is not just in the *Phaedrus* that he introduces such stories; this is a characteristic Socratic tactic. He frequently uses stories (which include dialogical passages) to introduce positive content; one good example is the exchange with the priestess Diotima in the *Symposium*, another is the discussion with the laws of Athens in the *Crito*. In the *Charmides* Socrates describes how he was told of a charm for curing headaches that naturally involves curing the soul with "fair words."[33] When Socrates presents his cave analogy he asks his interlocutors to imagine what the freed prisoners would say to being told everything they thought they knew was an illusion. These stories are part of the cure along with the purgative questioning.

Using stories to introduce ideas also fits nicely with Socrates' claim to ignorance. Given that he has publicly stated that he knows nothing, and that such a stance is often central to his conversational tactics, the only way he can introduce ideas is to report them as belonging to someone else or as stories in circulation that do not belong to anyone.[34] It is not hard to imagine how Plato might take this example a step further and compose stories about Socrates to replace the compositions of oral epics that were being gathered and archived around that time.[35] Socrates fought oral stories with new oral stories; Plato was displacing archived epics with new composed stories.

So let us take the story of writing at face value. In it are presented two opinions about the value of writing. That of Theuth is that writing will (1) improve the memory of Egyptians and (2) make them wiser. It is not clear if he felt the two virtues of writing were connected by a causal link. His argument, as Thamus takes it, is that by improving memory, writing will make people wiser. Thamus counters this by arguing that far from improving memory, users of writings will no longer have to internalize what they have learned, trusting it to external marks. Writing will replace careful memorizing while giving the illusion that one still possesses that which has been written. The result will be people who remember less but think they are wiser. People will also avoid having to internalize what they memorize; in other words, they will not have to think about what they memorize; they can possess it without understanding it. Those who trust their memorandum will not only be less wise but will be deceived as to their wisdom. Wisdom will be replaced by its semblance—a pale imitation.

The connection between memory and wisdom that is taken for granted in this story is no longer obvious. We tend to think of memory as a knack of little value except when shopping without a list, but that is only due to the wealth of information tools we have access to. It was not so long ago that even books were luxury items that few could afford. Memory has been devalued in our culture partly due to this proliferation of memory aids. We all can now afford to carry phone books, appointment books, and notebooks. Now there are even electronic memory aids the size of pocket calculators that are replacing the traditional paper tools. The average household has an unprecedented number of storage systems: books, tape decks, CD players, record players, VCRs, and refrigerators. At the institutional level there are archives and libraries, which are the centers of today's universities (along with computing services). The computer promises even more efficient storage and retrieval with software agents that can remind you of information before you even see it, making decisions about what you want to be reminded of and when. In the Socratic world, however, memory was an important ability as few of these aids existed. As I pointed out in chapter 2 on oral dialogue, in an oral culture the ability to remember is necessary to most occupations, including philosophy. The structure of oral discourse reflects the need to be able to remember it. One cannot gather a complex argument without the ability to remember the parts so the parts have to be arranged in a memorable fashion. One can understand how a god like Theuth could argue that writing would contribute to wisdom. But that doesn't change the fact that memory is not all. What Thamus points out in response to

Theuth is something that is obvious to us today: possession of information is not knowledge or wisdom. It does not matter how many books you have, or even how much you have memorized. To understand something you have to internalize it in some fashion, and only then can a written work remind you of what you know.[36]

Socrates' critique of writing does not stop with the story of Theuth and Thamus. In typical Socratic fashion, the story is the occasion for further discussion. Just as the speeches of the *Phaedrus* are followed by dialogue, so the story of writing is followed by discussion. Socrates compares the written discourse to one of "unquestioned legitimacy,"[37] that discourse which is "written" in the soul and goes with knowledge. The written discourse is a representation of the living discourse in the soul, and should not, like an optical illusion, be confused for the original. From this it follows that the most appropriate type of composition would be the planting of a discourse in another soul, not on paper. The writer plants his discourse in a dead medium, while the lover plants his discourse in a soul where it can live and grow.

The sign of life is the ability to answer questions. The discourse planted in writing cannot adapt to answer questions. This is illustrated by the fate of Lysias's thought: written down his discourse on the lover cannot answer Socrates. At best a written work can remind us of what we know so that we can answer the questions we bring to the text. The discourse planted in the soul of the beloved is alive in a way that a text will never be. It can give birth to other discourses, and most importantly it can ask and answer questions. We should remember that all the stories in Plato's dialogues about achieving knowledge involve the asking of questions. In the cave story in the *Republic* it is by asking questions that the philosopher constrains people to identify the illusions projected for them.[38]

The ability to answer questions of a discourse and its authority are connected. When Socrates introduces stories and snatches of dialogue, he deliberately avoids introducing content that can be ascribed to anyone. The discourses are either stories attributable to some magical source or dialogues that do not belong to anyone. His truths have to stand on their own, whoever was responsible for them (though they have the advantage of being defended by Socrates). Socrates introduces a new way of evaluating the value of a discourse. Rather than looking at the authority of a discourse's author, one should question it. If it cannot even begin to answer appropriately, it condemns itself. The authority of living discourse is not only its ability to answer questions, but also its ability to adapt itself to different ethical situations. A living discourse can modify itself to different characters and situations. In an earlier chapter I pointed out how in the *Gorgias* Socrates insisted that he had to be personally convinced and that every argument had to be tailored to him rather than simply guaranteed by another. All that listening to a report of conviction can do is purify one of opinions so that one is ready for a living discourse. In the *Phaedrus* he shows how the art of rhetoric is the adaptation of discourses (including written ones) to individual characters. Questionability and adaptability go hand in hand. Because the living discourse is not simply a memorized or written work, but is knowledge recollected by the soul of a person, it can adapt itself to new situations and deliver messages that can ask and answer questions. The living discourse can deliver messages faithfully and answer for them just as Phaedrus can, by the end of the dialogue, deliver a message suited to Lysias, unlike the composition Lysias left in the hands of Phaedrus.

For Socrates the difference between a written work and the living discourse of conviction is the difference between the truth and its imitation.[39] The truth is not a set of propositions that are true for eternity, but a person capable of speaking and acting truthfully in any situation. The truth is not passive, but an active response to the world. A written work is obviously incapable of acting (though readers might act as a result of their reading), therefore it is not truth. It follows that those who write and believe their writings are the truth, are mistaken about writing in general, and their writing in particular. For this reason Socrates repeatedly says that the only writers who are not to be reproached for writing are those who make it clear that their writings do not contain permanent truths.[40] Writers have a responsibility to apologize for their writing and point out its limitations. Writers have a responsibility to undermine their writing in favor of the living discourse. Writers, in effect, have to be willing to question their writings, and be questioned about them—and in that questioning be prepared to abandon the imitations of truths therein.

For Socrates, composition, be it in writing or teaching, is an ethical act. You are responsible not only for what you compose and for whom, but for the very decision to compose and the choice of compositional practice. To choose to write is to choose to compose in one fashion over another, to plant ideas in one place over another. Socrates suggests in his life and in his stories that the best composition is that on the soul of a living person—teaching, if you will. A written composition is written for more than one person; it cannot be adapted to a particular soul, and therefore can never convince in the way that dialectical rhetoric can, which by his definition is designed for individual souls. Writing can only work in a dispersed fashion, being adapted for a wide variety of people—the lowest common denominator. It is a blunt hermeneutic instrument that more often goes wrong, getting misinterpreted or overinterpreted.[41] Plato would have us compare the composition of Lysias and its history to the message Socrates sows in the soul of Phaedrus for Lysias.

What Is Left to Writing

What role then is left for writing? If writing is an ethical choice of activity, there might be situations for which it is the right choice. Socrates in the final summary of the message for Lysias identifies some situations where writing is an acceptable alternative:

- Compositions like writings can serve to remind those who have already been dialectically convinced of what they know, especially the truth about writing—i.e., that it is no substitute for teaching. Socrates opens room for a discipline where students are taught the living truths and writings serve to remind the academy of what it knows. One wonders what he would say about a discipline that only promotes teachers who write.

- Composition is an acceptable activity only at times of leisure. It is an activity that should have a low priority, lower than teaching the living discourse, but nonetheless acceptable during times of leisure when others are drinking.[42] Even Socrates is willing to leave Athens and compose speeches when others are napping or drinking.

- Compositions are acceptable if they are delivered in a larger context where questioning can undermine and replace them. For example Socrates delivers two composed speeches, but follows them with a living dialogue.

CONCLUSIONS ON WRITING AND ORALITY

It remains to show that the character of the model author that we summarized by looking at the prefaces of Ciceronian dialogues fits with the Socratic position on writing as presented in the *Phaedrus*. I cannot prove that all authors of dialogue held something like the Socratic position, though I believe one can show that many were aware of it and one could trace it through the history of dialogue. Here I am trying to show that the Socratic position is consistent with the character traits outlined in the first part of this chapter. Moreover, though I will not demonstrate it here, the Socratic position is the best available explanation for these character traits. Due to the absence of the empirical authors, we will never know with certainty who they are and, specifically, why they wrote dialogues. We can, however, provide a model that fits the evidence found in Ciceronian prefaces. The model gives a credible explanation for the behavior of the author, drawn from one of the most significant dialogues ever written. The concerns of Socrates could lead to dialogues written like those of Cicero and Hume.

Absence

The model author is best characterized by his absence. This absence can now be fleshed out. The author is absent when, like Socrates, he does not care to share his convictions in written form. The author professes ignorance in his absence as Socrates did with his words. It is the authorial equivalent to Socratic ignorance. He does not claim to know anything but stories that he can pass on, the truth of which we have to judge for ourselves.

The absence of the author makes sense for those who believe written compositions cannot replace living ones. The author who is absent may, like Socrates, teach in other ways. Writings would serve certain functions but not all. They might be designed to remind students of what they have been taught in other ways, or, more importantly, they may be designed to be overheard. Just as Socrates staged some dialogues for his audience (and not the interlocutor), so a written dialogue could serve as bait for further dialogue. In the chapter on oral dialogue we saw a progress of dialogue from conversations designed to be overheard to those directly with the interlocutor. The first type was not designed to teach content, but to intrigue and humble the target. They are composed in preparation for an audience. The written dialogue is really no different if we believe Socrates. It is prepared to be overheard (or read). It cannot replace the second type of living dialogue, but it can serve instead of the first where there is a community of philosophy that can question itself.

Authority and Character

This absence has an effect on the authority of the text. The absence of the author makes it difficult to identify the text with a single position belonging to a single authority. There are instead competing positions linked with different characters. None of these characters have all the authority, though some like Socrates are subtly positioned to be more attractive by the end. The author, if he does appear in a dialogue, is a character with no more authority than the protagonist. The authority of the work is ultimately like that of Socrates' story of writing—it could have come from a tree or a god and we have to judge it by itself (by questioning it).

For Socrates misinterpretation and overinterpretation are major problems that writing exacerbates. Writing dialogue reduces misinterpretation through the absence of the author. The author of a dialogue cannot be accused of presenting opinions that he cannot defend from misunderstanding when he does not present anything except other characters, who again do not speak to the reader but to each other. Authors like Cicero take great pride in surveying all the important positions of philosophers, so that the reader can hardly take the work as uncontroversial support for one or another position. The written dialogue is peculiarly suited to authors who do not want to trust their beliefs to writing.

The absence of the author is mirrored in the absence of the reader. The reader is not addressed in the dialogue; no one says, "believe this. . . ." Thus the reader cannot misunderstand in the sense of believing he was told something. The reader, because he is an eavesdropper, does not have the same authority to report what he was told. No one has told the reader of a dialogue anything, hence he cannot, strictly speaking, have misunderstood anything. With his authority as reader ignored, the reader cannot misinterpret or overinterpret with the same confidence. The reader is forced into circumlocutions or humility.

This sounds like sophistry, but it is borne out in the history of the interpretation of Platonic dialogues. Plato's dialogues are remarkably resistant to the type of interpretation that goes, "Plato says such-and-such." Any reporting of Plato's words tends to be couched today in frames of humiliating interpretative heuristics. If one wants to speak boldly one has to speak of what Socrates said. This resistance to interpretation, which can be interpreted as an invitation to thought, but does not always play out as such, is testimony to the effect of the withdrawal of the author. No author has been interpreted in such a variety of ways and with such interpretative uncertainty. I am arguing that this is the direct result of an attempt to compose works that were consistent with the Socratic discussion of writing. Plato is absent because he takes his beliefs seriously enough to not want to commit them to a medium that is so susceptible to misinterpretation. The irony is that he puts Socrates, who did not write, in the position that he cannot defend what he is portrayed as saying.

Apology

The apologetic character of the author is understandable given the way the Socratic writer is supposed to undermine his own work with his own words. The Socratic writer, who believes that writing is dangerous and less likely than other types of focused composition to inspire others, cannot be reproached if he shows his uncertainty about writing in his own words. Socrates makes it quite clear that anyone who writes should be the first to critique it.

The apologetic prefaces of authors of dialogue are their way of showing the problems of writing when compared to other ways of acting. Apology is consistent with an ethic that takes seriously the choice to write. It considers the choice to write as one of many possible ways of composing messages to the other in an imperfect world where willful misunderstanding is often the case. It chooses to write in the context of other possible activities to which writing is a reluctant alternative. Moreover, it draws our attention to those other activities, specifically the living dialogue where one can focus one's message to the individual. It is a written gesture in the direction of something other than writing, and thus must always appear apologetic or withdrawing.

Leisure

Given the limitations of writing, it is an activity best pursued at times of leisure, when you aren't called to other forms of action. It is interesting that Socrates himself did not start composing written works until in prison—enforced leisure of the sort that Boethius and Cicero also experienced.[43] The author who, like Socrates, believes that writing is likely to do little good compared to dialectical questioning, is likely only to allow himself to write when everyone else is off drinking or asleep. Writing is for when you cannot engage others in more effective ways.

Not only should we write when we have the leisure, but we should write for times of leisure. You write for yourself when you are older, when you will want to be reminded of what you knew. You write for the leisure of old age or for the leisure of others who are properly taught. You write for those who have the leisure to pursue philosophy once an interest is aroused. The written work of leisure should be appreciated at comparable times of leisure by those who also have other ways of learning. Writing fits when there is a culture of philosophy that can undermine the writings with living dialogue. The written dialogue works like the oral dialogue that was designed to be overheard; it is designed to precede a culture of questioning that can overtake it.

Culture

For this reason there is central to dialogue a concern for the culture of philosophy. At the end of the day Socrates cares about how the love of wisdom is cultured in others and the culture that promotes (or does not promote) the love of wisdom. Writing is one of many activities that promote philosophical culture, though a relatively ineffective component. Without a culture of philosophy written works are as wasted as seeds on barren rock.

That does not mean that all dialogues are written in the context of perfect dialogical cultures. Many dialogues show us philosophical cultures as they should be. They specifically imagine the oral and dialogical aspects of the culture. They depend on a culture that they are trying to imagine. They are, in modern terms, creating the need for the culture that would satisfy the questions they raise. Like an advertisement they show something that may not be the case, but should be so, in the mind of the author.

The Story of Dialogue

There is in the *Phaedrus* a story that provides a conclusion to this chapter, and that is the story of the message from the gods to Lysias. The end result of the excursion Socrates and Phaedrus take is a message from the gods of the spot to Lysias and Isocrates. This message is conceived through dialogue; it does not come whole from either Socrates or Phaedrus. It is a composition that is designed to beckon toward the path of dialectical rhetoric rather than present a polished position. It should unsettle Lysias and encourage him to set aside vain writing for philosophy. It is a gesture that replaces the insult Phaedrus was planning for Lysias.

The source of this message needs to be clearly identified, not because it is important in terms of the dialogue, but because we are so concerned these days with sources and resources. The source of the message is the divine love that Socrates has for Phaedrus, and hence it is fair to say that the message was inspired by the gods. Socrates is an example of the sort of love that he describes in his second speech that sees his god in the beauty of the other and makes love to the other by bringing out the divine in them. Socrates is not responsible alone for the message; he is assisted by Phaedrus. They are the two steeds that pull the chariot. The message that lies in the nature of divine love is delivered by the characters, pulled by a team in dialogue. To search for an author for such a message makes a mockery of our fascination with authors and sources. The model author is a messenger, absenting himself so that we do not confuse him with the source of the message or attribute the authority of the message to him.

This message is composed at a time of leisure when most others are resting for later moments of leisure. Socrates allows himself to be led outside the city walls when nothing much is happening in the city to prepare messages for later such moments when people will have the leisure to recall such stories. The message is a composition in response to a previous composition by Lysias, also composed at his leisure. Leisure needs to be understood as a time of retreat or play, when one goes outside the walls. It is the time perfectly suited to composition as it is the time when public life does not call. Such leisure can be enforced and unwelcome, as it was for

Cicero and Boethius. It is, in sum, the time when one is removed from public life—there is no one you must talk to, no one to answer to.

We can see in the story of the message a positive side to leisurely composition. During times of leisure, messages can emerge that are addressed to those who are absent. The message that emerges in public need not be delivered to anyone, because they are all present. The message born in leisure needs to be delivered. The delivery is a reluctant responsibility for one sensitive to the opportunities for misinterpretation, which explains the apologetic character of writers of dialogue. One delivers it in a way that indicates this reluctance and points to that from which it was a message. One delivers it with apologies and then one absents oneself so as not to distract the reader.

Writers of dialogue are the deliverers of such a message. They compose a written work much as Socrates scripted events to be overheard by others. They compose the work to be witnessed. The work bears a message that points, not at the work, nor at the message-bearer, nor at their intentions, but in the direction of thinking. A message like a hint points beyond it, to a god or a tree. It is a gesture that beckons in one direction over another, often down a path, giving directions for those who want to follow that path. (The message for Lysias should point him down the path of dialectical rhetoric, as should the message to us.) Both the written dialogue, and the oral dialogue that is arranged to be overheard, point to the possibility for living questions sown in a culture of philosophy.

The written dialogue is a story that should be taken at face value. It can remind us of what we know, but it cannot teach us as direct questions can. It is written in acknowledgment of this fact and deliberately distances itself from claims to conviction. It points instead to a focused oral dialogue which is capable of turning our head so that instead of the phantom images we see the forms that generate those images.

Being questioned in a Socratic fashion can be uncomfortable. Questioning can be a violent act when it is designed to constrain us to look at the blindingly bright truth. Written dialogue is written to prepare us for such questioning, or to remind us that we should be questioning. In this way, the written dialogue parallels the overheard oral dialogue. It is not a representation of such oral dialogue. Both the scripted oral dialogue and the written dialogue deliver similar messages. They both point to living and questioning dialogue. Perhaps the story of the message is what Heidegger and others mean when they talk about dialogue being that through which meaning comes.

We have looked at the stakeholders of the written dialogue, the reader and author. The reader of dialogues has a role remarkably similar to the role of the audience of oral dialogue. The reader overhears the dialogue much as an eavesdropper. The text of the dialogue does not attempt to convince the reader so much as show characters interacting in a way that can lead the reader to reject the character that is unprepared for philosophy. In certain cases the rejection can be a traumatic experience similar to a religious conversion where one is emptied of one's previous beliefs in order to be redefined. Written dialogue tends to be less effective, but we can't all listen in to Socrates. Rather we can say that dialogue prepares philosophical character by holding some traits up as acceptable and showing how others are distasteful under stress. Both written and arranged oral dialogue can be crafted to prepare us for philosophy; they are not positive philosophy itself, and hence their uncertainty. Their preparation is to point us in the right direction. Both oral and written dialogue are really the same genre of persuasion where the composer does not directly address the audience, but arranges a conversation that the audience overhears. As they both work the same way, the oral and written dialogue deserve the same name, dialogue. Let us now see if we can define this dialogue.

NOTES

1. Umberto Eco, "Between Author and Text," *Interpretation and Overinterpretation* (Cambridge: Cambridge University Press, 1992), p. 69. The work nicely supplements his delightful novel on overinterpretation, *Foucault's Pendulum*. The overinterpretation of texts is especially a problem with dialogues where the intention of the author is obscured by their withdrawal leading to imaginative reconstructions of what "Plato must have meant."

2. As I mentioned before, I am sticking to dialogues for evidence in this work. If one were to go further afield one could look at the correspondence of dialogue writers like Plato, Diderot, and Hume.

3. Exactly what the text is in this context depends on the will of the

readers. If they choose to treat three of Plato's dialogues and a letter as a whole text, that in effect becomes the single text through which to see the author.

4. Anthony Ashley Cooper, Earl of Shaftesbury, *Characteristics of Men, Manners, Opinions, Times, etc.*, vol. 1 (Gloucester, Mass.: Peter Smith, 1963), p. 132.

5. Cicero in the preface of *Laelius, On Friendship* gives his reason for the shift from reported to direct dialogue: "I committed to memory the substance of the discussion, and I have set it out in this book after my own fashion: I have, as it were, brought the characters on stage to speak in person, avoiding the frequent insertion of 'I said' or 'he said', and giving the impression of a conversation between persons actually present" (1:3). The direct form is not only more efficient, saving the reader from the apparatus of reporting, it also brings the characters closer to the reader, obscuring the author.

6. For some authors there might be a perfection to disappearing. The dialogue through which friends and exemplary characters speak could be for some the most creative way to express themselves.

7. "This type of dialogue, grounded in the authority of eminent men of past generations, seems somehow to carry more weight; and indeed, I sometimes get the feeling, when I read my own work, that it is Cato who is speaking, not myself." *Laelius, On Friendship*, 1:4. While this could be a vanity on Cicero's part, I suspect the dialogue form appeals to certain writers because it allows them to listen to voices that may be within, but are nevertheless better heard when characterized.

8. The cynic would argue that the cynical view is manifested not in the accessibility of intentions but in their inaccessibility. One could not covertly manipulate readers if one said one was going to do so. Therefore we have to look elsewhere for evidence of manipulative intention. By confining myself to a respect of the text, I doom myself to a view that is sympathetic to the model author and ignorant of his "real" intentions as manifested elsewhere. By looking only at the model author we cannot see any incompatibilities between the character of the model author and the intentions of the empirical. My point, however, is that the empirical author's intentions are for the most part inaccessible and problematic for reasons beyond the scope of this paper. Given their inaccessibility we cannot really assume they set out to manipulate us in the face of evidence within the text (and our hearts). The cynics assume manipulation when the evidence gets dense as the cynical assumption is safe. I believe the simplest explanation is the best one—if authors disappear it is because they wanted to disappear. I would also argue that in the assumption of manipulation we tend to ignore the evidence in the text which is accessible and interesting. Some of this internal evidence even points at manipulation though not all of it. In the last

chapter we explored some of the manipulation of the reader. Here we are going to focus on the other evidence about the author.

9. David Hume, *Dialogues Concerning Natural Religion* (New York: Bobbs-Merrill, 1970), pp. 3–4. I have clipped a longer passage to highlight the reasons for not writing a dialogue. Later, I will look at the reasons for such a move.

10. Cicero, *The Making of an Orator*, trans. E. W. Sutton (London: Heinemann, 1942), p. 5 (3–4).

11. Cicero, *The Nature of the Gods*, trans. Horace C. P. McGregor (Harmondsworth, England: Penguin, 1972), p. 72 (6–9). The single man is the Emperor Augustus.

12. J. M. May in *Trials of Character: The Eloquence of Ciceronian Ethos* (Chapel Hill: University of North Carolina Press, 1988) discusses the way Cicero built his own character over time and the need for this self-inflation. He does not deal with Cicero's dialogues, but I think his discussion is relevant nonetheless. Cicero is not the only author to use the dialogue to reflect back on his philosophical career. There is an element of this in Heidegger's dialogue with a Japanese.

13. Cicero, *The Nature of the Gods*, p. 71.

14. Ibid., p. 69.

15. Ibid.

16. Boethius, *The Consolation of Philosophy*, trans. V. E. Watts (Harmondsworth, England: Penguin, 1969), p. 35.

17. Ibid., p. 36.

18. Today Cicero is relegated to Classics departments. His dialogues are rarely taught in philosophy. Likewise ignored are the philosophical traditions that look back on Cicero for their inspiration like the Renaissance humanist philosophy of Italy. I suspect this is due to two things. (1) It is due to the frank connection between oratory and philosophy which is important to a statesman/philosopher engaged in politics but not to an academic philosopher who is presumably supposed to be removed from the hurly-burly of local politics. Cicero's works today seem tainted by his political agenda which in turn has a lot to do with glorifying his achievements, including his oratorical ability. There is also an unfashionable imperialist smell to Cicero, which may have made him popular in like-minded cultures but is not likely to today. (2) It is also due to the fact that Cicero himself seemed content to borrow much of what he put forward. He does not seem so original now that we have access to much of Plato's and Aristotle's thought.

19. Plato, *Phaedrus*, trans. R. Hackforth, in *The Collected Dialogues of Plato*, ed. Edith Hamilton and Huntington Cairns (Princeton, N.J.: Princeton University Press, 1961), 276d.

20. Ibid., 228a.

21. Ibid., 228b–c.

22. Ibid., 278b–c.

23. Socrates compares compositions to "those lessons on justice and honor and goodness that are expounded and set forth for the sake of instruction, and are veritably written in the soul of the listener." *Phaedrus* 277e–278b. I suspect that this contrast is not meant to cover all the possibilities. Socrates would agree that not all lessons that are not composed are equally valuable. After all, Gorgias and Protagoras offered to teach by answering questions instead of lecturing. Thus I contrast the composition with improvised persuasion of which Socratic lessons on the soul are the paradigm.

24. Ibid., 259e.

25. Ibid.

26. Ibid., 274b.

27. Ibid., 274c.

28. Ibid., 274e.

29. Ibid., 274a–b. I find it intriguing how Socrates' story shows a human, albeit a king, critiquing a god. A generous interpretation would be that gods are potentials which have to be properly exploited by people. Writing is a potential which is eternally there; we have to decide how to use it or not.

30. Ibid., 230a.

31. Ibid., 275b–c.

32. One can find the same connection in the work of Umberto Eco. On the one hand, in his academic work he has argued against overinterpretation; on the other hand, he has acted by creating new stories that are plausibly about overinterpretation, notably *Foucault's Pendulum*.

33. Plato, *Charmides*, trans. Benjamin Jowett, in *The Collected Dialogues of Plato*, 157a. In the *Phaedo* Socrates also talks about the use of spells and charms to relieve the anxieties that his followers have about his death (77d–78a). The extended story of the soul after death that starts at 107d could be the final charming story.

34. A more cynical explanation is that Socrates like Protagoras used stories to talk down to his juniors who could not understand ideas otherwise. As Protagoras puts it to Socrates, "Now shall I, as an old man speaking to his juniors, put my explanation in the form of a story, or give it as a reasoned argument?" (320c). In this case the stories are not the sign of ignorance but one of patronizing vanity.

35. The Athenian archives were established in 400 B.C.E.

36. The problem of memory and its relationship to wisdom is a theme that runs through a number of dialogues. In the *Meno* there is the suggestion that we

know everything, but have forgotten it. Learning is a matter of recollecting what we know. This can be done through questioning of the sort that Socrates shows Meno when he elicits mathematical knowledge from the slave boy (82–85). In the *Phaedo* the theory of recollection is recovered explicitly as proof of the immortality of the soul (73–76).

37. Plato *Phaedrus* 276a.

38. Plato, *Republic*, trans. Paul Shorey, in *The Collected Dialogues of Plato*, 7.515d. It is interesting that the process of philosophical liberation, in this story, is viewed as a painful one for the student. Questions are used to force the student out into the open and away from the shadows. This fits with the descriptions we have of the Socratic method of questioning, which as I pointed out earlier, was usually a humiliating experience.

39. Socrates compares writings to the works of painters, whose "products stand before us as though they were alive, but if you question them, they maintain a most majestic silence." Plato *Phaedrus* 275d.

40. He that believes "writing will provide something reliable and permanent, must be exceedingly simple-minded; he must really be ignorant of Ammon's utterance, if he imagines that written words can do anything more than remind one who knows that which the writing is concerned with." Plato *Phaedrus* 275c–d.

41. George Grote, in *Plato, and the Other Companions of Sokrates* (London: John Murray, 1865) suggests that one of the reasons Plato set up a school was to ensure the correct interpretation of his dialogues after he was dead (vol. 1, p. 134). This might have been one of his answers to the problems raised by Socrates in his own dialogue.

42. What to do during the long drinking binges that were common practice seems to have been a preoccupation of Plato's. In the *Symposium* he tries to show how such parties could be redirected to entertaining philosophical discourse. In the *Laws* he suggests that the parties could be used as an occasion to test the young. Here he suggests that one should just leave and go write.

43. Plato, *Phaedo,* trans. Hugh Tredennick, in *The Collected Dialogues of Plato*, 60c–61b. Cebes and others note the turn to writing that Socrates takes in his last days. Cebes relays the question for them all, "Evenus asked me a day or two ago, as others have done before, about the lyrics which you have been composing lately by adapting Aesop's Fables and 'The Prelude' to Apollo. He wanted to know what induced you to write them now after you had gone to prison, when you had never done anything of the kind before." Socrates' answer is that he is writing verses in response to a recurring dream that encouraged him to practice the arts. Until then he had thought that doing philosophy was practicing the highest art, but in his final days he decided to try other arts just in case.

5
The DEFINITION of DIALOGUE

When Sperone Speroni (1500–1588) heard that his dialogues had been denounced he requested and got an audience with the Master of the Sacred Palace, who could give the *nulla osta* needed for publication in Rome. In the meeting, as he describes it in his *Apologia dei dialogi*, he tried to defend his dialogues by defining the literary dialogue and the author's responsibilities in such a way as to excuse the questionable passages of his works. His defense was in vain; despite his willingness to change passages and write an *Oration Against Courtesans*, his collection of dialogues was put on the Index of Forbidden Books. The popular dialogues that he had written in his youth (1520s to 1540s) were, by the 1570s, no longer acceptable in the ever more repressive atmosphere of Counter-Reformation Rome.[1] His written apology, which was not published, but was circulated among friends to deal with the danger of the denunciation, did not have the desired effect, nor did his meeting with the Master of the Sacred Palace.

In this chapter we will look at the context of Speroni's defense and the theory of dialogue he proposes. We will move from this defense to a working definition of dialogue inspired by the work of Mikhail Bakhtin, the Russian literary theorist. Until now we have been answering the question: Is dialogue one thing or many? In the last three chapters we have seen that oral and written dialogue are surprisingly similar to the major stakeholder, the reader/auditor not to mention the author/composer. The experience of overhearing an oral dialogue (designed to be overheard) and reading a written one are similar enough for us to treat dialogue as one thing for the purpose of definition. The question then for this chapter is: What is dialogue? We will approach this question obliquely, returning to earlier definitions of literary dialogue.

BREAD, FISH, AND ANCHOVIES

The trouble with Speroni's dialogues started when an anonymous "gentleman" submitted a copy of the dialogues to the Master of the Sacred Palace with the dangerous passages marked and annotated. Speroni did not know who the gentleman was who denounced his work, but he was sure the man could not be a gentleman; on the cover of the copy of the annotated dialogues was written, "bread, fish, anchovies, flour, pepper, tuna."[2] Speroni saw this shopping list as a sign that the man was a "cook, even a good cook, but a gentleman, never."[3] That Speroni's accuser would be a cook is strangely appropriate as the theory of dialogue which Speroni uses to defend his works in the first part of his *Apologia* is one of delightful mixture. A dialogue, Speroni argues, is like poetry (in the larger sense of fiction), specifically like *commedia*, where the audience is entertained by the combination of different characters, many of whom are unsavory taken alone, but delightful when mixed with each other. In the hands of a good cook, bread, fish, anchovies, flour, pepper, and tuna might make a delightful meal; similarly in the hands of a good dialogue writer, characters like courtesans and moneylenders might make an enjoyable symposium.[4] The author of the mixture (*satura*) should not be confused or blamed for the words of the ingredients who speak according to their nature.

The Return of Dialogue

To understand the original flavor of Speroni's *Apologia* we need to step back and get a sense of the context of the work. The first point that should be noted is the extraordinary resurgence of the dialogue starting with

Bruni's *Dialogi ad Petrum Paulum Histrum* (1401). The dialogue had never disappeared during the Middle Ages (witness the importance of Boethius's *Consolation*), but in the fifteenth and early sixteenth centuries it became the dominant form of learned discourse in Italy. Why was this? For humanists like Bruni, the Ciceronian dialogue was a way of defining a new culture based on conversation among gentlemen that was the humanist answer to the barbarous hair-splitting disputations of scholasticism. Dialogue was not just an alternative literary form in the Renaissance, it was also an alternative philosophical activity. In dialogue the character and oratorical skills that the humanists were cultivating could be displayed in the community they imagined. The Renaissance writers were interested in forming a new culture around learned and courtly dialogue; the literary form, especially the Ciceronian style, could be used to evoke the culture they were creating just as Cicero set out to create a Latin philosophical tradition. Bruni, unlike Petrarch who had earlier written a dialogue that is closer to the soliloquy of Augustine or Boethius, turned back to Cicero for inspiration, with a dialogue between Florentine characters designed to evoke a polished culture for Florence comparable to the classical culture of Athens and Rome. (It is no surprise that the relative merits of classical culture and Florentine culture are at stake in the dialogue.) In his dialogue there are neither the short questions and answers of the Socratic dialogue, nor the self-examination of the soliloquy.[5] In the dialogue you have an admirable set of leading men and their students, men who respect each other and enjoy arguing both sides of the issue in an academic fashion that shows off their social and oratorical skills. All the characters represent the author in a fashion, not just the narrator, because Bruni is proud of the entire community he was recreating in the classical fashion with dialogue.

This Ciceronian style of dialogue was later adapted to other ideals as in Castiglione's *Cortegiano* where courtly life is celebrated and codified. Castiglione set an example of learned courtesy in conversation; including women in the community of dialogue for the first time, his work became a textbook of conversational manners for both sexes. The Ciceronian style of dialogue was also versatile enough to also be adapted to uses that later the essay or treatise would be used for: Galileo's *Dialogo dei massimi sistemi* for example, where scientific issues are popularized by putting them into dialogue, showing incidentally how learned men should discuss science.

This is not to say that the Ciceronian model was the only model of dialogue that Italian Renaissance writers returned to. Lucian's satiric dialogue of the dead was picked up by writers like the architect and writer Leon Battista Alberti. The Socratic dialogue was also adapted by writers like Valla, as we pointed out in a previous chapter. The symposium or *convito*, where there is a round of speeches around a meal, was also popular (witness Ficino). All said, this often ignored chapter of the philosophical dialogue was not only remarkable for the quantity of works and their application to the changing culture of letters, but also for its variety and invention. When philosophers bemoan the end of the dialogue after Plato they overlook this exceptional period when the dialogue was a fully exploited and dominant literary genre.[6]

The Turn to Theory

It is not surprising, given the explosion of dialogue and a growing interest in literary theory, that someone would become interested in the poetics of dialogue. What is surprising is how long it was before there were any works on the theory of dialogue. This was in part because of the value placed on dialogue as an activity, and the relationship of the literary form to the activity. The literary dialogue was tied to the culture of conversation and *convito*. The written dialogue was the humanist way of theorizing the culture of civil conversation they were creating. A dry treatise on the theory of literary dialogue without characters and situations would have missed what was at stake and would have been viewed as crude and scholarly. Literary dialogues like Bruni's and Castiglione's can be seen as the Renaissance way of writing about conversation in a fashion appropriate to the conversation imagined. They are, like Plato's *Phaedrus*, examples of what they discuss.

By the second half of the sixteenth century with the exploration of other types of dialogue (other than the Ciceronian) the literary dialogue had come of age and detached itself from the oral and cultural issues it was tied to earlier. The translation of, and commentaries on, Aristotle's *Poetics* brought that work and literary theory to the forefront. It was inevitable that someone like Sigonio noticed that Aristotle had left open the question of the nature of the literary dialogue.[7] In a relatively short time from 1561 to 1585 there was a burst of works about the poetics of dialogue by three scholars associated with Padua. Three significant works on dialogue were written in this period, that of Carlo Sigonio (*De Dialogo Liber*, 1561), Sperone Speroni (*Apologia dei dialogi*, 1574), and Torquato Tasso (*Discorso dell'arte del dialogo*, 1585).[8]

It is significant that these theories of dialogue of the late sixteenth century came at a time when open dialogue was being suppressed and closed down in the name of orthodoxy.[9] Sigonio's work, the first theoretical work on the literary dialogue, is a manual telling people how they should write dialogues; Speroni's *Apologia* is triggered by a denunciation and attempts to reopen a space for free dialogue. Tasso's work was written when he was confined to an asylum and paranoid about the very real dangers associated with expressing unorthodox opinions. In sum, this burst of theories about dialogue came at a time when the literary dialogue was exhausted and under increasing scrutiny. The theories reflect in different ways the change in climate that brought an end to the extraordinary output of literary dialogues in Italy. Some of these theories reflect the new orthodoxy, while others like Speroni's try to leave room for a dialogue wedded to comedy.

The Climate of Interpretation

Speroni, when he meets his Master and later writes his defense, has the immediate problem of distancing himself from the works of his youth and clearing his name, but his deeper problem is dealing with an anonymous accusation. Like Socrates he isn't defending himself against an openly articulated position but must deal with a suspicious interpretative climate that increasingly sees the dialogue as a sneaky way of delivering unorthodox ideology which therefore needs to be disciplined. His answer is to respond to the interpretative tendencies that misread his dialogues by suggesting how dialogue works, what type of work it is, and thus how it should be read. To understand this interpretative climate we can look to the other two theorists of dialogue, Sigonio and Tasso, though neither of them can be held responsible for the atmosphere Speroni encountered in Rome.

In Sigonio's model of the dialogue, which fits the Ciceronian works of Bruni, all the characters of the dialogue have to be great and admirable men; there is no room for wits, courtesans, and moneylenders.[10] The dialogue should show the best of the community discoursing in one of their few moments of leisure together, usually a feast day,[11] because otherwise, if they discoursed when there was work to do, they would not, by definition, be serious gentlemen. (Shopping and cooking, needless to say, are unworthy of such leaders.) All of these men and women represent the author as an ideal community. The author chooses the dialogue form both to make the message easier to assimilate and to show how gentlemen discuss such issues (in their few moments of leisure together).

Renaissance literary theorists were fond of classifying and a major issue around the dialogue after Aristotle left it hanging was where it fit in the order of discourse. The key to the reading of dialogue is what sort of work it is; all three theorists bother far more with the classification of dialogue than we would. In fact, a major defensive tactic of Speroni is to try to dislodge the classification of dialogue as a form suited to the representation of serious discussion. We can best see the competing classification of dialogue that Speroni has to deal with in Torquato Tasso's "Discourse on the Art of the Dialogue," a short clear work that nicely summarizes the conservative position on the place of the written dialogue and the types of dialogue.[12]

Tasso mentions the classical distinction that there are three types of dialogues: (1) representative or dramatic ones that can be performed on stage where the reasoning is done by the characters, (2) historical or narrated dialogues where the narrator reports his thoughts and what people say, and (3) mixed dialogues where there is a mixture of narration and direct representation.[13] This classical distinction depends on the way the words of the characters are reported. In a narrated dialogue the narrator will report that then so-and-so said this, while in the direct representative dialogue, and in parts of the mixed dialogue, the speeches alternate with no such reporting. This formal distinction seems petty to us now, but it hinges on the presence of the narrator which in many cases has an effect on the openness of the dialogue. Where there is a strong authorial presence through a narrator the other characters fade to the point where one wonders whether the work is a dialogue or just a discourse with a few quotations. Conversely where there is no narrator the author is most distant and the comic possibilities of incongruous characters are greatest. One might add that when there is a strong authorial presence the possibility of an ineffable meaning coming through is also endangered. Needless to say, the formal distinction does not always hold; there are direct dialogues where the characters are so similar that they really seem like ornamental variations of the author's wishes. Likewise there are reported dialogues where the narration does not affect the lively differences between reported characters.

Tasso is not, however, happy with the classical distinction and introduces one modeled on Sigonio. He summarizes it nicely:

> We shall say, then, that the dialogue is an imitation of discussion, written in prose, without representation, and designed for the benefit of civil and speculative men. We shall set it down that there are two kinds—one contemplative and the other moral—and that the subject of debate in the first is infinite while in the second it can be infinite or finite. What the plot is to a poem, moreover, the question of debate is to a dialogue: its form and, as it were its soul. And just as a plot must possess unity, so too must the subject about which questions are raised in a dialogue.[14]

For Tasso there are two types of imitation, that of action, and that of discussion or reasoning. Verse and drama imitate action; dialogue imitates the reasoned discussions of men, though, as he points out, you can't have one without the other. Rather than dividing dialogues by their formal features, Tasso categorizes them by their subject matter or question. There are those dialogues that discuss contemplative matters and are aimed at knowledge and truth, and then there are those that deal with actions in which case they are moral, and directed at praise and blame. While his classification allows for the imitation of frivolous conversations by disreputable men directed to entertainment, Tasso clearly thinks the dialogue proper imitates only the reasoning of the speculative men on serious philosophical questions.

Tasso identifies four parts to the dialogue: the question or subject matter, the opinions, the characters, and the style. He spends a large part of his discourse on the subject matter and the importance of the unity of the question. For Tasso the plot that unifies the dialogue is the flow of questions and answers that make up the dispute over the subject. He remarks that "because questioning is the particular business of the dialectician, it seems that he is the one who ought to undertake to write dialogues."[15] Later he grumbles about the habit of giving the questioning in a dialogue to the less-informed interlocutor rather than the Socratic figure because that leaves the plot in the hands of ignorant interlocutors. For Tasso the core of dialogue is a series of dialectical questions aimed at eliciting the truth or at least purifying error. Wandering dialogues that touch on a number of subjects without resolving anything are not his idea of the ideal dialogue. Around this core there can be ornamental settings and conclusions, but it is the chain of Socratic questions that define the dialogue.

As for the opinions and characters this is where Tasso sees the need for poetic skill. In a dialogue the opinions and the character of the interlocutors have to be faithfully imitated with poetic skill. By this he means that a writer of dialogues has to be able to imitate the language and actions of the characters he chooses. For this reason Tasso concludes that the "writer of a dialogue must be an imitator no less than the poet; he occupies a middle ground between poet and dialectician."[16] As for style, Tasso believes that the dialectical passages with questions and answers should be simple, but the openings and conclusions can be as ornate as any other work.

We can conclude this section on the interpretative climate faced by Speroni by summarizing thus the unexpressed expectations that he had to confront:

1. The dialogue is a serious form suited to the presentation of truths or at least the purification of error. The entertaining (poetic) character of the dialogue should enhance but not drive the dialogue.
2. The dialogue is best suited to the representation of reasoning that leads to truths for which the author is responsible. To put it another way, the dialogue is a way of showing the convincing reasoning that leads to the truths that the author wishes to expound.
3. For this reason the movement of questions through a dialogue is the equivalent of a plot, providing unity to the work. The author is responsible for the choice of subject and the movement of the questioning (and answering).
4. This means the author is responsible for the choice of characters and situation. The characters should all be worthy of the author

and likely to discuss the issue in a serious fashion. (If there are to be disreputable characters they should be soundly refuted in the course of the dialogue.) Given that the characters should be realistic they should be examples of good men who in the right situation are disposed to serious discussion and learned reasoning leading to approved ends.

5. Therefore the author is responsible for the words of all the characters, especially their conclusions unless those opinions are clearly refuted. In addition the author can be identified with the primary speaker or narrator when there is one.

Needless to say this is a limiting view of dialogue that leaves very few acceptable dialogues. Even Plato would not fare well if tested this way, and Speroni for this reason makes much of the example of Plato in his defense. These interpretative tactics were not codified anywhere unless one looks to the works of Sigonio, and later Tasso, but Speroni has to deal with the worst case, a suspicious and conservative climate that is intolerant of poetic license. Speroni has to draw out these interpretative tendencies where they were never written down and confront them over and over. He has to resort to theories, examples, and analogies to make conviction difficult. It doesn't really matter if one agrees with all of Speroni's wandering thoughts, or that they contradict each other, so long as one leaves the meeting (or reading) unsure that one can condemn the author for the words of his characters.[17]

Speroni's Defense

Before going into detail about Speroni's defense it is best that we comment on the peculiar form of his apology. The work has four parts. The first, and the most important for our purposes, reads like a random collection of thoughts on the interpretation of the dialogue addressed to the Master of the Sacred Palace. In the second part he goes over the questionable passages defending them, addressing the reader rather than the Master. In the third part he is engaged by his conscience (his Socratic *daimon*) who calls him to critique his youthful work, which he does in the first reversal of the work. Whereas in the first and second part he ingeniously defends his work by concentrating on the distance of the author, in the third he finally admits the author's responsibility. Finally in the fourth part, addressed to god, there is a second reversal where he concludes that the author is really only responsible to god and that all literature that is not devotional is vain. Thus, what he had conceded in the third part, showing his good will by critiquing his own work, is trivialized as he concludes piously that only god can judge his work.

The work, like Plato's *Apology*, is hardly a dialogue.[18] In parts it becomes dialogical, and it is interesting to chart the different interlocutors that Speroni engages, not to mention the different postures Speroni takes as he conducts his defense. In the first part where Speroni recounts what he said to the Padre Maestro we feel the presence of this judge and on one occasion Speroni even reports his words.[19] Further on he addresses his unknown accusers admonishing them to listen to his lengthy defense (as if they were there to interrupt).[20] In the second part we have a similar direct challenge to the reader to pay attention to the context of the passages he is dealing with. This is a young and combative Speroni. Then in the third part we have the reported dialogue with his conscience and finally the fourth part is addressed to god—*Signor Dio omnipotente*.[21] Speroni in these last two parts gets older, more conservative, and less interested in his dialogues.

In each of the parts Speroni begins engaged with an interlocutor but slides into straight prose. There is a unifying thread to the character of the interlocutors addressed that is mentioned at the very beginning, when Speroni complements the listening Father, who he says is an "example to him who doesn't know how to pay attention when it is a matter of the honor of others."[22] Like Valla, he sets up the possible character of his audience, who can in this case either listen quietly (and let a gentleman defend himself), or rudely interrupt like someone just out of a kitchen. Throughout the work there is the presence of these two possible listeners, the patient judge-conscience-god, and the kitchen mob that threatens to interrupt. The judge is the ideal auditor, and the mob is reminiscent of the jury heard through Socrates' defense. Speroni's work tries to encourage the reader to reject the latter and listen patiently like the former, slipping into an attitude that becomes involved in the feast of ideas, reversals, and images to the point of forgetting the original issue, i.e., the condemnation of Speroni's youthful dialogues.

This is not the place to wander down the delightful path of comparing the defense of Socrates and that of Speroni, nor am I going to do justice to the second, third, and fourth parts of the *Apologia*, though I agree with Virginia Cox that the work has not been dealt with adequately as a whole. (She points out that concentrating on the first part does Speroni a disservice.[23]) Instead, like Jon Snyder, I am going to concentrate on defensive tactics of the first part because they include the first attempt to articulate a definition of dialogue that fits the variety of dialogue and captures the open character of dialogue. Speroni's first position on dialogue is remarkably similar to the position I believe emerges from the evidence I have so far gathered on the oral and written dialogue.

One of the features that stands out in the first part of the *Apologia* is its wandering and labyrinthine character. The defense is not presented methodically, but in a fashion compatible with the comical type of dialogue that he is defending. Snyder put it thus:

> Speroni's theory of dialogue emerges in a text that is a *satura*, a mélange of many things ranging from parable to oration to literary pastiche to dialogue itself. This protean critical rhetoric or metalanguage constitutes a defensive maneuver in its own right, masking Speroni's own stake in his text. . . . Speroni says so much about dialogue in so many ways that only with considerable difficulty can he be pinned down to a single position.[24]

Before trying to extract his defensive arguments we should look at some of the many analogies he gathers to his defense. For example, Speroni compares the writer of dialogue to a doctor who uses poisons (disreputable characters) to do good,[25] or a painter who might include monsters in a composition.[26] Elsewhere, to emphasize the artistry needed for such *commedia,* he compares the author to a general who has to organize troops in war and guests at a *convito* in peace.[27] One of Speroni's more interesting analogies comes when he is comparing the philosophical works of Aristotle, which he calls contemplative fields (they are flat and only produce one crop), to the gardens of dialogue that surround rural villas with their mix of fountains, statuary, and plants. The garden is the place of leisure not work, and produces a variety of herbs and spices that can be mixed with the nutritious produce of the fields to add flavor. While the fields feed the philosopher, the gardens add spice to the plain fare of the intellectual. Another image he uses for the dialogue is that of the rose bush, that while it has delightful flowers, it also has thorns, just as the dialogue may have inspiring moments among prickly characters.[28] He doesn't do so, but he could have compared the author of dialogue to a chef who marshals ingredients, but cannot be blamed for the bitterness of pepper if taken out of context, to say nothing about anchovies and their fishy character.

We can now return to how Speroni deals with the interpretative tendencies that I summarized above. To begin, he classifies the dialogue as prose that is like *poesia*, the Italian word for fiction that, taken from Aristotle, covers everything from drama to verse. The dialogue as such is an imitative form, in this case the imitation of what people say, and it is thus well formed when what the characters say is what they would be likely to say, and not what the author might want them to say. Central to his defense, however, is the next move, where he narrows the classification and compares dialogue to *commedia* whose effect depends on the novelty and variety of the characters who speak according to their different natures. Speroni is trying to get his dialogues read as if they were light farces not intended to deliver truths but meant to delight through lively misunderstandings and absurd characters. By shifting the classification Speroni hopes to achieve six things:

1. First he wants to legitimize his choice of disreputable characters. In comedy one expects unsavory characters, not just old wise men. (The old wise men in comedy tend to look rather silly.) If he can get his dialogues read as comedy then that frees him from the responsibility to only portray the best people in the best light.
2. A second expectation of comedy is that it should represent a diversity of characters who are different from each other. Traditionally the entertainment of comedy comes from the contrast of diverse characters. Thus one expects, in comedy, people of all sorts, from noblemen to courtesans to be combined in ways that highlight their differences. Much of the humor of comedy comes from this incongruous combination where often the most respectable characters taken out of context are made strange. Plato was not adverse to the comic possibilities of the combination of reputed wise men with an uncommon

character like Socrates. Representing people out of context is a classical parodic tactic to ridicule the serious and established ideology.

3. In comedy the author is expected to match the opinions and manners of his interlocutors to the type of person they represent. "Thus the well formed dialogue, like that of Plato, has many and different interlocutors who reason in the fashion of the character and life that they represent."[29] A writer of dialogue, like Plato, should not be blamed if disreputable characters say disreputable things, but should be admired for the poetic skill displayed if what they say is in keeping with their type. This is the crux of his defense—that the first responsibility of the dialogue writer is to the realistic imitation of types of people even if disreputable. (It should be noted that in the third part of the *Apologia* Speroni amends this position by assigning to the author responsibility for the whole.)
4. The classification of dialogue as comparable to comedy should also answer the temptation to expect dialogue to deliver truth. In comedy one does not expect an orthodox truth but a variety of contrasting opinions, especially novel ones, even if all are flawed.[30] A comedy is made of errors that do not necessarily lead to truth, except in so far as the reader might notice its absence. The dialogue writer should, like a painter, concentrate only on the appearances—the manner and speech of characters—not the truth of the matter.[31]

   Speroni goes further and suggests that representing the opinions of people who think they know, but do not, is a particularly delightful tactic, one that Plato was fond of.[32] He also singles out dialogues that combine characters who are all ignorant but refuse to be silent or confess their ignorance. Speroni compares this combination of ignorance in dialogue to the striking of flint with iron, where two cold and serious substances can be used to produce hot sparks which could light up the soul of the right reader.[33]
5. Speroni makes much of the fact that when he wrote his comedies he was young and ignorant. A young author of comedies cannot be expected to know the truth, but only to imitate character, a twist on Socratic ignorance and love of *logos*. The author, like the painter, need almost be deliberately ignorant of whatever underlying truth there is in order to capture the appearance of people. The painter

manipulates the visible appearance while the dialogue writer imitates their oral display. Thus Speroni grabs the bull by the horns, and deliberately claims the mantle of ignorance in his defense, claiming it a virtue for the young dialogue writer.[34] (The hint, if we remember the Socratic precedent, is that those who are judging Speroni do not even know they do not know. This is part of the thrust of the fourth part where Speroni damns all writing that is not devotional as vain and ignorant—at least he has the wit to admit it.)

In a pretty touch Speroni, now old, comments on how he will critique his dialogues as the severe father of comedies lectures his son.[35] Though he doesn't do that in the first and second part, there is a degree to which the third and fourth parts seem like the useless lectures of the old patriarchs in a farce, lectures which no one listens to anyway, *pace* Cox.[36]

6. If the dialogue is not expected to deal with serious truths and the reasoning that achieves those truths, then we should not expect the dialectical movement of questions and answers to move the dialogue. Instead it is the artistic combination of very different characters that provides the delightful unity of the work. "Certainly the contrast of people, because that is full of novelty, is the heart and soul of dialogue."[37] (One of the questions we have to ask of the artist is how he combines these incongruous characters while making the dialogue look natural and unforced.)

This comical defense pulls together a number of the themes we have dealt with in previous chapters. To begin, Speroni draws on the Socratic idea that dialogue is tied to leisure. He distinguishes *ozio* and *negozio*, Italian for "leisure" and "business," which he says includes the business of contemplation (professional philosophy).[38] Leisure is the time of recovery from work and has types of literature appropriate to it like the comical dialogue. The work of leisure should not be judged by standards of the time of work. Dialogue is not suited to hard philosophical work, but philosophical play, when we want to be entertained and have suspended our judgment.[39] Aristotelian treatises, on the other hand, are philosophical works suited for instruction and the serious transmission of ideas. Speroni, no doubt, has the discussion of leisure in the *Phaedrus* in mind when he defends his works thus, but the time of leisure is no longer the time when others are drinking, but the time of youth, followed by the serious work of wise old age.

Speroni makes hay from the absence of the author. The dialogue delights us by presenting us with variety and novelty and to do this the author must withdraw in favor of the different characters (as Plato did). When writing, the author "silences his own voice, and fills those [dialogues or gardens] with various new names and manners, and with new and different arguments."[40] The absence of the author is linked to the ability to delight. The greater the presence of the author the less the variety and hence the less the diversion. In addition Speroni ties the authorial presence to the responsibility of the author. The greater the presence of the author the easier it is to disentangle the author's opinions and judge them. This in turn puts a damper on the entertainment value of the work, as an author, when present, becomes answerable for the tenor of the conversation as a whole. An author if present can be judged by the company he keeps and if he values his reputation will steer the conversation toward serious subjects or stay away entirely.

This allows Speroni to give new life to the classical classification of dialogues. He distinguishes the reported dialogue from the representative one. The reported dialogue is like the epic where the author narrates (like a historian) the actions and words of others. In the representative dialogue others are allowed to speak for themselves. Since the epic dialogue (which he associates with Cicero and Xenophon) is like history where one does not report all facts but only the important ones, it should only report the worthwhile words of serious people. By contrast the representative dialogue, associated with Plato and Lucian, is free to entertain through the imitation of the ridiculous and ignorant.[41]

He also comments on the responsibilities and place of the reader. It is up to the reader to know how to read dialogues written for leisurely entertainment. It is the fault of the reader if he pricks himself on the thorns of a rose bush by trying to grasp it. The reader should know not to expect instruction from a genre suited to entertainment. Nor should the reader expect resolution from a dialogue; rather, the author presents characters who have their say and leave the dialogue all believing they have won the dispute, to the amusement of the reader and author who have not missed this. The dialogue is thus not for the instruction or delight of the characters, but for the audience who is entertained by the contrast of ignorance. The author and reader together can laugh at the play of the posturing of characters. The reader is not expected to identify with an unrepentant interlocutor, learning as he is questioned, but can delight in the ignorance of those who think they know.

To conclude with Speroni, his feast of ideas on dialogue are not as incompatible with Tasso's as they appear; they offer a different type of dialogue as paradigmatic. For Tasso the serious narrated dialogue is paradigmatic; for Speroni it is the comic dialogue without narration. Both their theories of dialogue leave room for the other: Tasso comments that one can have the dialogical equivalent to comedy, and Speroni talks about the serious work of Cicero's dialogues. In Speroni's case his garden of thoughts is not designed to be a coherent theory that excludes others so much as a defensive labyrinth of ideas, while Tasso's work has a normative aspect that could be used to critique the comical dialogue as unworthy. In conclusion it is interesting to compare these two paradigms conveniently in a table:

	Tasso's Serious Dialogue	**Speroni's Comic Dialogue**
Direct or Reported:	Reported or Mixed Dialogue	Direct Representation
Characters:	Serious and Important Men	Variety of People, including Women, Disreputable People, and Fools
Subject:	Speculative or Ethical Issues	Anything (Does not necessarily have a coherent subject)
Resolution of Dialogue:	Purification of Error or Resolution of Truth	Comedy of Errors
Audience:	Civil and Speculative Men	Men and Women of Wit and Letters
Responsibility of Author:	To Instruct and Benefit	To Delight

A DEFINITION OF DIALOGUE

Given the limiting effect theory was put to in the late Italian Renaissance it would be unseemly if I were to use Speroni to propose a definition of dialogue that can be used to delimit dialogue today, as tempting as that may be given the growing fascination with dialogue in all quarters. Rather I will present, courtesy of Speroni, a theoretical position that tries to keep open the possibilities for dialogue and suggests ways of discussing the close connection of form and content. What I am going to propose is a working definition, buttressed by M. M. Bakhtin's theory of the novel, intended to show what the dialogue is capable of and how we can appreciate its artistry. It is a working definition in that it is supposed to provide work for the lover of dialogue.

Why choose to define dialogue at all? Definitions have a reputation for limiting discourse. The etymological roots of *define* lie in *definire*, the Latin for "to end" or "to terminate." It is no surprise that one definition of "define" is "to determine the boundary . . . to settle the limits of . . ."[42] But there is another sense of the word *define*, "to bring something into focus," which is what this definition is designed to do. Definitions can be treated as hints that guide one back in the direction of the sought. So without further ado let us propose a short form of the definition:

A dialogue is a unity of diverse voices.

The reader familiar with Bakhtin will notice how I have borrowed from his definition of the novel. In his essay "Discourse in the Novel" he writes: "The novel can be defined as a diversity of social speech types (sometimes even diversity of languages) and a diversity of individual voices, artistically organized."[43] My borrowing is not without reason. Bakhtin himself, in another essay "Epic and Novel," calls the Socratic dialogue the "authentic predecessor of the novel."[44] The Socratic dialogue for Bakhtin had many of the defining characteristics of the novel: laughter in the form of Socratic irony, the combination of different styles and dialects, a hero like Socrates, and closeness to everyday life and its language.

The key to Bakhtin's definition and mine is that the dialogue is a combination of different voices, each with its own form and content. It is a meal made of many ingredients like fish, bread, and anchovies. The ingredients have not been melted in a pot until the result has a single color and flavor; they have been instead mixed into a garden salad leaving the ingredients distinct. All other genres have their own particular form, but the dialogue (and even more so the novel) is a mixture of these.[45] The paradigmatic dialogue has no single language, nor a single form, but is made up of the artistic combination of others. "The style of the novel is to be found in the combination of styles; the language of a novel in the system of its 'languages.'"[46]

It would be tempting to call the dialogue a metagenre that encloses within it other forms of discourse, but that would give it a status it doesn't deserve. If anything it is beneath the other genres, closer to the everyday confusion of voices from which literary genres rise. I prefer to consider it a genre at the threshold of others, parasitic on the authoritative voices of the age, capable of parodying them, but not of determining them. The dialogue, like any form of parody, depends on the voices it contrasts. It is woven out of the distinct threads that have been spun by others.

Voice

Let us begin at the end of this definition and work our way through its words. A voice is a combination of form and content. Most of the voices in dialogue are the speech of a character which carries opinions (content) in the language appropriate to his or her background and personality. Dialogue, however, can be used to combine voices other than those of characters. We can find in dialogues the voices of gods, the voices of artificial entities like Dialogue and the Laws of Athens, and voices that are of a different genre like the verses that introduce each part of Boethius's *Consolation* or the prefaces to Cicero's dialogues.

Often one voice will come through another. The most obvious example is in narrated dialogues where the narrator writes in his own voice and then slides into direct reporting of others so that you can hear them through him. You can also have characters that impersonate others, as Socrates does when he argues with the Laws of Athens or represents the positions of others in the *Theaetetus*. (The conversational ability of Socrates to represent the voice of others makes him particularly suited to dialogue; he can organize within himself voices in a fashion similar to Plato when writing. Socrates is the oral analog to the dialogue writer.)

Bakhtin takes this a step further and suggests that all voice is the reorganization of other voices. "The ideological becoming of a human being, in this view, is the process of selectively assimilating the words of others."[47] This leads to an interesting problem: if a dialogue is a unity of voices and a voice is itself a unity of voices, one gets an infinite regress of voices. It also means that in some way all discourse is dialogical as there is no such thing as a simple voice. Bakhtin would undoubtedly not be bothered by this regress, because he is fascinated by the ways we can include the voices of others within ours. The difference between a voice and a dialogue, however, lies in the degree of assimilation of the enclosed voices. A dialogue is a unity where the voices are not assimilated, but left clearly distinct; in a voice the assimilation is an ongoing process where most of the differences have been sanded down. (The exception to this is the Socratic hero who speaks in different voices like dialogue, but he has a special role in dialogue comparable to that of the author outside.)

Bakhtin talks about language where I have chosen to focus on voice. A language is a broader category than a voice. "We are taking language not as a system of abstract grammatical categories, but rather language conceived as ideologically saturated, language as a worldview, even as a concrete opinion, insuring a *maximum* of mutual understanding in all spheres of ideological life."[48] A voice is a particular instance of the use of a language, for example a character choosing what to say within the possibilities offered by the conceptual scheme and distinctions offered by the language. In philosophical dialogues, where the contrast of the ideological dimension of different languages is important, characters tend to be exemplary representatives of the languages (social, professional, and regional background) they speak in. Characters tend to be simplified so that they become pure voices identifiable by the reader as belonging to a certain class and profession. This is especially true when we have characters who represent abstract entities like Philosophy or Justice. This simplification highlights the contrast of the characters and their ideological backgrounds. This also explains why we have slipped into talking of dialogue between communities.

To be fair, most of us speak many languages, switching languages even in mid sentence. Therefore, just as there can be different voices using the same language, an individual can switch languages or speak in different voices. Thus in dialogue one also finds certain characters like Socrates who are not simple voices, but themselves a unity of voices in different languages. These characters, because they have the same ability to represent different voices that dialogue has, are typically the heroes of dialogues, and the closest we have to a representative of the author. It should be noted that these heroic speakers do not necessarily represent the opinions of the author; they represent the capability to compose their voice that is parallel to the author's ability to compose a unity of voices. Socrates can manage oral dialogue the way Plato manages written dialogue. The symmetry of Socrates and Plato we have mentioned before. What Plato did with written dialogue can be seen as an application of the Socratic oral practice.

By languages Bakhtin does not mean the traditional national languages like French, English, German, and Japanese; he is interested in the ways of discoursing particular to different social, professional, and regional groups. Languages for Bakhtin also have an ideological character; they are not content independent. A language has a horizon of possible opinions that can be expressed within it. Among other things it is difficult to critique a language from within it, using only its distinctions. This was the danger Heidegger felt so acutely. While for Heidegger the ideological dimension of a language is a problem as it makes understanding between languages difficult (not to mention the difficulty of reaching beyond the concepts of one's language), for Bakhtin this is not a problem as it is not the characters who have to understand each other. The novel and dialogue, intended for the audience not the interlocutors, can delight and instruct even if the interlocutors do not reach an understanding. If anything, to paraphrase Speroni, the dialogue delights most when the interlocutors talk at cross-purposes misunderstanding each other because of subtle differences in meaning. In Hume's *Dialogues* we see this at work. Philo deliberately voices his skepticism in the language of Demea thereby convincing him that they understand each other and are united in their critique of Cleanthes. Cleanthes alerts the reader that the agreement masks a much deeper difference than that between him and Demea, but it is not until the end that Demea realizes the extent of the difference and leaves.

Heidegger's hesitation and awareness of the danger of dialogue between languages is particularly interesting because it is a problem within dialogue, not a problem for the auditors outside of dialogue. Within his dialogue Heidegger worries about his ability to understand the other and resorts in his hesitant way to defining terms. The defining of terms, be it in the roundabout fashion Heidegger takes, or the direct way Socrates imposes on his interlocutors, is one mechanism for overcoming language differences and forging a communal language that will maximize understanding. (This is not the only tactic for entering into dialogue; others are to make the conversation itself a topic of conversation, to agree on "rules" of discussion, or to periodically review what has passed.) Heidegger is not innocent of the ways languages can be adapted to meet; he himself was a master at borrowing from the language of poetry and religion to overcome limitations in the language of metaphysics, thereby altering the very language of metaphysics we now use. But all these tactics are for those within dialogue who wish to understand each other (which is not always the case). From the distance of the author and auditor, understanding between characters is not always desirable as it erases the contrast of the characters. The comic dialogue and its ironic variant thrive on certain misunderstandings. The Socratic hero often takes advantage of the ambiguities to eject characters rather than educate them or include them in the understanding. Particularly in representative dialogues, where the comic contrast is highest, we find characters sacrificed rather than included in understanding. This is often the fate of orthodox voices whose authority is made strange when contrasted with other voices that they, in their ignorance, refuse to acknowledge. If the hero of dialogue is the voice that can adapt to other voices, the villain is the brittle unchanging voice, convinced that it is the universe of truth.

Diversity

A dialogue that combines voices that are indistinguishable in their opinions and language is hardly a dialogue at all, for it reads like a treatise artificially rendered as a dialogue. A treatise, after all, also has content and form. What distinguishes the dialogue is the diversity of opinions and characters. A dialogue is a way of bringing different opinions together while preserving the voice of those opinions. In Hume's *Dialogues*, we do not have the dry comparison of positions on the nature of god, all represented in the same voice, and therefore losing the particular character of some of the voices; instead we have incarnated opinions expressed in the fashion that suits the type of person who would hold those opinions. In the *Phaedrus* it is not an accident that the speechwriter Lysias is not present, since that is in the character of the speechwriter; he writes for others rather than for himself, absenting himself from the declamation.

A dialogue that simply mixes voices at random is also rarely successful. As Speroni says, it is the contrast of these voices that delights. Dialogue is particularly suited to the contrast of positions that are rarely confronted and are fundamentally unreconcilable if one takes seriously their expression. That which is a problem when you are in dialogue, is a virtue when you audit the represented dialogue. Within dialogue you have to beware of the differences between your language and that of your interlocutors, especially when the difference is subtle enough to be overlooked. For this reason the process of entering into dialogue, defining your terms and setting out the rules of the dialogue, is so important to participants. Outside of the dialogue, as an auditor, reader, or author, you can take advantage of this diversity in a number of ways. You can use it to parody a language and those who speak in it. You can choose to use one language to highlight the inadequacies of another, thereby critiquing it, or you can admire the persistence of those who are adapting to find a middle ground.

The traditional philosophical work extracts positions from voices, translating them to the voice of professional philosophy with its jargon and character. The voices once depersonalized can be compared as objects of the same sort. This reduction in certain cases fails to grasp what is at stake, especially in cases when it is the character of the community of discourse which is at issue. Dialogue by contrast can preserve the situated expression of ideas, but rarely works when one wants to resolve differences because it thrives on diversity and therefore tends to maintain diversity. To paraphrase Hume, dialogue is not suited for the delivery of complex systems that reconcile everything, but is suited to issues where there is no clear resolution.

Bakhtin is at his best when he shows the dialogical character of all works, even those that on the surface seem monological. As he points out, "Our speech is filled to overflowing with other people's words."[49] To some extent all discourse includes a diversity of voices. The extent to which a work is a dialogue is a matter of the degree to which either the work contains dialogue or is situated within a larger one. A monological work is addressed to an audience; it enters into a larger dialogue that is already taking place, identifying its interlocutors through references.[50] A dialogue, by contrast, encloses its own dialogue and thus its own audience. It is no coincidence that so many dialogues spend time building up the character of the auditors among whom the reader (and author) can sit. The dialogue, rather than entering an existing community of discourse, tries to imagine its own community of discourse. For this reason the dialogue is particularly suited to situations when what is at stake is the community of discourse, its language, the character of the participants, and its possible subjects. The traditional work enters an existing community of discourse and therefore cannot stand outside it to offer alternatives. The philosophers who take advantage of the dialogue either mock the existing community or try to imagine a utopian community, be it a small circle or a republic, where new configurations of voices gathered can join.

The failure to account for the diversity of the voices in a dialogue (or novel) leads to interpretative strategies that isolate some feature from the whole. Especially in philosophy, where our professional discourse is built around the comparison of ideas in the voice of a recognized professional language, it is tempting, and not altogether unwarranted, to try to extract from a dialogue a single voice with one content. This is done in two ways: (1) you extract a single voice from within the dialogue, like that of Socrates, and treat it as the essence of the whole, or (2) you take the whole as the single voice of the author, ignoring the differences between the voices. Neither of the strategies is entirely unwarranted, for the dialogue lends itself to being treated as an encyclopedia of voices on a subject which can be mined for positions that when extracted can be answered elsewhere. (Certainly Cicero intended to provide a collection of acceptable positions from which Latin philosophy could start.) The problem arises when one tries to establish exactly what the author believed in this fashion. Plato scholarship has struggled with this problem for centuries; one is tempted to think that this struggle is the real legacy of Plato. Readers can never be confident in their reading, so they must continually reinvent Plato through increasingly complicated interpretative moves.

What is of particular interest to us is what Bakhtin calls the stratification of languages in literary works. These strata are the different dimensions on which different voices can be plotted. It is a rough, three-dimensional taxonomy that we can use to appreciate not only the differences between voices of the same background but the differences across backgrounds. For Bakhtin there are three dimensions of languages:

1. *Generic languages* are the languages of different literary forms, for example the language of the epic, the letter, the oration, or the manual. The novel, and on occasion the dialogue, combine different genres with their particular languages. So, for example, in dialogue we find not only direct speech, but epistolary prefaces which are in the language of letter writing, fragments of verse, and composed speeches.
2. *Social or Professional languages* are the second dimension of languages, and this is the one most exploited in dialogue. Different professions have their particular jargon and ideological background as do different social classes. The dialogue allows the combination of characters who speak different professional and social languages, using the same vocabulary in subtly different ways. It is no coincidence that Socrates was always out in the market talking to the tradesmen.
3. *Regional languages* are the third dimension of languages. In addition to the differences between genre of voice and social/professional background, we have to listen for the sometimes subtle geographic differences.

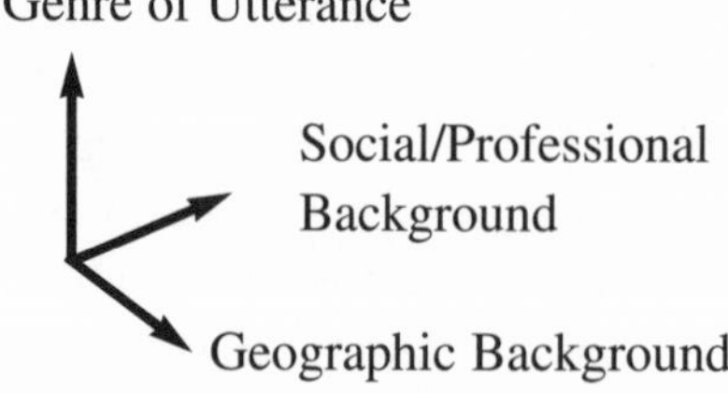

These three dimensions give us a starting point for identifying the types of voices of a dialogue. Each voice has a genre, a social and professional background, and a regional dialect. If the dialogue is a unity of these voices, we can begin to appreciate a dialogue by identifying the types of differences between voices, plotting them in this three-dimensional space. For example, in epistolary dialogues, the voice of the narrator is couched in the language of letter writing; it is of a different genre than the others in conversation. Cicero, the letter writer, is a character who, though of the same social, professional, and regional background as the other characters, is expressing himself in a different genre of utterance. The work of appreciating a dialogue involves appreciating the variety of voices within.

Unity

If dialogue preserves diversity, the challenge for an author is to create a unified work that can be called *one* dialogue. While in traditional philosophical works the language and content can provide unity to the work, this cannot by definition be the case with dialogue, as it is a unity of many languages and opinions. For this reason the strategies that dialogue writers use to create unity out of the diversity of voices have to be different from the ones used by the essay writer. A philosophical reader might be tempted to throw up his or her hands and consign the unity of dialogue to the broad category of "art," that divine inspiration that cannot be discussed further but only located. This, however, misses some obvious mechanisms for forging unity out of contrasting voices, mechanisms which have philosophical relevance, not only because they are the concrete expression of the author's composition, but also because they are tied to the issues of philosophical culture that are central to many dialogues. Identifying these mechanisms allows us to appreciate the artistry of a dialogue, but that doesn't lessen their hermeneutical significance to the philosophical reader.

Formal Clues

The least interesting and most obvious mechanism for providing unity is to use formal clues that indicate to a reader the beginning, end, and parts of the dialogue. Prefaces and postfaces can work this way, wrapping up the dialogue into a unity bracketed by these devices. Especially important can be the finalization clues that indicate the end of the dialogue. Dialogue is like any utterance; there are hints that indicate when the utterance is over so that the audience can respond or go home. In dialogue these mechanisms can be internal to the conversation or external to it. To give a few examples: in Socratic dialogues it is not unusual for the Socratic character to take advantage of the confutation of the interlocutor to deliver a longer speech that wraps up the debate. In narrated dialogues, like those of Cicero, a final reversal can be a closing mechanism, unwinding the careful reasoning as a final act.

Occasion

The occasion of the dialogue also provides a unity to the work. A dialogue between characters usually involves some sort of meeting that brings them together. The reason for their meeting I will call the occasion and it often has its own logic. The occasion should not be confused with the setting, though the two are obviously tied. The occasion is the explicit chain of events that brought the characters together and will inevitably take them apart, back to their own worlds. It is the action of the dialogue, what little there is. In Lucian's dialogues of the dead we find an unearthly occasion—meetings in hell. In the *Phaedrus* the desire of Phaedrus to learn Lysias's speech by heart, out of hearing of others, takes him outside Athens where he meets Socrates who notices the half-hidden speech.

Setting up a believable occasion is one of the challenges that faces the author or arranger of dialogue. If the characters are people who do not usually meet in everyday life, or if they do meet, they haven't the time to philosophize, then the author must craft a meeting where they all have an excuse to stay and talk. The arranger of an oral dialogue also has to make sure his audience is around to hear. One can see how the occasion, especially where the characters involved are busy men, must be an exceptional moment of leisure like a religious holiday when it would be unseemly to work. The choice of occasion is not simply a matter of setting up a believable meeting, the occasion, in the finest dialogues, is in harmony with the rest of the dialogue. Socrates meets Euthyphro because both are involved in court cases that revolve around a younger generation trying its elders. In the *Phaedrus* the discussion of writing and rhetoric is nicely illustrated by the fate of Lysias's speech in the hands of Phaedrus and Socrates.

Chronotope

In "Forms of Time and Chronotope in the Novel" Bakhtin introduces a useful idea for understanding the unity of dialogue, the idea of the *chronotope*. The chronotope is the time and space of a work of literature. It is more than the physical setting, it is the "intrinsic connectedness of temporal and spatial relationships that are artistically expressed in literature."[51] The chronotope is the type of place and the pace of life in that place that characterizes a dialogue. It is a major constituent of the culture of the dialogue which in turn, I have been arguing, is often the point of dialogues. Thus the chronotope may be our best device for categorizing dialogues philosophically. Discussions of chronotope make more sense if we give examples of the most important ones in philosophical dialogues. These chronotopes should be compared to the space and time mentioned at the end of chapter 2, "The Orality of Dialogue."

Villa Time: One of the most common chronotopes is the rural estate with its leisurely villa pace. The villa is a country estate far from the city and work. It is a place of relaxation with gardens that provide spices and herbs to dress up the business of city life. When gathered at a villa you have all day, and sometimes more than a day, to discuss anything. The amount of uninterrupted time naturally encourages long speeches.

In that the villa is a private space, one can say things that one could not in public. The privacy encourages play, especially the oratorical play where characters take both sides of an issue reversing themselves to show off their rhetorical skill. The privacy of the villa means that there is no audience outside the collection of friends gathered, which means the author has to use a narrator to let us in on what we would otherwise never hear of. Unlike public dialogues there is no place for us sitting at the edge, so we hear of the dialogue through a reporter like Pamphilus in Hume's *Dialogues*.

The villa is where friends gather; thus the competition among characters tends to be friendly, without the combative dialectic of public dialogue. Discussions in the villa rarely have the clear resolution of a dialectical dispute; friends do not bully each other into humiliating capitulation, nor do friends impose rules for discourse on each other. Finally, at a villa you tend to have gathered people of similar social and economic background. There is less diversity among friends—people tend to spend their leisure with people who have similar interests.

Symposium: The space of the symposium is the dining room; the time is the leisurely pace of dinner punctuated by dishes. The pace of a meal conditions the pace of the speaking, the speaking is the meal for the mind, each speech has its time and contributes to the complete feast. Being in the home, the symposium space is private, like villa time, but the home is often in the city, so the symposium is a shorter break from work, and therefore closer to everyday business. As it is private you again have people who know each other and generally respect each other. Since there is also the issue of the reader's access to the private home, the symposium is therefore often reported; we gain access through someone who was there.

Public Space: After villa time the second major chronotope of the dialogue, closely tied to Socratic dialogue, is that of the public space. The public space can be a piazza, the steps of a court, a gymnasium, or the coffee house. In public space the interlocutors are on show, so they tend to talk for others, which is why there are more possibilities for irony in public dialogues. This type of dialogue is often representative, not narrated, because the public is right there; we the auditors need no excuse to listen in. Characters in public have to nurse their reputation and this conditions what they say. In public people are not likely to play with words, try new ideas, or express private beliefs. The public space thus encourages the discussion (and embarrassment) of orthodox (public) opinion. When in front of others the discussion tends to be aimed not at the instruction of the interlocutors but at the silent audience, the interlocutors speak at each other, but for the audience as in a debate. Interlocutors compete as if the silent majority were a jury and their reputations were at stake.

In public space the interlocutors need not be friends. This is where any citizen can discuss issues of public concern. This is where important public figures are challenged before others. It is where people who would not normally meet at home or at their villas encounter each other, often people from different social and economic groups. The public dialogue can thus offer the greatest diversity of characters (with the exception of the dialogue of the dead).

The encounter in public space is rarely planned. People with other business happen to run into each other, and this sets the pace of the dialogue. When you have other affairs, and did not intend to spend time chatting, the dialogue is fast and short, crowded by the important business of the interlocutors. The time of the public dialogue, because it is sandwiched between other events, is closely tied to the affairs of the city. It is a time situated in the history of the characters and polis, not a leisure time apart and unconnected to its history. Public dialogues are part of the history of the community as they can make reputations, so the subject of the dialogue tends to be serious and politically relevant.

Along the Path: A less common chronotope is the road along which the interlocutors wander. The path usually leads from somewhere to somewhere (even if in a circle back to home) and thus the dialogue along the path often moves from topic to topic. Heidegger nicely uses the rhythm of the day to pace his dialogue along a country path. The path followed usually leads through the countryside so the dialogue has some of the private character of villa time with people who respect each other wandering over ideas at their leisure.

Limbo: An important literary chronotope is the space of the dead, be it Hades, Heaven, or Limbo. This is a space and time entirely disconnected from human history where characters can be brought together who could have never met in real life. The dialogue of the dead is like public dialogue in that this space allows for unlikely combinations of people in front of others. In limbo these characters should have all the time in the world to talk, yet these dialogues are often short and paced like those that take place in public space. This is partly because Limbo is a public space where people meet before others in contest. It is also because dead characters are often stereotypes; their death has fixed them as a type. The dialogue of the dead achieves most of its effect through the incongruous combination of these characters in a way that mocks one or another type, and this effect does not take long to achieve if the mix of characters is right. Such a dialogue is almost over before it has begun; once the comic combination is clear to the reader so that they can see its potential there is no reason to continue.

Soliloquy: A chronotope at the edge of dialogue is the solitary space of contemplation, be it in a study, a dream, or a prison. In this space the narrator enters into dialogue with spiritual advisors, be they daimons, one's conscience, Philosophy incarnate, gods, or saints. The space is isolated and private to the extreme, and there is no one but the narrator and the advisor they conjure up. While during the soliloquy the time seems eternal, the meditation is often triggered by a personal crisis. The time of the soliloquy is an interruption of eternity into the personal life of the narrator. The soliloquy takes as long as it has to, and when it is over, the normal course of events starts up again. It is the long night before death.

Because the soliloquy is often triggered by a crisis of some sort and it is a dialogue between characters within the narrator, this type of dialogue is often autobiographical. It is a type of dialogue that represents the thinking of the narrator at some critical moment. In the soliloquy the hero gathers up his life and prepares philosophically for day.

This chronotope extends beyond the dialogue. The diversity of characters is always tenuous in a soliloquy. The soliloquy is properly a genre of its own including such works as Descartes's *Meditations.* Some soliloquies are dialogue in the sense that there is an alternation of voices, but most do not qualify as there is not the diversity between the voices.

What all these chronotopes have in common is that they are all places and times of discussion, and interludes in the life of work. They are times of leisure when people have time to think and talk. The only chronotope that involves any action is that of the path when people are walking while talking. (This is what distinguishes the novel from the dialogue; the novel includes places and times of action not just leisure.) Most of these times are within history. Most dialogues are particular moments in the history of the community of discourse, a good example being the set of dialogues around Socrates' death: the *Euthyphro*, which takes place before the trial; the *Apology*, which shows the trial; the *Crito*, which takes place after the trial; and the *Phaedo*, which recounts his death by hemlock. The place of these dialogues is also a specific spot in the community accessible to the participants. While the place may not be public, it is rarely an intimate spot unlikely to be the site of a conversation (that could be reported) like the bedroom or bathroom. For this reason I consider the soliloquy a different genre from the dialogue. Its private meditative space and time is what distinguishes it. The exception to these general rules would seem to be the dialogues of the dead, those that take place in Hades or Limbo, but even they are in a specific place in the afterworld. Though they do not take place in the history of the living, they do, however, take place in the history of the dead. For example, they have to take place after the death of the participants, and in many of such dialogues one senses that there is a "history" of sorts for the gods of the afterworld. My point is that dialogue always seems to take place in a specific context, something a treatise does not, for example. Even the dialogue of the dead has this sense of context—that it is in a particular time and place and is not a work that is eternally true.

The chronotope can be used not only to differentiate the varieties of dialogue, but also to differentiate genres. We have seen a hint of this with the soliloquy, which overlaps with the dialogue, and with the awkward fit of the dialogue of the dead. In the conclusion I will discuss the varieties of philosophical writing at greater length using the chronotope to distinguish three major genres. Those who are interested in the differences between dialogues and the differences between dialogues and other genres do well to use the chronotope as the distinguishing feature.

Themes

The last unifying mechanism that needs to be mentioned is the theme. I use the word theme because not all dialogues, even philosophical ones, have only explicit subjects, and even when they do, there are other themes that, like strands stretching through the dialogue, help keep it together. Themes can be explicit subjects of discussion recognized by the speakers as an issue that keeps them talking, or they can be implicitly carried in the images, examples, and manner of the characters. The most interesting themes have a way of being both a subject for discussion and turning up transformed in other ways. In Socratic dialogues these themes are often driven by the movement of questions that acts like the plot of a novel. This is not, however, the case with all dialogues, even ones clearly philosophical.

Any discussion of themes in a dialogue needs to consider (a) the explicit issues that are discussed openly, (b) the implicit issues, and (c) those issues that are both. Often the most interesting issues, like that of the relationship between the younger generation and their elders that runs through the *Euthyphro*, are developed both explicitly and implicitly by the author. The theme is discussed as an issue while also being shown in the interaction of Socrates and Euthyphro. For this reason it is important to trace themes through an entire work rather than extracting the explicit discussion and ignoring other developments of the issue. If we are interested in the just individual as discussed in Plato's *Republic*, we should follow the discussion on the just state. For example, the proposal to purify the state by evacuating it of all older citizens can be compared to the traumatic purification of the individual that was discussed in the chapter on oral dialogue. A proposal to get rid of unwanted voices might seem extreme for a state, but therapeutic for the individual.

Another aspect of this is that it is important to understand how a theme emerges in the social context of the dialogue. We should not treat themes only as arguments that can be represented by a series of questions and answers unattached to people. We have to understand the conversational context of each theme. Why and how does someone raise an issue? Why did it come up at that point? To generalize, careful attention needs to be paid to (a) how and by whom a theme is launched, (b) interventions on the theme through the work (be they explicit or implicit), and finally (c) how the theme is concluded. We can think of a theme as the trajectory of an issue through the space of the dialogue. It is important to note who launches the theme and where it is launched. It is important how the course of the theme is altered by other characters and themes, and finally, it is important where the theme is going when the dialogue ends. Only then can we appreciate how a theme holds the diversity of people together.

There is a tendency in philosophy to follow a theme only when it is being discussed explicitly. If we isolate moments in the development of a theme we miss the unifying nature of that theme. For example, in Hume's *Dialogues*, skepticism is an explicit issue at the beginning (especially dialogue 3) and at the end of the dialogue (dialogue 12). What happens to the issue in the middle? In the dialogue by Heidegger discussed at the beginning of this book we noted how issues would hesitantly wind their way through the work. Questions are asked only to be answered obliquely or much later. To understand how such a theme is a unifying mechanism one has to ask what happens to it throughout the dialogue, including the middle parts when it is not discussed. Are there really two discussions of skepticism, or are the two explicit discussions part of a single trajectory of the issue through the dialogue that picks up baggage in the long traverse through the parts that do not explicitly deal with skepticism? If the latter is the case, how is the issue modified by the intervening parts? This is not to say that all themes must traverse an entire dialogue; my point is that we have to be sensitive to those that do.

Not only do we have to pay attention to how themes traverse a dialogue, but we need to be sensitive to how the themes interact. Certain themes can be difficult to extract and discuss as a single thread because they merge with other themes, are modified by others (intervene in the trajectory of each other), or change into new themes. It is therefore important that individual themes not only be followed through a dialogue, but that attention be paid to how they work together to make a dialogue a thematic unity. To understand how themes unify a dialogue a careful interpreter might:

1. Identify the major themes in a dialogue, both those that are explicitly discussed and those that are not.
2. Follow each theme through the dialogue paying careful attention to:
   2.1 the context in which the theme is launched,
   2.2 the interventions on the theme as it moves through the work, and
   2.3 the concluding direction of the theme when the dialogue ends.
3. Consider the interaction of the major themes and how they affect each other.

Interpretation of Dialogue

I said at the beginning that the definition proposed was a working one. One way we can use this definition is to help us read dialogues appreciatively. We can take the definition of dialogue proposed here and use it to identify questions that the interpreter of a dialogue should consider. If the features I have discussed, especially the unifying ones, are really relevant to the dialogue, they should provide a framework of things to look for and describe in a dialogue. This framework should not limit interpreters; it should help them focus on the dialogue, and remind them of features they might have missed. We can repurpose the definition as two sets of questions designed to elicit the nature of a particular dialogue:

1. *Diversity of Voices:* Who are the principal voices in the dialogue? How is the form of their expression related to the opinions they express? What is the generic, social, and geographical background of each voice? How are the voices different? What voices might be missing?
2. *Unity of Dialogue: Occasion*—What is the occasion of the dialogue? How do the characters happen to meet? *Chronotope*—What is the setting and pace of the dialogue? What type of space and time does the dialogue take place in? *Theme*—What are the major themes? How do they move through the dialogue, and how do they interact?

Oral Dialogue

To conclude this chapter we need to ask if this definition can illuminate the oral dialogue. We have conducted this discussion of the definition of dialogue in the context of literary dialogues, but the larger context of this work has been the search for commonality between the oral and written dialogue. We found that both the oral and written dialogue are composed for the delight of the auditor or reader, that the dialogue was not directed to the participants, but to those in the audience. I have also commented, in the context of this definition, on the concerns of those in dialogue against those auditors at the periphery. Heidegger, the character in dialogue, wants to overcome the difference in language, while Heidegger the author wants to use it.

To digress for a moment, this definition is not a manual for those who want to enter into dialogue. The needs of those in dialogue are different from those of interpreters who wish to appreciate it from the outside. The auditor and reader can enjoy a misunderstanding that would be counterproductive for those within. Something can be a dialogue for those outside that is frustrating or humiliating for those within. One of the implications of the unity of dialogue is precisely that one has to be outside to name it as such. One has to have a distance from an event to call it a dialogue. The distance can be that of the participant after the fact reflecting on it, or that of the auditor listening in, or that of one who hopes for a dialogue coming. My point is that distance is a feature of our relationship to dialogue, something can only be so named at the distance from which it can be seen to be a unity. That said, we could work our way back from this definition to guidelines on how to encourage dialogue. I will do so briefly in the conclusion. What remains now is to see if this feature can help us understand the oral dialogue.

One feature of oral dialogue is its hesitant character. We hesitate to say we are in dialogue; rather, we talk about entering dialogue. We hesitate to call something a dialogue while it is ongoing; rather, we call for dialogue to come, or recognize it as such after the fact. One reason for this is our expectation that a dialogue be a unity comparable to those exemplary dialogues we have heard or read. Our expectations of dialogue are such that we hesitate to call something a dialogue unless it is completed and we can look back on it and find it worthy, just as we would hesitate to call a life just before it is over. As in literary dialogue we have to achieve a distance comparable to that of the reader before we can call something a dialogue. Even the participants in a dialogue, when they recognize it as such, see the dialogue from a peripheral perspective, that of a reader or auditor; they step outside their role in the dialogue and look at it as an auditor. I have noted earlier the importance of the negotiations about how to proceed, and the reflections by characters on the course of the dialogue. These negotiations and reflections within dialogue are the "stepping back" that we all do to think about the value of the conversations we are in and their possible direction. This negotiation and reflection is characteristic of friendly dialogue.

But how do we recognize something as a unified and completed dialogue, even if we do so only after the fact? The characteristics that I suggested above for appreciating the written dialogue are the features we look for in the oral dialogue. We look for the bringing together of diverse voices. Where everyone is of the same background and agrees about everything you don't have a dialogue. It is rather the bringing together of difference that we admire in oral dialogue. To change the focus of this discussion, the political dialogues we call for tend to be between groups that have significant differences. Nobody would consider a discussion a dialogue unless significant social, professional, ideological, or regional differences are overcome. This is the healing power of dialogue that we call for, its ability to gather difference. As for the mechanisms that we use to bring our voices together in oral dialogue, the unifying strategies noted above also apply. We have to pay attention to the formalities of conversation, there has to be an occasion (preferably one congruent to the issues discussed), we need a setting and pace that is appropriate (and the setting and pace chosen will affect the character of the dialogue, especially the publicity surrounding the dialogue), and finally there are themes and subjects that tie dialogue together. These unifying strategies are an analytical tool for the interpreter of dialogue, but they can be refocused to allow us to imagine what the conditions for dialogue are, or to allow us to appreciate what brought diverse people together in something we want to call a dialogue after it happened.

NOTES

1. By 1563 the Council of Trent had ratified the proposals that gave the Inquisition power to control opinion in the name of religious orthodoxy.

2. Speroni, *Opere*, ed. Marco Forcellini and Natal dalle Laste (Padua, 1740), p. 313. I have used two versions of Speroni's *Apologia*. Where I could, I used an annotated and modern edition prepared by Mario Pozzi which is in *Trattatisti del cinquecento*, vol. 1, pp. 683–724. This I refer to as "Speroni, in Pozzi, *Trattatisti*." Unfortunately Pozzi only chose to include the first part of the *Apologia*, so I also used a reproduction of the 1740 edition of the *Opere* of Speroni. The complete *Apologia* appears in this collection in the first volume, pp. 266–425. This I refer to as "Speroni, *Opere*."

3. Speroni, *Opere*, p. 313.

4. To be fair to Speroni, he does not make this comparison between the

dialogue writer and cook; he compares the dialogue writer to a host at a *convito* (symposium) who arranges an agreeable collection of characters for a discussion. Giordano Bruno does, however, make this comparison in a dialogue entitled "De la causa, principio e uno": "Just as in the material and physical meal, likewise happens in the verbal and spiritual; thus this dialoguing has its various and diverse parts, just like the other; nor otherwise does this one have its proper conditions, circumstances, and means, just as the other does." "De la causa, principio e uno," in *Dialoghi italiani* (Florence: Sarsoni, 1972), p. 197. This is my translation from the Italian.

5. Two works of interest on the Italian Renaissance dialogue are David Marsh, *The Quattrocento Dialogue* (Cambridge, Mass.: Harvard University Press, 1980), and Virginia Cox, *The Renaissance Dialogue: Literary Dialogue in its Social and Political Contexts, Castiglione to Galileo* (Cambridge: Cambridge University Press, 1992). Marsh is good on the origins of the humanist dialogue. He sees Augustine as a crucial figure in the period between the classical dialogue of Plato, Lucian, and Cicero, and the return to the classical of the Italian Renaissance. Augustine rejected the academic evenhanded Ciceronian dialogue that tries to show both sides of an issue for the soliloquy. Boethius's *Consolation* and Petrarch's *Secretum* are in this tradition of internal dialogue. It is Bruni who shrugs off the spiritual model where there is one correct answer and returns to the classical Ciceronian model. Cox on the other hand deals with the way literary dialogue responded to and often attempted to imagine intellectual culture—a topic I discussed in the context of Cicero in the preceding chapter. She nicely charts the politics of the dialogue.

For an accessible abridged translation with commentary, see Galileo Galilei, *Galileo on the World Systems*, trans. Maurice A. Finocchiaro (Berkeley: University of California Press, 1997). It should be added that Galileo may have also used the dialogue form to protect himself by representing the Copernican views as those of a character. See section 3 of the Appendix by Maurice Finocchiaro.

6. I can think of three reasons why the Italian Renaissance dialogue has been ignored in English-speaking philosophical circles. First, many of the works have not been translated out of Latin or Italian (the second of which is not one of the languages normally considered important for philosophers). Second, this was not a period of professional philosophy with concerns similar to ours and is thus better studied in departments of Renaissance Studies or Italian Studies where the eclectic mix of issues, languages, and history can be dealt with as a whole. Third, the popularity of the dialogue makes these thinkers difficult to assimilate into a history of philosophical positions.

7. Luisa Mulas in "La scrittura del dialogo" (Oralità e scrittura nel sistema

letterario. Atti del convegno, Cagliari, 14–16 aprile 1980, ed. Giovanna Cerina, Cristina Lavinio, and Luisa Mulas [Rome: Bulzoni Editore, 1982]) discusses the late appearance of theories of dialogue and the possible reasons for this. She finds it surprising how few and how late the theories of dialogue are given the predisposition to write dialogues and the theoretical interests of the Cinquecento.

8. For a more complete discussion of the theories of dialogue of the late Italian Renaissance see Jon R. Snyder's *Writing the Scene of Speaking: Theories of Dialogue in the Late Italian Renaissance* (Stanford, Calif.: Stanford University Press, 1989). This excellent work covers the works of Sigonio, Speroni, Tasso, and Castelvetro (whose commentary on Aristotle's *Poetics* discusses the dialogue).

9. Virginia Cox, in *The Renaissance Dialogue*, charts the shift from open dialogue to closed dialogue. She finds the change gathered in Speroni's apology. The first two parts celebrate the open dialogue, the last two reflect the effects of the new orthodoxy. "How intentionally we cannot be sure, the third and fourth parts of the *Apologia dei dialoghi* give us a shrewd indication of the path that the dialogue was to travel. . . . The tradition of the open dialogue, he suggests, was set on a collision course with secular and religious authority." *The Renaissance Dialogue*, p. 76.

10. This discussion of Sigonio's theory is largely based on Snyder's discussion in *Writing the Scene of Speaking*.

11. See Snyder, *Writing the Scene of Speaking*, p. 62.

12. It should be mentioned that Tasso studied under both Speroni and Sigonio and his *Discourse* follows Speroni's even though I am using it, too, as an example of the classifications of dialogue Speroni is responding to. I do this because Tasso is accessible to the English reader, is close to Sigonio, and in his clear exposition seems to best capture the interpretative waters that Speroni is navigating his apology through. For an introduction to Tasso see *Tasso's Dialogues: A Selection, with the "Discourse on the Art of the Dialogue"* (Berkeley: University of California Press, 1982). This collection contains English translations and an introduction by Carnes Lord and Dain A. Trafton.

13. Tasso, "Discourse on the Art of the Dialogue," in *Tasso's Dialogues*, p. 19.

14. Ibid., p. 25. I have adapted the translation of Lord and Trafton to highlight the normative character of the passage. The translator chose to translate "senza rappresentazione" with "not intended for performance" where it could be translated literally "without representation," which suggests that for Tasso the narrated dialogue is paradigmatic. Also, Tasso uses the word "quistione" which Lord and Trafton translate "subject" (of discussion) and I have chosen to leave as "question" because it emphasizes the importance Tasso put on questions to the plot of the dialogue.

15. Ibid., p. 25.

16. Ibid., p. 33.

17. Snyder makes the interesting point that the wandering character of the first part is a deliberate strategy. See *Writing the Scene of Speaking*, p. 91.

18. Snyder makes the comment that it is a dialogue "between Speroni and his own writings or, rather between Speroni and the writing of dialogue itself." Snyder, *Writing the Scene of Speaking*, p. 95.

19. Speroni, in Pozzi, *Trattatisti*, p. 689.

20. Ibid., p. 698.

21. Speroni, *Opere*, p. 392.

22. Speroni, in Pozzi, *Trattatisti*, p. 685. My translation.

23. Cox, *The Renaissance Dialogue,* pp. 70–71.

24. For an excellent treatment of Renaissance theories of dialogue, Speroni, and the labyrinthine in Renaissance dialogue, see Pugliese, *Il discorso labirintico del dialogo renascimentale*, 1995.

25. Snyder, *Writing the Scene of Speaking*, p. 92.

26. Speroni, in Pozzi, *Trattatisti*, p. 685.

27. Ibid., p. 699.

28. Ibid., p. 695.

29. Ibid., p. 684. My translation.

30. Ibid., p. 691.

31. Ibid., p. 699.

32. Ibid., p. 707.

33. Ibid., p. 708.

34. Speroni draws on Plato's *Ion*, where Socrates shows the ignorance and inspiration of the poet. As the dialogue is like poetry the dialogue writer is like the poet/rhapsode of the *Ion*, and hence knows nothing. Speroni, in Pozzi, *Trattatisti*, p. 710.

35. Ibid., p. 689.

36. One is tempted to reply to Virginia Cox that the last two parts are such lectures of the severe patriarch, and therefore do not deserve any attention. There is however a deeper way in which all the parts, and all the characters of the author taken on in each part, make up a comedy of defense. This serves both the purpose of complicating the issue of Speroni's guilt beyond simple calculation, and turns the whole work into a mixture of authorial positions. The whole work is, in effect, a mix of the possible characters of the author, from the young defensive youth to the pious old man who just wants to make his peace with his maker.

37. Speroni, in Pozzi, *Trattatisti*, p. 707.

38. Ibid., p. 690.

39. Ibid., pp. 690–91.

40. Ibid., p. 694. My translation.

41. Ibid., pp. 696–97.

42. This is from the online version of the *Oxford English Dictionary* 2: http://www.oed.com/. See entry for "define."

43. M. M. Bakhtin, "Discourse in the Novel," in *The Dialogic Imagination: Four Essays by M. M. Bakhtin*, trans. Caryl Emerson and Michael Holquist (Austin: University of Texas Press, 1981), p. 262.

44. Bakhtin, "Epic and Novel," in *The Dialogic Imagination*, p. 22.

45. Benedetto Croce would disagree that one can clearly distinguish the form and content of any work of art. See Croce's *Æsthetic as Science of Expression and General Linguistic*, trans. Douglas Ainslie, 2d ed. (London: Macmillan, 1929), p. 15.

46. Bakhtin, "Discourse in the Novel," p. 262.

47. Ibid., p. 341.

48. Ibid., p. 271.

49. Ibid., p. 337.

50. "All rhetorical forms, monologic in their compositional structure, are oriented toward the listener and his answer." Bakhtin, "Discourse in the Novel," pp. 280–81. It should be pointed out that Bakhtin's project is much more ambitious than mine. For him dialogue is the principle of all discourse. He approaches what might be called a philosophy of dialogue that understands thought, speech, and literature in terms of its interaction with the other.

51. M. M. Bakhtin, "Forms of Time and Chronotope in the Novel," in *The Dialogic Imagination*, p. 84.

CONCLUSION

In this work I have presented a definition of philosophical dialogue. We began with the question of its unity—Is dialogue one thing or many?—by looking at the two important candidates, oral and written dialogue. I concluded that the relationship between the organizer of oral dialogue and his audience is the same as that between the writer of dialogue and the reader. Oral and written dialogue are one genre of relationship between the persuader and his audience. I then looked at some Renaissance definitions of dialogue, finally proposing a working definition that allowed me to identify the parts and types of dialogue. I concluded that both oral and written dialogue are a unity of diverse voices, showing that we could categorize dialogues best by the time and place that are the ground for the unity of those voices. This definition, while it says something about dialogue in general, does not by itself help us understand the place of dialogue in the larger field of philosophical persuasion. In this conclusion I will place this work in the flow of discussion around "philosophical style" and philosophical writing, discussing the differences between dialogue and other forms of philosophical writing. This will allow me to conclude with some observations on the question of the relationship between philosophical expression and doctrine and in particular the philosophical constraints and possibilities of the genre dialogue.

PHILOSOPHICAL STYLE

The issue of philosophical style has for a long time been confused with the question of clarity, a question often used to dismiss authors, especially those from the "Continental Tradition," as being too obscure to be worth reading. Writers like Brand Blanshard, author of *On Philosophical Style*, are concerned with what it is that makes philosophical writing as clear as possible, for example, the appropriate use of examples. Such manuals on expository writing, while sometimes useful, obviously are too limited in their scope to help us with the place of dialogue in philosophical expression. Recently, however, the issue has been redirected from such petty concerns by philosophers like Berel Lang and Mark D. Jordan. Philosophical style has become the generic name for questions of philosophical writing, philosophical genre, or more generally the poetics of philosophy. Berel Lang has been working on this issue for some time publishing two basic works in the field: *Philosophical Style: An Anthology about the Writing and Reading of Philosophy* and *The Anatomy of Philosophical Style: Literary Philosophy and the Philosophy of Literature*. We will return to Lang later and begin with an introductory article by Mark D. Jordan that nicely surveys the field.

Philosophical Genre

Jordan begins "A Preface to the Study of Philosophic Genres" by distinguishing his project from other projects that are frequently confused with the study of philosophical genres. He mentions the long history of philosophy's strained relationship with rhetoric and the relation of philosophy and language. Language in this history is something that is "treated" as an object for study and not the body of philosophy itself. A second history that he traces from Aquinas to Blanshard is the topic of writing philosophy, which, he points out, often deteriorates into "helpful remarks about writing expository prose."[1] A third approach, which comes close to the study of genres, is found in the work of philosophers like Louis H. Mackey who look at individual works by moving from their content to the embodiment of that content.[2] For Jordan the study of genres is the opposite movement: "The study of genres would move, instead, from the structure to the possibilities for doctrine."[3] Jordan calls Mackey's connection of doctrine to structures a *material* correlation, while the question of genres is a *formal* correlation.

Along the same lines, and of greater interest to us, Jordan discusses an essay by philosopher Albert William Levi on the dialogue which was the first of a series of articles published by *Philosophy and Rhetoric* on "philosophy as literature" entitled, "Philosophy as Literature: The Dialogue."[4] Levi poses the question thus: "What I am interested in is the fact that Malebranche should have chosen the dialogue form for his philosophizing, and the way in which he utilizes its possibilities. . . ."[5] As Jordan points out, Levi starts with the biographical question of why particular authors like Malebranche chose the dialogue form for their content. While the biographical reasons behind the choice of the dialogue are interesting, this question does not really address the possibilities of the genre. It assumes that authors have a doctrine in their head and they choose among the genres at their disposal—an assumption which may be true of some authors, but does not throw light on the possibilities for a genre in general. The choice of a particular author does not exhaust the possibilities for a genre; after all, authors can choose a genre for the wrong reasons, or choose a genre that is at odds with their doctrine, a juxtaposition that Levi himself draws our attention to. Jordan's formal question precedes the biographical. Only if we have some idea what dialogue can do can we comment on how the choice of genre runs counter to the doctrines held by it.

Levi moves from the biographical approach to sociological conclusions about the effect of professionalization on the choice of genre of philosophers: "For I think one can safely say that *philosophy's literary involvement is almost directly inverse to the degree of its professionalization*. The dialogue form is clearly unsuited to a parade of scholarship or the symbolic demonstration of one's mastery of the conventions of logical rigor."[6] Jordan feels Levi is missing the point; all philosophical forms are literary, though some, like expository writing, have as a generic feature the pretense that they are not literary genres, but clear expositions.[7] Nonetheless Levi's point still stands, if modified; philosophy's involvement today in certain literary genres, like the dialogue (that have as a generic feature an explicit literary aspect) is almost directly inverse to the degree of its professionalization. The professionalization of philosophy creates a climate where philosophers are trained in and expected to produce certain types of writings like the essay and the commentary. The structure of the profession encourages certain forms and not others. Jordan is objecting to the distinction of certain genres as literary and others as not, while Levi is making a sociological point about the culture of professional philosophy today.[8] Levi is making a natural leap from the question of genres of writing to the genres of professional philosophy. In this he is joined by Berel Lang who believes that the analysis of philosophical style "bears directly on the practice or 'doing' of philosophy itself."[9] If it is true that genres like the dialogue correlate with certain doctrines then would it not be even more true that the organization of the discipline would also tend to encourage certain doctrines over others? This is, of course, one of the possibilities for dialogue as a genre: that it can discuss the relationship of culture to doctrine. Dialogue as a genre of philosophical writing is suited to the critique of the culture of the discipline.

After distinguishing his project from others Jordan turns to the question he thinks is interesting: "The question is not, Why should a dialogue be chosen? It is, What thought thinks itself as dialogue?"[10] Jordan wants the issue to be what possibilities and constraints for thought exist for a genre like dialogue, not how to write a clear essay. Jordan is opening the space for the exploration of the formal correlation between genres and thought. Jordan connects this topic to the larger question of the genres of persuasion. "The ultimate ground for the plurality of genres in philosophic discourse may be the plurality of modes in persuasion."[11] Thus the genres he is looking at are not simply literary genres but modes of persuasion that might cross from the oral to the written, which is what I have shown in the case of dialogue. If what is important is the way of persuasion, not the oral or written character, the key is the relationship between author/teacher and their audience. This is the issue of the *Phaedrus*; and also what distinguishes genres: the art of the dialectician is to know, among other things, the types of persuasion and the characters they are suited to.

This is the extent of Jordan's preface to the study of philosophical genres: setting up a question and suggesting that it will be what Northrop Frye calls "the radical of presentation" that will allow us to unwrap the correlation between genre and thought. The rest of his paper reflects on the dangers of such an approach: that it can lead to a discussion of "genre as such," or to a "Table of Generic Categories."[12] He ends with the challenge of the ineffable to philosophical expression:

> The claim of antiquity that there is something of vital importance to philosophic discourse which cannot be enunciated by it touches the study of genres in many ways. It might suggest a ranking of genres according to how closely they approach what they cannot reach. . . . Yet, finally, the question of the ineffable serves to keep the analysis of genres in check by reminding one that there is something beyond. . . . The study of genres might show why that *other* thinking of discourse is needed still.[13]

Generic Relationships

Berel Lang, who Jordan tells us commented on an earlier version of his paper, picks up where Jordan leaves off, trying to map out the basic genres of philosophical discourse by looking at the relationship between author and reader.[14] In "Towards a Poetics of Philosophical Discourse" he proposes to use a model of literary action to identify the major genres.[15] In this model a text is a transaction between an author and a reader. The implied or explicit author has a point of view from which he or she communicates to the implied or explicit reader. The differences in point of view allow Lang to build a simple schema of philosophical writing. The following chart shows the point of view of the author and reader of three of the genres Lang proposes in this schema.[16]

Genre	Author	Reader
Dialogue Reflexive Writing	Absent or problematic author whose point of view is dispersed through many characters.	Reader is also absent and, like the author, is eavesdropping. Reader has to create an authorial point of view from those of the characters.
Confession Performative Writing	Author's point of view is a subject of the text.	Reader invited to follow author's narrative, and to duplicate the experience of the author regarding the object of discussion.
Treatise Expository Writing	Detached author whose point of view is presented as an objective view accessible to all.	Reader invited to share objective point of view from which all can contemplate a fixed object of study.

In another essay, "Space, Time, and Philosophical Style," Lang connects the point of view with the space and time created by a work. While he doesn't mention Bakhtin in the essay he comes to a similar conclusion about the importance of the chronotope to the identification of genres. Extending the visual metaphor of "point of view," every genre for Lang presents a space and time within which the author and reader are points with views. The type of space determines the possible relationship between the different points within, and the possibilities for direction of view and movement of these points. Thus we can, by looking at the space and time created by works, identify the major genres and their philosophical capacity.[17]

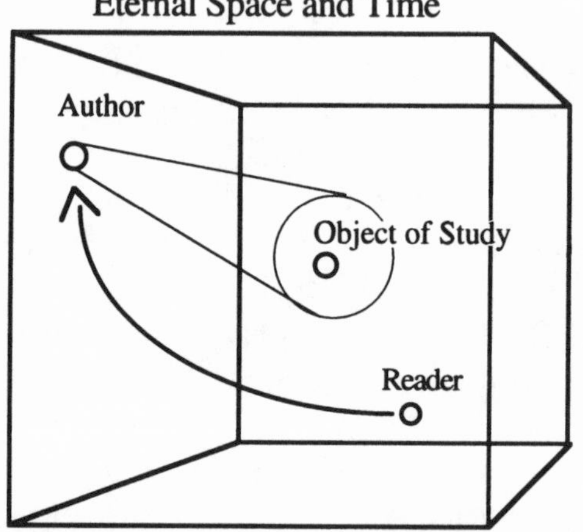

Expository writing presents us with a fixed objective space and time where the author, reader, and object of study are all points. This eternal space and time is presented as if it were a given shared space that we all have access to, not a space created by the author. (This intellectual space is often the world of presuppositions shared by the profession.) The author presents himself as one who exposes the given object of study by, in effect, shining a light on it, within a space he did not create. The point of view from which the author exposes the object is accessible to the reader; the author invites readers to look at the object from that view. Lang points out that in such works the author's "act is one of discovery rather than of invention."[18] It isn't the case that the object and authorial perspective are created by the author so much as an eternally given object

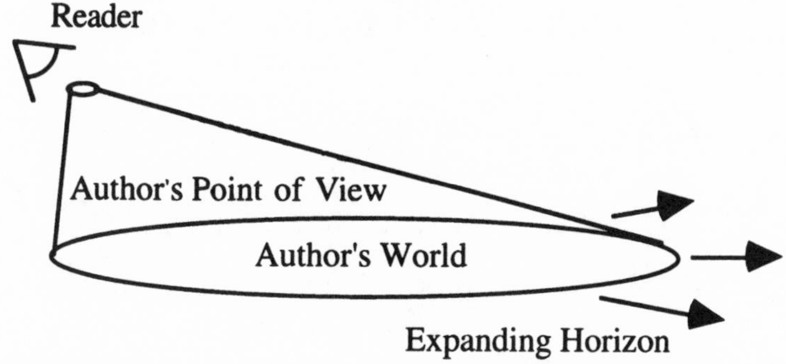

is illuminated from a certain eternally available angle. Nor is there much movement through this space except in so far as the reader is encouraged to move to the author's illuminating point of view.

By contrast, performative writing presents us with a subjective time and space where everything is measured from the view of the author. The space and time of works like Descartes's *Meditations is* the view of the author and to some extent defines the author. The author is not a point that moves within universal space to find the best perspective, but the center of a particular space (like a study) from which the world unfolds. The author's point of view is a personal history, not an eternal perspective. It is a time of life (the author's) that we might also experience. The reader gets to see the world through the eye of the author and thereby experience the unfolding of that view so that they can recreate the experience. There is movement, not within the space, so much as *of* the space as it spreads out to include the subject of study. Rather than there being an object of study which one moves to view within an all-embracing space, the world that the space expands to uncover is the subject of study. The moving horizon (or limit) of this expanding view is where our attention is at any one point of the story.

In reflexive writing the space is a particular space, just as it was in performative writing, for example, a particular garden or courtyard, but it is not a space defined by the experience of the author (or reader). It is a communal space chosen by the author for the setting. Likewise the time of reflexive writing is also a particular time in history, but not a personal time unfolding from the author. It is also a communal time when people are likely to meet. Reflexive writing differs from expository in that the chronotope is a particular place and time within the space and history of

Interlocutors' Points of View

Author/Reader

the community. It differs from performative in that there is not a single authorial point of view from which everything unfolds. In dialogues there are multiple points of view, one for each character. The author and reader are absent as a point of view (they are just listening in) and thus are forced to build a point of view from those within the work. As Bakhtin puts it the author is refracted through the characters. If readers want an authorial point of view they have to reassemble it from the characters.

The particular space and time of a dialogue is what holds the points of view of the characters together. It is the stage within which the voices play and, as such, is the most visible presence of the author. The chronotope of dialogue, however, must also be a communal space and time, as it has to be believable that the characters gather at that place and time. As for the object of study in reflexive writing, having multiple points of view allows individual points of view to fall under the gaze of others. Points of view, or if you wish, characters and their interaction, are one of the subjects of reflexive writing, which is precisely why it is reflexive; it is writing capable of holding itself up for discussion. This was one of Bakhtin's points: that the novel is, by virtue of the multiplicity of voices within, the only genre capable of discussing itself (and the process of genre making). As the individual points of view held within a dialogue can be voices of different persuasive genres, reflexive writing can have as its subject other genres. The *Phaedrus* is an example of this, in that it holds other genres of persuasion within it in a way that allows them to become objects of discussion. This is different from the way expository writing deals with other genres. This book, while it is about dialogue, does not have dialogue within it as one voice. This work depends on your having read dialogues in a way that a dialogue on dialogue would not.

We can summarize the differences in chronotope of Lang's three major genres of philosophical discourse with the following chart.

Genre	Space	Time
Dialogue Reflexive Writing	Meeting space—the stage of discussion where people could meet. It is a specific space in the world of participants.	A time in the history of the community of discourse. It is usually a leisure time when people can meet and discuss.
Confession Performative Writing	Private space where the author retreats to recreate himself and the world.	Biographical time—the subjective time of the author. A time within a life that the reader can experience.
Treatise Expository Writing	Universal space, fixed and accessible to everyone from which all can be seen.	Eternal time, accessible to all for all time. Nothing changes in this time; it is the time of eternal truths.

THE CAPACITY OF DIALOGUE

Keeping in mind the dangers that Jordan and Heidegger warn of when grasping something like dialogue and squeezing it for content, I will conclude by commenting on the philosophical capacity of dialogue. By philosophical capacity I mean the possibilities and constraints the genre puts on the doctrine(s) enclosed within. I should begin by pointing out that I am not a generic determinist. I do not believe there is a hard connection between genre and doctrine, i.e., that the choice of genre of expression does such violence to the content that one cannot say anything but what the genre determines. In fact I believe one can swim against the current of a genre, contradicting its tendencies if one wishes. At the same time I do not believe that there is no connection between genre and doctrine, i.e., that ideas can be casually translated from one form of writing to another without suffering any change. The truth is more complex: a genre puts constraints on and opens possibilities for what is said. So, to present a system of thought in a genre like dialogue would result in something hardly a dialogue at all, or it would result in a situation where the very system of thought is undermined by the different voices that make the dialogue. It is not impossible to use a genre for that to which it is not suited. The history of the dialogue is filled with awkward and basically bad dialogues, but, where one goes against the capacity of the genre, one either risks writing something that is not recognizable as a good example of that genre, or one risks having one's writing undermined by the ideological tendency of the genre. I would even go so far as to say that in certain cases the repurposing of a genre against the grain of its possibilities can result in a work of art, exceptional precisely because of its ability to stretch the constraints of the genre. Such works are the exceptions that rule the genre.[19] The recent turn to the ineffable dialogue, like the opening of dialogue to comedy by Lucian, may be such an exceptional moment of change for dialogue.

In addition to placing constraints and opening possibilities, genres also carry specific ideological baggage. By ideological baggage I mean specific, and often minor, points of doctrine that are implied by the genre. These ideological points are tied to the constraints and possibilities, but they are less of a force acting on everything that is said, than a supplement to what is said. These points can be overcome by the text, but they nonetheless accompany it as baggage. These remarks are best understood in the context of a specific genre, so I will turn to my conclusions about the capacity of dialogue.

The Culture of Dialogue

As I have commented above, the dialogue cannot avoid being about the culture of dialogue. Whatever the object of discussion is, the dialogue presents us with an image of how people talk about such issues, and thus the way people talk about an issue becomes a supplementary issue. Only the driest of dialogues gives us nothing to reflect on in this fashion. This feature of dialogue is also a possibility that can be exploited by the author of dialogue who wishes to imagine an alternative culture of philosophy or contrast ways of participating in the culture of discussion. Unlike the anthropological treatise that makes culture and how people interact an object of study, the dialogue can illustrate the possibilities, thereby both commenting on the present culture and changing the culture by showing what could be the case as if it were the case.

It is in this context that we can speculate about the fascination with dialogue since the Second World War. Dialogue as a genre of interaction is suited to the discussion of culture. One of its possibilities is the ability to present a unity of different voices representing different cultures. At the same time it is constrained in that it is difficult to represent in dialogue the assimilation of these voices. Dialogue is thus suited to those who wish to create a culture that maintains the differences among subcultures and their voices. It is, if you will, better suited to the Canadian model of a multicultural salad bowl, than the American melting pot.

We can see this on a small scale at work in the university. When Cicero decided to encourage the growth of a Latin philosophy, he chose to gather the dominant philosophical schools of his time into dialogues.[20] In the same fashion the North American university has gathered philosophies from the cultures it recognizes into departments and conferences. With the proliferation of imported ideologies and the growth in academic output, comes the need for a paradigm or ritual for tolerant coexistence. The desire to encompass the other leads to the desire for dialogue. To hold all the schools of thought in an academic equivalent of a garden salad we need a wide and theoretically neutral receptacle. Dialectic doesn't work once the variety grows past a certain point, so we turn to a more neutral playground like dialogue, which we hope is open enough. As it was for Cicero, dialogue is an activity we hope is capable of gathering the different voices into a new tolerant whole that fits our self-image as open to the other and supposedly does not oppress those gathered. If this is the case we should now ask if dialogue has hidden ideological constraints such that it actually excludes or misrepresents certain positions, especially those that are themselves intolerant. Is the call for dialogue truly neutral? Does it not reflect a desire to consume or enter the other? Should we be ashamed of this desire or should we simply be aware of it?

The Vocalization of Dialogue

Because the dialogue represents a culture of discussion and not action, it is constrained in its imagination to the oral interaction among people. The dialogue shows people talking, not fighting or lecturing. Part of the baggage of dialogue is a subtle legitimization of discussion as an activity. The meditation inevitably glorifies meditation as a philosophical way; likewise the dialogue generally sets up conversation as an important part of what it is to do philosophy, even when the characters say nothing explicitly about the importance of talk (as they do in many dialogues anyway). The point is that if something important is shown happening in dialogue, one cannot help but think the author is also hinting that that is the way important work is done in dialogue. To connect this with the previous point about the culture of philosophy, this is one feature of the culture of philosophy which dialogue inevitably presents as valuable. It is conceivable that one could write a dialogue that showed the uselessness of talk: Valla in his dialogue "On Free Will" seems to be attempting something close to this, but you always run the risk of people feeling the conversation, despite its end, was worth it just so that one could get to that end. Perhaps a novel could introduce dialogue between a torturer and his victim such that the reader left the work nauseated by talk, but such a novel would depend on the action that accompanies the dialogue to achieve its effect. My point is that most dialogues set up as exemplary the talking philosopher, not the meditating, reading, or writing philosopher. This is one of the items of philosophical baggage that accompanies the dialogue as a genre.

Not only does dialogue value the voice but it values the voice as it chooses to express itself in oral dialogue. By this I mean two things: first, that dialogue encourages the inclusion of voices as they choose to express themselves, and second, that it tends to favor those voices that are themselves dialogical. There is a tension between the dialogue's encouragement of diversity and the dialogue's encouragement of voices that works well in conversation. On the one hand dialogue represents voices as they would speak themselves, rather than translating them into a common language for comparison; on the other hand, those voices that are themselves predisposed to dialogue tend to stand out.

To look closely at the first point, dialogue by being a unity of voices tends to preserve the character and language of voices. It therefore suggests that there is something philosophically valuable about the character and language of different voices. Dialogue is, as a genre, a subtle critique of the tendency of other genres to eliminate differences in favor of solutions. The dialogue suggests that the way people talk about their ideas is an important part of the ideas and should be preserved (as it is in dialogue). Even when voices are embarrassed or contradict themselves the net effect of most dialogues is that it is nonetheless worth preserving those voices in their contradiction. The dialogue becomes for the discipline of philosophy an archive of voices.

To look at the second point, it is no coincidence that the heroes of philosophical dialogues tend to be voices that themselves are capable of deploying different voices as the occasion warrants and are those voices capable of interacting effectively with other voices. Both Plato's Socrates and Hume's Philo are characters who can impersonate other voices and are skilled conversationalists. Dogmatic voices that expect to be treated as authorities do not fare well in dialogues, because their character is at odds with the character of the genre. Socrates and Philo share the ideological baggage of the genre in which they appear. They are interested in the culture of philosophy and are willing to operate in an environment where authority is not given but earned. They can imitate other voices when necessary and love conversation.

We can look at the issue of vocalization in dialogue from a different perspective—that of the participant in dialogue and ask what makes for a successful participant. This perspective can be derived from the definition proposed. Doing so helps us understand the types of voice favored by the genre. To enter in dialogue you have to be willing to:

1. Discuss the dialogue itself. This means you have to be willing to negotiate the conditions of the dialogue rather than dictate them, and then reflect on the progress of the dialogue. That is to say, the conduct of the dialogue is one of the legitimate themes of the dialogue. In this context one should discuss the occasion, the space and pace (chronotope), and the themes that are the subject of the dialogue.
2. Respect the other interlocutors in their diversity. This means one

must be willing to give them a chance to speak, and listen to them when they speak. It follows from this that one should:

2.1. Respect the other interlocutor as other. This means one must accept that other interlocutors could be profoundly different, and not simply confused versions of what one knows. You have to begin with an openness to the possibility of difference that might never be overcome. You have to beware believing you understand what the other really is and means; you have to avoid interpreting the others' experience for them.

2.2. Respect the other as they choose to represent themselves. Part of respecting the other is respecting their choice of voice. Respecting them involves letting them speak in the character and language they choose.

2.3. Respect the other's opinions. This means that one not only respects their voice but what they say. This does not mean that one has to agree with the position of the other, but that one has to be willing to listen to it seriously in order for the dialogue to proceed. This ultimately means that one has to be open to the possibility that they are right (otherwise they would not be open to the possibility that you are right).

3. Present your opinions honestly and in your own voice. If the other is to learn about your position just as you do about theirs, then it is your responsibility to honestly present the truth as you see it in the voice that best characterizes you.[21]

There is a tension in points 2 and 3. If one seeks to enter into dialogue with someone who does not respect your position or your manner of expression, it becomes difficult to respect that aspect of their position. Dialogue doesn't happen between intolerant positions; they can be expected never to get to the point of entering into dialogue unless they are willing to alter their position to the point of conceding that there is something worthy of respect in the other. This puts limits on all the participants in a dialogue, namely that they must, to some degree, present themselves as respectful of the process of dialogue and the others involved. We can see here the way in which dialogue is not ideologically neutral. To enter into dialogue inevitably involves an openness and respect. Ideologies that are unwilling to respect others cannot be brought seriously into dialogue, one can only mock them with dialogues for others to hear or read. While a dialogue can be an effective way of portraying intolerance in a way that encourages the reader to reject it, it is difficult to enter into meaningful dialogue with that intolerance in a way that leads to reconciliation.

The Authority of Dialogue

With the disappearance of the author goes the authority typical of a monological work. As Hume points out, it is difficult to use a dialogue to forcefully expound a single system of thought. This is because a dialogue contains different voices that in their difference undermine the authority of any one voice. This does not mean that in dialogues there are not dominant voices; it means that no voice can dominate to the point of being the sole authority. Where there is a sole authority there is no dialogue, just exposition. We can see this at the level of characters and how they succeed in dialogue. Characters that present themselves as authorities and expect respect for what they have to say due to some status that is not displayed in the dialogue, tend to appear ridiculous in a dialogue. This is one of the comic possibilities of dialogue, amply discussed by Bakhtin and used by Lucian: the satirical presentation of tired authoritarian ideologues so that they appear pompous windbags. Within the dialogue the characters are all on a level playing field; their ability to convince those listening depends on what they say within the dialogue. They have to earn their authority. This does not mean that the author cannot manipulate things so that certain characters acquire in the dialogue greater authority. There are all sorts of devices whereby the author can set up the scene so that one character becomes an authority during the dialogue in ways that if the reader were aware of them they might not seem so convincing.

The undermining of authority is part of the ideological baggage of dialogue. Not only are authorities questioned, set up so that they seem out of place, and undermined by dialogue, it is also the case that dialogue carries the hint that authority is problematic unless renewed through conversation. Another way of putting this is to say that dialogue tends to favor a mild form of skepticism that is suspicious of dogmatic positions and their authority. It is no coincidence that many dialogue writers, from Cicero to Hume, are perceived as being skeptical. The dialogue leaves us with the impression that the author does not think there is a single correct position on the issue, and that the truth is best represented as a unity of positions around an issue (and in continuing dialogue to renew themselves). I would even go so far as to say that dialogue is the genre best suited to skepticism as it shows the skepticism in addition to showing the skeptic. Hume's *Dialogues* reinforce the position of Philo within. The hero of the dialogue has the same capacity for dialogue that the author has. Even Philo's recantation in the last part is an example of the ability of the skeptic to carry many voices within, just as Hume the author does when he writes.

If there is an authority that is transmitted through dialogue it is the authority of ageless wisdom—the authority of the tradition of which the voices are part. This is not an authority that is "authored" or owned by an individual. Therefore it cannot be incarnated in a voice in dialogue or referenced in an exposition. It is the wisdom that collects in dialogue and remains after the reading. It is what comes through dialogue. This is the wisdom which is dangerous to name or define. It is what Jordan calls the ineffable and what Heidegger and he remind us is important. Jordan suggests one could rank genres by their ability to approach the ineffable without reaching it, their ability to hint at it without grasping it. One might define dialogue, as Heidegger wants to, as that ineffable that comes through *logos*, in which case dialogue would have a special status. But that is not the sense of dialogue that I have been defining, nor is that the sense of dialogue as a genre of persuasion among others. I believe all genres have their ways of approaching the ineffable; they all have a way of allowing the ineffable to come through. The dialogue has no special place among genres in this regard. The undermining of authority that accompanies dialogue is a feature of dialogue that can be exploited to enhance the coming through of the ineffable. Other genres have other such features. That does not mean it is always exploited or that there are not other features that can be exploited this way. It is simply a hint as to how one can approach the ineffable through dialogue.

THE MODE OF DIALOGUE

Dialogue, as Jordan and this work discuss it, is a pattern of interaction (and persuasion) that works at different levels. In this book I have looked at dialogue at two levels: as an oral event, and as a genre of writing. While I have not done so here, I believe it is possible to extend the discussion of dialogue to include two other levels: thought and communal interaction. By this I mean that, just as we talk about dialogue as an oral activity, we can discuss it as a genre of thought and, at the other end of the scale, as a genre of relationship between communities. This position is different from saying that we can talk about what happens in thought (or among communities) *as if* it were a dialogue—using dialogue as a model or metaphor for thought and communal interaction. I am suggesting that dialogue is more importantly a mode of interaction that manifests itself at many levels, not just between people. This mode can be found in the thoughts of an individual, among individuals, written down, or among communities. In this context one could look at the soliloquy as a related genre of writing that teaches us about the dialogue of thought, or one could look at the utopian dialogue for more about communal dialogue.

It is not, however, the case that dialogue at any one level is unconnected to dialogue at the others. Our understanding of dialogue at each level informs our understanding of dialogue at the others. The written dialogue presents us paradigms for oral dialogue. The written dialogue also combines voices that represent ideologies, i.e., voices representing groups of people or communities when they talk. We could go on to map the ways that each register of dialogue influences the other, but that is another project. The point is that the mode of dialogue is not separable from the levels at which it manifests itself as if it were an abstract idea. Dialogue, to be understood, has to be understood as a mode that manifests itself in a particular way, at particular levels of human interaction. It is interesting at which levels it is meaningful to talk about dialogue and it is important how dialogue at any one level echoes though others while registering echoes from them. The understanding of dialogue at one level cannot be cleanly separated from that of other levels as they all resonate with voices from other levels. This is one of the features of dialogue that makes it such an attractive paradigm. Expectations for dialogue at one level can be inherited from another. For example, in the call for political dialogue between communities, there can be echoes of the intimacy of a garden dialogue between friends, or echoes of the rigor of a written Socratic dialogue. It is tempting when defining dialogue to sever the connection between levels of dialogue so that one can grasp one type of dialogue at a time. Doing so grasps dialogue in a way that damages it. It may be a necessary first step, but eventually one has to return to a view of the whole of dialogue resonating through its different levels. The danger of an exposition such as this work is that it has focused on two levels, grasping the oral and written dialogue. I hope the reader can release this grasp and hear that which echoes through the other dialogues.

The End

Death is a Dialogue between,
The Spirit and the Dust.[22]

NOTES

1. Mark D. Jordan, "A Preface to the Study of Philosophic Genres," *Philosophy and Rhetoric* 14, no. 4 (1981): 201. Along with Berel Lang's anthology *Philosophical Style* (Chicago: Nelson-Hall, 1980), the first pages of this article provide a good overview of the way writing has been discussed in philosophy.

2. Louis Mackey, "On Philosophical Form: A Tear for Adonais," *Thought* 42, no. 165 (1967): 238–60. Mackey deals with Plato's *Euthyphro*, Aquinas's *Summa Theologiae*, and part of Hume's *Enquiry Concerning Human Understanding*. To be fair to Mackey he argues for a symmetrical relationship between literary (formal) analysis and logical (content) analysis—that each should inform the other. Where I think Mackey and Jordan are different is that Mackey looks at individual works moving back and forth from form to content, while Jordan is proposing a study of a genre as a whole.

3. Jordan, "A Preface to the Study of Philosophic Genres," p. 203.

4. It is not clear whether Jordan's article, which also appeared in *Philosophy and Rhetoric*, was considered by the editors to be part of the same series begun five years before. Another series of articles of note on this subject is a 1980 issue of the *Monist* (63, no. 4) dedicated to "Philosophy as Style and Literature as Philosophy" of which I discuss Berel Lang's contribution "Towards a Poetics of Philosophical Discourse" later in this chapter.

5. Levi, "Philosophy as Literature: The Dialogue," p. 2.

6. Ibid., p. 19.

7. Jordan, "A Preface to the Study of Philosophic Genres," p. 207.

8. If there is any truth to Lucian's complaints about the number of philosophers and the use of the dialogue by them it could be that professional philosophy after Plato encouraged the dialogue genre in the same way that we today tend to expository writing in our professional capacity. The same might be said to be true of the brief period in the Italian Renaissance before the Inquisition when dialogues were one of the most popular forms. It would follow that dialogue is just as capable of professionalization as any other genre.

To the best of my knowledge the larger question of the effect of the organization of the discipline on the produce of the discipline has not been dealt with adequately in the English sources. There is a pathetic book by D. W. Hamlyn, *Being a Philosopher: The History of a Practice* (London: Routledge, 1992) that is full of generalizations about how French philosophy is different from serious English philosophy because the French don't have the tutorial system. A far more serious discussion of these issues is found in recent French philosophy.

9. Lang, "Space, Time, and Philosophical Style," p. 146.

10. Jordan, "A Preface to the Study of Philosophic Genres," p. 205.

11. Ibid., p. 205.

12. Ibid., pp. 207–209.

13. Ibid., p. 209.

14. In a footnote Jordan mentions how they cover much of the same ground, but warns that, "Lang gives too much weight, I think, to the categories of his stylistic and generic analysis. He may also be assuming that he has found a fixed, Newtonian point from which he can describe quite objectively the varieties of philosophic speech." "A Preface to the Study of Philosophic Genres," p. 211, n. 32. I believe the only way to avoid that danger is to be rooted in particular works, moving from individual works to generic observations (and then back). Jordan, given the limitation of the article form, does not have the time for this, but it also runs counter to his preface, that focuses on the movement from generic structure.

15. "The model of literary 'action' . . . has, in this respect, at least the advantage of simplicity; it presupposes a model of communication as a transaction only among speaker (implied or explicit), audience (again implied or explicit), and the referent of what is said." Lang, "Towards a Poetics of Philosophical Discourse," p. 450.

16. In "Towards a Poetics of Philosophical Discourse" Lang actually proposes a fourfold schema with the commentary as the fourth genre. I have stuck to the threefold schema he proposes in "Space, Time, and Philosophical Style"

(p. 452). The commentary is similar to the treatise having a detached author, the difference is that there is a referent to which the author defers, the primary text and its implied author.

17. In the following discussion I have departed slowly from the points made in Lang's article, especially in my discussion of reflexive writing. While I do not think my discussion is incompatible with Lang's, I just don't want to burden this conclusion with the work of commenting on how Lang could be adapted to make sense of the dialogue, which is my focus.

18. Lang, "Space, Time, and Philosophical Style," p. 150.

19. If one believes that the use of the dialogue form undermines the critique of poetry in Plato's *Republic*, it might be an example of such an exceptional work. It is worth noting that its exceptional character depends on our expectations of the genre while stretching them. Lucian's repurposing of a form associated with philosophy to mock philosophy would be another example of such exceptional dialogue.

20. The prefaces of Cicero's dialogues contain explicit discussions of why one would choose dialogue. For a commentary on Cicero's prefaces and approach to dialogue, see Michel Ruch, *Le Préambule dans les oeuvres philosophiques de Cicéron* (Paris: University of Strasbourg, 1958).

21. For an interesting discussion of how "people should reason together" see D. L. Hitchcock, *Some Principles of Rational Mutual Inquiry* (Amsterdam: International Society for the Study of Argumentation, 1990). This short essay presents principles for friendly dialogue as an alternative to adversarial disputation. Adversarial disputation would seem to be the prevalent model for resolving differences of opinion in North America; witness the use of courts, elections, and referendums to deal with differences. The disadvantage of the adversarial model is that it encourages participants to play to win, not to compromise. Hans-Georg Gadamer's *Truth and Method* (New York: Crossroad, 1985) is also interesting on openness to dialogue.

22. Emily Dickinson (1830–1886), *The Complete Poems*, no. 976 (1955). Taken from the *Microsoft Bookshelf, 1994* (Redmond, Wash.: Microsoft, 1994).

BIBLIOGRAPHY

Alberti, Leon Battista. *Dinner Pieces*. Translated by David Marsh. Binghamton, N.Y.: Medieval & Renaissance Texts & Studies in conjunction with The Renaissance Society of America, 1987.

Allinson, Francis. *Lucian Satirist and Artist*. New York: Langman's, 1927.

Aristophanes. *The Clouds*. In *Aristophanes; with the English Translation of Benjamin Bickley Rogers*. 3 vols. Cambridge, Mass.: Harvard University Press, 1924.

———. *Clouds*. Translated by Kenneth James Dover. Oxford: Clarendon Press, 1968.

Aristotle. *Poetics*. In *The Basic Works of Aristotle*. Edited and translated by Richard McKeon. New York: Random House, 1941.

Armstrong, C. J. R. "The Dialectical Road to Truth: The Dialogue." *French Renaissance Studies, 1540–70*. Edited by Peter Sharratt. Edinburgh: Edinburgh University Press, 1976.

Bakhtin, M. M. "Discourse in the Novel." In *The Dialogic Imagination: Four Essays by M. M. Bakhtin*. Translated by Caryl Emerson and Michael Holquist. Austin: University of Texas Press, 1981.

———. "Epic and Novel." In *The Dialogic Imagination: Four Essays by M. M. Bakhtin*. Translated by Caryl Emerson and Michael Holquist. Austin: University of Texas Press, 1981.

———. "Forms of Time and Chronotope in the Novel." In *The Dialogic Imagination: Four Essays by M. M. Bakhtin*. Translated by Caryl Emerson and Michael Holquist. Austin: University of Texas Press, 1981.

———. *Speech Genres and Other Late Essays*. Translated by Vern W. McGee. Austin: University of Texas Press, 1986.

Benardete, Seth. *The Rhetoric of Morality and Philosophy: Plato's Gorgias and Phaedrus*. Chicago: University of Chicago Press, 1991.

Blanshard, Brand. "Selections from *On Philosophical Style*." *Philosophical Style: An Anthology about the Writing and Reading of Philosophy*. Edited by Berel Lang. Chicago: Nelson-Hall, 1980.

Boethius, Ancius. *The Consolation of Philosophy*. Translated by V. E. Watts. Harmondsworth, England: Penguin, 1969.

Box, M. A. *The Suasive Art of David Hume*. Princeton, N.J.: Princeton University Press, 1990.

Branham, R. Bracht. *Unruly Eloquence: Lucian and the Comedy of Traditions*. Cambridge, Mass.: Harvard University Press, 1989.

Bruni, Leonardo. "Dialogi ad Petrum Paulum Histrum." *Prosatori latini del Quattrocento*. Edited by Eugenio Garin. Milan and Naples: Ricciardi, 1952.

Bruno, Giordano. *Dialoghi italiani*. Florence: Sansoni, 1972.

Buber, Martin. *Between Man and Man*. Translated by Ronald Gregor Smith and Maurice S. Friedman. New York: Macmillan, 1970.

———. *I and Thou*. Translated by Ronald Gregor Smith. 2d ed. New York: Charles Scribner's Sons, 1958.

———. *Pointing the Way*. Translated by Maurice S. Friedman. New York: Schocken Books, 1974.

Cain, James M. *The Baby in the Icebox and Other Short Fiction*. New York: Penguin, 1984.

Carabelli, Giancarlo. *Hume e la retorica dell'ideologia*. Florence: La Nuova Italia Editrice, 1972.

———. *Uno studio dei "Dialoghi sulla religione naturale."* Milan: Publicazioni Della Facoltà di Lettere e Filosofia, 1972.

Carruthers, Mary. *The Book of Memory: A Study of Memory in Medieval Culture*. Cambridge: Cambridge University Press, 1990.

Cartledge, Paul. *Aristophanes and His Theatre of the Absurd*. Bristol, England: Bristol Classical Press, 1990.

Castiglione, Baldesar. *The Book of the Courtier*. Translated by Charles S. Singleton. Garden City, N.Y.: Anchor Books, 1959.

———. *Il libro del cortegiano*. Milan: Mursia, 1988.

Cherniss, Harold Fredrik. *The Riddle of the Early Academy*. Berkeley: University of California Press, 1945.

Cicero, Marcus Tullius. *De Finibus Bonorum et Malorum*. Translated by H. Rackham. London: Heinemann, 1961.

———. *De Oratore: The Making of an Orator*. Translated by E. W. Sutton. 2 vols. London: Heinemann, 1942.

———. *The Nature of the Gods*. Translated by Horace C. P. McGregor. Harmondsworth, England: Penguin, 1972.

———. *On Friendship, and the Dream of Scipio*. Translated by J. G. F. Powell. Warminster, England: Aris & Phillips, 1990.

Classen, C. Joachim. "The Speeches in the Courts of Law: A Three-Cornered Dialogue." *Rhetorica* 9, no. 3 (summer 1991): 195–207.

Cosentini, John W. *Fontenelle's Art of Dialogue*. New York: King's Crown Press, 1952.

Cox, Virginia. *The Renaissance Dialogue: Literary Dialogue in Its Social and Political Contexts, Castiglione to Galileo*. Cambridge: Cambridge University Press, 1992.

Croce, Benedetto. *Æsthetic as Science of Expression and General Linguistic*. Translated by Douglas Ainslie. 2d ed. London: Macmillan, 1929.

Davis, Robert Con, and Ronald Schliefer, eds. *Contemporary Literary Criticism: Library and Cultural Studies*. 2d ed. New York: Longman, 1989.

De Crescenzo, Luciano. *The History of Greek Philosophy*. Vol. 2, *Socrates and Beyond*. Translated by Avril Bardoni. London: Picador, 1990.

Descartes, René. *Descartes: Philosophical Writings*. Translated by Elizabeth Anscombe and Peter Thomas Geach. Rev. ed. Indianapolis, Ind.: Bobbs-Merrill, 1971.

Diderot, Denis. *Diderot's Writings on the Theatre*. London: Cambridge University Press, 1936.

———. *Oeuvres complètes de Diderot*. Edited by Jules Assézat and Maurice Tourneux. 20 vols. Paris: Garnier, 1877.

———. *Rameau's Nephew and Other Works*. Translated by Jacques Barzun and Ralph H. Bowen. Garden City, N.Y.: Doubleday, 1956.

Dorey, T. A., ed. *Cicero*. London: Routledge & Kegan Paul, 1964.

Dover, Kenneth J. *Aristophanic Comedy*. London: B. T. Batsford, 1972.

———. "Socrates in the Clouds." *The Philosophy of Socrates: A Collection of Critical Essays*. Edited by Gregory Vlastos. New York: Anchor Books, 1971.

Eco, Umberto. *Interpretation and Overinterpretation*. Cambridge: Cambridge University Press, 1992.

Ferroni, Giulio, ed. *Il dialogo: scambi e passaggi della parola*. Palermo: Sellerio Editore, 1985.

Feyerabend, Paul K. *Three Dialogues on Knowledge*. Oxford: Basil Blackwell, 1991.

Ficino, Marsilio. *Sopra lo amore*. Milan: Celuc, 1973.

Fontenelle. *Jugement de Pluton, sur les deux parties des nouveaux dialogues des morts*. Paris: Michel Brunet, 1704.

Foucault, Michel. "What Is an Author?" Translated by Josué V. Harari. *The Foucault Reader*. Edited by Paul Rabinow. New York: Pantheon Books, 1984.

Furbank, P. N. *Diderot: A Critical Biography*. London: Secker & Warburg, 1992.

Gadamer, Hans-Georg. *The Idea of the Good in Platonic-Aristotelian Philosophy*. Translated by P. Christopher Smith. New Haven: Yale University Press, 1986.

———. *Philosophical Apprenticeships*. Translated by Robert R. Sullivan. Cambridge, Mass.: MIT Press, 1985.

———. *The Relevance of the Beautiful and Other Essays*. Translated by Nicholas Walker. Cambridge: Cambridge University Press, 1986.

———. *Truth and Method*. Translated by W. Glen-Doepel. 2d ed. New York: Crossroad, 1985.

Garin, Eugenio. *Italian Humanism: Philosophy and Civic Life in the Renaissance*. Translated by Peter Munz. New York: Harper and Row, 1965.

———, ed. *Prosatori latini del Quattrocento*. Milan and Naples: Ricciardi, 1952.

Gilder, George. *Life After Television*. Rev. ed. New York: W. W. Norton, 1994.

Grassi, Ernesto. *Renaissance Humanism: Studies in Philosophy and Poetics*. Binghamton, N.Y.: Centre for Medieval & Early Renaissance Studies, 1988.

Griswold, Charles L., ed. *Platonic Writings, Platonic Readings*. New York: Routledge, 1988.

———. "Style and Philosophy: the Case of Plato's Dialogue." *Monist* 63, no. 4 (1980): 530–46.

Grote, George. *Plato, and the Other Companions of Sokrates*. 3 vols. London: John Murray, 1865.

Gumpert, Gary, and Robert Cathcart, eds. *Intermedia: Interpersonal Communication in a Media World*. Oxford: Oxford University Press, 1979.

Guthrie, W. K. C. *Socrates*. Cambridge: Cambridge University Press, 1971.

Hackforth, R. *The Composition of Plato's Apology*. Cambridge: Cambridge University Press, 1933.

Hamlyn, D. W. *Being a Philosopher: The History of a Practice*. London: Routledge, 1992.

Harasim, Linda M., ed. *Global Networks: Computers and International Communication*. Cambridge, Mass.: MIT Press, 1994.

Havelock, Eric A. "The Orality of Socrates and the Literacy of Plato: With Some Reflections on the Historical Origins of Moral Philosophy in Europe." *New*

Essays on Socrates. Edited by Eugene Kelly. New York: University Press of America, 1984.

———. *Preface to Plato*. Cambridge, Mass.: Belknap Press, 1963.

Heidegger, Martin. "Conversation on a Country Path about Thinking." Translated by John M. Anderson and E. Hans Freund. In *Discourse on Thinking*. New York: Harper Torchbooks, 1966.

———. "A Dialogue on Language." In *On the Way to Language*. Translated by Peter D. Hertz. New York: Harper & Row, 1982.

———. "The Nature of Language." In *On the Way to Language*. Translated by Peter D. Hertz. New York: Harper & Row, 1982.

———. *Unterwegs Zur Sprache*. Pfullingen: Günther Neske, 1959.

Heim, Michael. "Grassi's Experiment: The Renaissance through Phenomenology." *Research in Phenomenology* 18 (1988): 233–65.

Hiltz, Starr Roxanne, and Murray Turoff. *The Network Nation: Human Communication via Computer*. Rev. ed. Cambridge, Mass.: MIT Press, 1993.

Hirzel, Rudolf. *Der Dialog: Ein Literarhistorischer Versuch*. Leipzig: Verlag Von S. Hirzel, 1895.

Hitchcock, David L. "Some Principles of Rational Mutual Inquiry. International Conference on Argumentation." Edited by Frans H. van Eemeren et al. Amsterdam: International Society for the Study of Argumentation, 1990.

Horton, Donald, and R. Richard Wohl. "Mass Communication and Para-Social Interaction: Observation on Intimacy at a Distance." *Intermedia: Interpersonal Communication in a Media World*. Edited by Gary Gumpert and Robert Cathcart. Oxford: Oxford University Press, 1979.

Hume, David. *Dialogues Concerning Natural Religion*. New York: Bobbs-Merrill, 1970.

Jones, C. P. *Culture and Society in Lucian*. Cambridge, Mass.: Harvard University Press, 1986.

Jordan, Mark D. "A Preface to the Study of Philosophical Genres." *Philosophy and Rhetoric* 14, no. 4 (1981): 199–211.

Kahn, Victoria. "The Rhetoric of Faith and the Use of Usage in Lorenzo Valla's *De libero arbitrio*." *Journal of Medieval and Renaissance Studies* 13, no. 1 (spring 1983): 91–109.

Keener, Frederick M. *English Dialogues of the Dead: A Critical History, an Anthology, and a Check List*. New York: Columbia University Press, 1973.

Kerferd, G. B. *The Sophistic Movement*. Cambridge: Cambridge University Press, 1981.

Kristeller, Paul Oscar. *Eight Philosophers of the Italian Renaissance*. Stanford, Calif.: Stanford University Press, 1964.

Krol, Ed. *The Whole Internet: User's Guide and Catalog*. Sebastopol, Calif.: O'Reilly, 1992.

Kushner, Eva. "Le dialogue en France au XVIe Siècle: quelques critères génologiques." *Canadian Review of Comparative Literature* (spring 1978): 141–53.

Laertius, Diogenes. *Lives of Eminent Philosophers*. Translated by R. D. Hicks. 2 vols. Cambridge, Mass.: Harvard University Press, 1938.

Lang, Berel. *The Anatomy of Philosophical Style: Literary Philosophy and the Philosophy of Literature*. Oxford: Basil Blackwell, 1990.

———. "Space, Time, and Philosophical Style." In *Philosophical Style*, edited by Berel Lang. Chicago: Nelson-Hall, 1980.

———. "Towards a Poetics of Philosophical Discourse." *Monist* 63, no. 4 (1980): 440–53.

Lang, Berel, ed. *Philosophical Style: An Anthology about the Writing and Reading of Philosophy*. Chicago: Nelson-Hall, 1980.

Levi, Albert William. "Philosophy as Literature: The Dialogue." *Philosophy & Rhetoric* 9, no. 1 (1976): 1–20.

Lloyd-Jones, Hugh. "Becoming Homer." *New York Review of Books*, 5 March 1992, pp. 52–57.

Lucian. *Lucian: With an English Translation*. Translated by Austin Morris Harmon. 8 vols. New York: Macmillan, 1967.

Mackey, Louis H. "On Philosophical Form: A Tear for Adonais." *Thought* 42, no. 165 (1967): 238–60.

Marias. *Philosophy as Dramatic Theory*. Translated by J. Parsons. London: 1971.

Marsh, David. *The Quattrocento Dialogue*. Cambridge, Mass.: Harvard University Press, 1980.

May, James M. *Trials of Character: The Eloquence of Ciceronian Ethos*. Chapel Hill: University of North Carolina Press, 1988.

McLeish, Kenneth. *The Theatre of Aristophanes*. London: Thames and Hudson, 1980.

Merrill, Elizabeth. *The Dialogue in English Literature*. New York: Henry Holt and Company, 1911.

Michelfelder, Diane P., and Richard E. Palmer, eds. *Dialogue and Deconstruction: The Gadamer-Derrida Encounter*. Albany: State University of New York Press, 1989.

Misgeld, Dieter, and Graeme Nicholson, eds. *Hans-Georg Gadamer on Education, Poetry, and History: Applied Hermeneutics*. Albany: State University of New York Press, 1992.

More, Thomas. *Utopia.* Translated by Paul Turner. Harmondsworth, England: Penguin, 1965.

Mulas, Luisa. "La scrittura del dialogo." *Oralità e scrittura nel sistema letterario. Atti del convegno, Cagliari, 14–16 aprile, 1980.* Edited by Giovanna Cerina, Cristina Lavinio, and Luisa Mulas. Rome: Bulzoni Editore, 1982.

Oakeshott, Michael. *The Voice of Poetry in the Conversation of Mankind.* London: Bowes & Bowes, 1959.

Ong, Walter J. *Orality and Literacy: The Technologizing of the Word.* New York: Routledge, 1982.

———. *Ramus: Method, and the Decay of Dialogue.* Cambridge, Mass.: Harvard University Press, 1958.

Pallavicino, Sforza. "Trattato dello stile e del dialogo." *Trattatisti e narratori del Seicento.* Edited by Ezio Raimondi. Milan: Riccardo Ricciardi Editore, 1960.

Parry, Milham. *The Making of Homeric Verse.* Oxford: Clarendon Press, 1971.

Perelman, Chaim. *The Idea of Justice and the Problem of Argument.* Translated by John Petrie. London: Routledge & Kegan Paul, 1963.

Plato. *The Collected Dialogues of Plato Including the Letters.* Edited by Edith Hamilton and Huntington Cairns. Princeton, N.J.: Princeton University Press, 1961.

Pozzi, Mario, ed. *Trattatisti del Cinquecento.* Milano-Napoli: Ricciardi, 1975.

Rankin, H. D. *Sophists, Socratics, and Cynics.* Totowa, N.J.: Barnes & Noble, 1983.

Reeve, C. D. "The Naked Old Women in the Palestra." *Hackett Publishing Company: Fall 1992 Complete Catalogue.* Indianapolis, Indiana: Hackett, 1992.

Renault, Mary. *The Last of the Wine.* New York: Random House, 1956.

Robinson, Richard. *Plato's Earlier Dialectic.* Ithaca, N.Y.: Cornell University Press, 1941.

Robinson, Richard. "Elenchus." *The Philosophy of Socrates: A Collection of Critical Essays.* Edited by Gregory Vlastos. New York: Anchor Books, 1971.

Rockwell, Geoffrey. "The Desire for Dialogue." *Toronto Semiotic Circle Bulletin* 1, no. 3 (1993): 2–6.

Rossetti, Livio. "Il momento conviviale dell'eteria socratica e il suo significato pedagogica." *Ancient Society* 7 (1976): 29–77.

Rossetti, Livio. *Aspetti della letteratura socratica antica.* Chieti: 1977.

Ruch, Michel. *Le Préambule dans les oeuvres philosophiques de Ciceron.* Paris: University of Strasbourg, 1958.

Sallis, John. *Being and Logos: The Way of Platonic Dialogue.* 2d ed. Atlantic Highlands, N.J.: Humanities Press International, 1986.

Sauvage, Micheline. *Socrate et la conscience de l'homme*. Paris: Éditions du Seuil, 1956.

Scruton, Roger. *Xanthippic Dialogues*. London: Sinclair-Stevenson, 1994.

Seeskin, Kenneth. *Dialogue and Discovery: A Study in Socratic Method*. Albany: State University of New York Press, 1987.

Seigel, Jerrold E. *Rhetoric and Philosophy in Renaissance Humanism: The Union of Eloquence and Wisdom, Petrarch to Valla*. Princeton, N.J.: Princeton University Press, 1968

Senge, Peter M. *The Fifth Discipline: The Art and Practice of the Learning Organization*. N.Y.: Doubleday, 1990.

Shaftesbury, Anthony Ashley Cooper, Earl of. *Characteristics of Men, Manners, Opinions, Times, etc*. 2 vols. Gloucester, Mass.: Peter Smith, 1963.

Sherman, Carol. *Diderot and the Art of Dialogue*. Geneva: Librairie Droz, 1976.

Snyder, Jon R. *Writing the Scene of Speaking; Theories of Dialogue in the Late Italian Renaissance*. Stanford, Calif.: Stanford University Press, 1989.

Socrates in the Agora. Princeton, N.J.: American School of Classical Studies at Athens, 1978.

Speroni, Sperone. *Opere*. Edited by Marco Forcellini and Natal dalle Laste. 5 vols. Padua 1740. Volume 1 reprinted, with a foreword by Mario Pozzi. Rome: Vecchiarelli, 1989.

Steegmuller, Francis. *A Woman, a Man, and Two Kingdoms; The Story of Madame d'Épinay and the Abbé Galiani*. New York: Alfred A. Knopf, 1991.

Struever, Nancy. "Lorenzo Valla: Humanist Rhetoric and the Critique of the Classical Languages of Morality." *Renaissance Eloquence; Studies in the Theory and Practice of Renaissance Rhetoric*. Edited by James J. Murphy. Berkeley: University of California Press, 1983.

Svenbro, Jesper. *Phrasikleia: An Anthropology of Reading in Ancient Greece*. Translated by Janet Lloyd. Ithaca, N.Y.: Cornell University Press, 1993.

Tasso, Torquato. *Tasso's Dialogues: A Selection with the "Discourse on the Art of the Dialogue."* Translated by Carnes Lord and Dain A. Trafton. Berkeley: University of California Press, 1982.

Taylor, A. E. *Plato: The Man and His Work*. 7th ed. New York: Methuen, 1926.

Thomas, Rosalind. *Oral Tradition and Written Record in Classical Athens*. Cambridge: Cambridge University Press, 1989.

Valla, Lorenzo. "De Libero Arbitrio" (On free will). *Prosatori latini del Quattrocento*. Edited by Eugenio Garin. Milan and Naples: Ricciardi, 1952.

———. *Dialogue sur le libre-arbitre*. Translated by Jacques Chomarat. Paris: Librairie Philosophique J. Vrin, 1983.

———. *On the Profession of the Religious and the Principal Arguments from the Falsely-Believed and Forged Donation of Constantine*. Translated by Olga Zorzi Pugliese. Toronto: Centre for Reformation and Renaissance Studies, 1985.

———. *Scritti filosofici e religiosi*. Translated by Georgio Radetti. Florence: Sansoni, 1953.

Versényi, Laszlo. *Socratic Humanism*. Westport, Conn.: Greenwood Press, 1979.

Vlastos, Gregory. *Socrates, Ironist and Moral Philosopher*. Ithaca, N.Y.: Cornell University Press, 1991.

Walton, Douglas. "Argumentation in Dialogues." *Argumentation* 2, no. 4 (1988).

Walzer, Michael. "A Critique of Philosophical Conversation." *Philosophical Forum* 21, nos. 1–2 (fall–winter 1989–1990): 182–96.

Warnke, Georgia. "Rawls, Habermas, and Real Talk: A Reply to Walzer." *Philosophical Forum* 21, nos. 1–2 (fall–winter 1989–1990).

Wilson, K. J. *Incomplete Fictions: The Formation of the English Renaissance Dialogue*. Washington, D.C.: Catholic University of America Press, 1985.

Xenophon. *Xenophon in Seven Volumes*. Translated by O. J. Todd and E. C. Marchant. 7 vols. Cambridge, Mass.: Harvard University Press, 1968.

Yates, Frances A. *The Art of Memory*. Chicago: University of Chicago Press, 1966.

———. *Giordano Bruno and the Hermetic Tradition*. Chicago: University of Chicago Press, 1964.

INDEX